Architecture and Agriculture

Architecture and Agriculture: A Rural Design Guide presents architectural guidelines for buildings designed and constructed in rural landscapes by emphasizing their connections with function, culture, climate, and place. Following on from the author's first book, *Rural Design*, the book discusses in detail the buildings that humans construct in support of agriculture. By examining case studies from around the world, including Australia, China, Japan, Norway, Poland, Portugal, North America, Africa, and Southeast Asia, it informs readers about the potentials, opportunities, and values of rural architecture, and how they have been developed to create sustainable landscapes and sustainable buildings for rapidly changing rural futures.

After obtaining his Bachelor of Architecture from the University of Minnesota and Master of Architecture from Yale University, **Dewey Thorbeck** won a Rome Prize Fellowship and studied in Italy for two years. The recipient of a number of architectural design awards, he is a Fellow of the American Academy in Rome, Fellow of the American Institute of Architects and past president of AIA Minnesota. Thorbeck is an adjunct full professor of architecture at the University of Minnesota and founder of the Center for Rural Design. Currently he is a senior research fellow with the Minnesota Design Center in the College of Design.

"All urban civilizations have roots in historical rural civilizations. While dazzling and cutting-edge, urban designs epitomize our modern ambitions for conquest and scale, but rural design deserves more attention than ever. *Architecture and Agriculture: A Rural Design Guide* seeks to help people understand the underestimated value of balance, diversity, and dynamism in rural culture. Thorbeck's work provides people with appropriate methods to improve rural living and working conditions, which is a great benefit for more than half of the world's population who are still living in the rural areas."

Dr. Jiang Haoshu, founder of Beijing Rural Culture Renewal Volunteers Association and curator of World Rural Development Forum

"In *Architecture and Agriculture: A Rural Design Guide*, Dewey Thorbeck sets out a comprehensive treatise for the exploration and design of agricultural buildings in the 21st century, a time when the scale and intensity of agriculture requires new approaches to ensure appropriate responses to regional and global issues. Building on rural design, Thorbeck explores global rural land use and building patterns, reminding rural policy makers, land use planners, architects, and those working with and for rural communities that design can and must play a significant role in enhancing rural quality of life."

David R. Witty PhD, MRAIC, FCIP, RPP, Provost and Vice-President Academic, Vancouver Island University

"*Architecture and Agriculture* goes beyond the typical romantic view of rural landscapes and architecture to examine working rural landscapes in the past and present. Dewey Thorbeck provides a global view of the issues that challenge rural areas and shows through case studies and research how sustainable approaches for rural architecture and communities can be developed. As someone involved with rural design issues and communities, I would recommend this book to those trying to understand the challenges these areas face globally today."

Professor John Poros, Mississippi State University, Former Director, Carl Small Town Center

"The city has dominated the 21st century conversations about architecture and sustainability, yet the hinterland is fundamental to the realization of both. Not only do rural landscapes provide the necessary material resources for our buildings and bodies, but they also function as critical settings for the development of innovative architectural ideas. In *Architecture and Agriculture*, Dewey Thorbeck shares his infectious admiration for thoughtfully designed farming communities in various regions of the world. Part historical survey, part case study catalog, and part design guide, the book is likely to attract a wide variety of audiences interested in the past and future of rural architecture."

Blaine Brownell, Associate Professor of Architecture at the University of Minnesota and author of the Transmaterial *series*

Architecture and Agriculture

A rural design guide

Dewey Thorbeck

LONDON AND NEW YORK

First published 2017
by Routledge
2 Park Square, Milton Park, Abingdon, Oxon OX14 4RN

and by Routledge
711 Third Avenue, New York, NY 10017

Routledge is an imprint of the Taylor & Francis Group, an informa business

© 2017 Dewey Thorbeck

The right of Dewey Thorbeck to be identified as author of this work has been asserted by him in accordance with sections 77 and 78 of the Copyright, Designs and Patents Act 1988.

All rights reserved. No part of this book may be reprinted or reproduced or utilised in any form or by any electronic, mechanical, or other means, now known or hereafter invented, including photocopying and recording, or in any information storage or retrieval system, without permission in writing from the publishers.

Trademark notice: Product or corporate names may be trademarks or registered trademarks, and are used only for identification and explanation without intent to infringe.

British Library Cataloguing-in-Publication Data
A catalogue record for this book is available from the British Library

Library of Congress Cataloging-in-Publication Data
Names: Thorbeck, Dewey, author.
Title: Architecture and agriculture : a rural design guide / Dewey Thorbeck.
Description: Milton Park, Abingdon, Oxon ; New York, NY : Routledge, 2017. | Includes bibliographical references and index.
Identifiers: LCCN 2016011583| ISBN 9781138937666 (hardback : alk. paper) | ISBN 9781138937680 (pbk. : alk. paper) | ISBN 9781315676166 (ebook)
Subjects: LCSH: Farm buildings. | Sustainable architecture. | Vernacular architecture.
Classification: LCC NA8200 .T46 2017 | DDC 725/.37—dc23
LC record available at http://lccn.loc.gov/2016011583

ISBN: 978-1-138-93766-6 (hbk)
ISBN: 978-1-138-93768-0 (pbk)
ISBN: 978-1-315-67616-6 (ebk)

Typeset in Charter and FS Albert
by Keystroke, Neville Lodge, Wolverhampton
Printed in Great Britain by Ashford Colour Press Ltd

Contents

List of figures ix
Acknowledgments xv
Foreword by Thomas Fisher xvii

1   Introduction 1
Author's background   5
Architecture and agriculture   11
Rural change worldwide   11
Rural change in America   13
Linking urban design and rural design   14

2   Rural architectural heritage 18
Ancient roots and European origins   19
Farmsteads   23
Farm buildings   24
English influences in America   27
Rural Malawi and Tanzania (East Africa), and Mongolia   29
Ichiu rural village in Japan   36
Dong community in rural China   41

3   Rural architecture and rural design 45
Rural change   46
Models of farm architecture   49
An educational and economic dilemma in barn design and construction   58
Rural building design guidelines   62

4 Architecture and agriculture case studies   64
   Sokol Blosser Winery, Dayton, Oregon, USA   68
   Deepwater Woolshed near Wagga Wagga, Australia   72
   Dalaker/Galta Farm House on Rennesoy Island, western Norway   76
   Mason Lane Farm Operations Center, Goshen, Kentucky, USA   79
   House for All Seasons, Shija village, northwestern China   85
   Quinta do Vallado Winery, Durou Valley, Portugal   89
   Jade Valley Winery and Resort, rural China   93
   Fabric-roofed dairy barn, Minnesota, USA   96
   St. Paul Farmers' Market, Minnesota, USA   98
   Rural design and rural architecture   101

5 Worker and animal safety and health   104
   Farm worker hazards   107
   Building code issues   108
   Evidence-based design guidelines   110
   Research possibilities   113
   Sustainable animal housing   115
   Urban agriculture and building code   116
   Linking human, animal, and environmental wellness   118

6 Rural sustainability and green design   123
   United Nations and sustainable development   127
   Examples of innovative technology for rural areas   132
   Rural futures   145
   Challenge for higher education   148

7 In-between landscapes   150
   Design disciplines dilemma   155
   Urban agriculture   156
   Urban/rural edge projects   163

8 Rural futures   169
   Design as language   170
   City of 7 billion or farm of 10 billion   171
   Crossing borders   172
   Rural development clusters   174
   Net-zero buildings and global warming   176
   Design thinking   179

9 Epilogue 183

Slums as urban models? 187
Linking urban and rural issues 188
Innovation and new design thinking 191
Sketching and the design process 194
Shaping urban and rural futures 199

References 200
Illustration credits 203
Index 205

Figures

1.1	The Chiloe Islands in Chile, a Globally Important Agricultural Heritage System	4
1.2	The author's maternal grandparents, Olaf and Hilda Hanson, in front of their barn in northern Minnesota in the 1940s	5
1.3	Aerial view in 1954 of the farm of the author's paternal grandmother, Synevva Eri	6
1.4	Sketch of the Italian hill town of Montepulciano	8
1.5	Purina Farms interpretive center in Missouri	9
1.6	Sketch of the rural Chinese village of Chuan Di Xia outside of Beijing	12
1.7	Historic bank barn in Pennsylvania	13
1.8	Round barn in southwestern Minnesota	14
1.9	Contemporary swine barn in Minnesota	14
2.1	Roman mosaic from the second-century Liberii farm villa in Tunisia	19
2.2	Exterior view of the Coxwell Barn in England	20
2.3	Interior view of the Coxwell Barn	21
2.4	Sherping Farmstead in western Minnesota	23
2.5	Gable barn with silo in northern Illinois	24
2.6	John Eidem farmstead in rural Hennepin County, Minnesota	25
2.7	Dairy research barn now the Pomeroy Alumni Center	26
2.8	Rural Chinese village of Chuan Di Xia	28
2.9	Rural Norwegian village of Laerdal	28
2.10	Village in rural Malawi, East Africa	29
2.11	Farm on a ridge in rural Malawi	31
2.12	Typical corn storage structure in northern Malawi	31
2.13	Villager selling potatoes in a market in rural Malawi	32
2.14	Maasai village in northern Tanzania	35
2.15	Mongolian herdsman moving from one grassland area to another	35

2.16	Mongolian ger (yurt) tent structure	36
2.17	Remote Japanese village of Ichiu	37
2.18	Village of Kamiyama in Japan	38
2.19	Engwa house in Kamiyama, now an office space	39
2.20	Dong community of Dali in rural China	41
2.21	Villagers at a dinner during a funeral around a drum tower in Zhaoxing	42
2.22	Villagers sing and dance under a drum tower in Zhaoxing village	42
3.1	Local farmers selling products at the St. Paul Farmers' Market in Minnesota	46
3.2	Typical post-frame building with metal roof and walls used for animal housing	47
3.3	Rural image illustrating the spatial relationship between animal agriculture and residential dwellings and the potential for social conflict	48
3.4	Pine Lake Wild Rice Farm shop complex	50
3.5	Central Building of the Pine Lake Wild Rice Farm	51
3.6	The new chemical building	52
3.7	Shop buildings illustrating the architectural relationship with the landscape	52
3.8	Typical tractor and disc equipment used on the farm	53
3.9	Three generations of the Imle family	53
3.10	The breeding center on Taylor Made Farm	54
3.11	One of five stud barns on Taylor Made Farm	54
3.12	One of the horse stables on Taylor Made Farm	56
3.13	Interior of typical horse barn	56
3.14	Typical horse stall	57
3.15	Joseph Taylor and sons	57
3.16	Round metal grain bins typical of rural landscapes today	61
4.1	Amish farmer plowing	64
4.2	Stone house and barn in northern Iowa	65
4.3	Historic vineyard farm in Napa Valley, California	65
4.4	Wooden horse barn in Nashville, Tennessee	66
4.5	Typical corn crib in northern Iowa	66
4.6	Wensman Seed Company in northern Minnesota	67
4.7	Entrance to the visitor center at Sokol Blosser winery in Oregon	68
4.8	Deck view from visitor center to valley	69
4.9	Seating terrace in visitor center	70
4.10	Interior view of visitor center toward tree	71
4.11	Open space between buildings at the visitor center	71
4.12	Deepwater Woolshed in New South Wales, Australia	72
4.13	End view of Woolshed	73
4.14	Interior of Woolshed with sheep	74
4.15	Woolshed detail of roof	75

4.16	Dalaker/Galta house in Norway	76
4.17	Dalaker/Galta house with sheep grazing	77
4.18	Dalaker/Galta house with rock field	77
4.19	Dalaker/Galta house corner detail	78
4.20	Glacier Museum in Norway by architect Sverre Fehn	79
4.21	Mason Lane farm with Barns A and B and grain bin	80
4.22	Interior of Barn A with roof trusses	80
4.23	End view of Barn B with bamboo screen	83
4.24	Interior of Barn B with hay at other end	83
4.25	Barn B from adjacent hay field	84
4.26	Shija village in rural China	86
4.27	House for All Seasons as prototype	87
4.28	Prototype house from above	88
4.29	House interior courtyard 1	88
4.30	House interior courtyard 2	88
4.31	Construction sequence of House for All Seasons	89
4.32	Quinta do Vallado Winery in the Douro River Valley, Portugal	90
4.33	Entrance terrace of the winery	90
4.34	Entrance to the Visitor Center at the winery	91
4.35	Interior of the Visitor Center	92
4.36	Interior of the Production Room	92
4.37	Interior of the Aging Cave	93
4.38	Jade Valley Resort and Winery in rural China	94
4.39	Well House, designed for the father of the architect	94
4.40	Well House entrance	95
4.41	Jade Valley Resort and Winery	95
4.42	Fabric-roofed dairy barn for 2,500 cows	96
4.43	The historic St. Paul Public Market in Minnesota	98
4.44	Sketch of the exterior of the proposed market design	99
4.45	Sketch of covered selling aisle	99
4.46	Sketch of the exterior of the indoor market	100
4.47	Sketch of the interior of the indoor market	100
4.48	Interrelated performance metrics for environmental and human health	102
5.1	Page 1 of brochure by Midwest Plan Service for a swine building	105
5.2	Page 2 of brochure illustrating different plan arrangements	106
5.3	Sheep research center in the Abruzzi region of Italy	110
5.4	Aerial view of Riverview Dairy farm in west central Minnesota	111
5.5	Interior view of feeding aisle in the cow barn	112
5.6	Rotary milking parlor	112
6.1	CLOUD concept for bringing high-speed internet service to the remote Chinese village of Shang Shui Guo	134
6.2	CLOUD concept over village at twilight	135

List of figures

6.3	CLOUD concept over village at night	136
6.4	Early site plan drawing of the Hometown BioEnergy facility	137
6.5	Elevation drawing of the proposed Hometown BioEnergy facility	138
6.6	The front entry side of the Hometown BioEnergy facility	138
6.7	Rear view of Hometown BioEnergy facility in winter	138
6.8	Location of the study area in Poland	141
6.9	Proposed layout for the green infrastructure in the Wrocław Functional Area	142
6.10	Simplified map of the green infrastructure in the Wrocław Functional Area	143
6.11	Presentation board of the cultural landscape study of the City of Paczkow regarding the location of wind farms	144
7.1	Diagram showing the connection that the rural design process can make between rural science and rural society	152
7.2	Diagram illustrating the relationship between urban design and rural design in shaping the future peri-urban landscape	155
7.3	Aerial view of Mithun Architects proposal for urban agriculture farm in the State of Washington	157
7.4	Ground-level view of the Mithun Architects proposal	158
7.5	Aerial view of the Thermal Village of Blumau	160
7.6	Large industrial glass greenhouse in Australia	161
7.7	Location plan of historic Andrew Peterson Farmstead in peri-urban landscape of Carver County in the Twin City Metropolitan Area of Minnesota	163
7.8	Andrew Peterson and his family in front of their home in 1885	164
7.9	The Andrew Peterson Concept Master Plan	165
7.10	The Entry Building to the historic Andrew Peterson Farmstead	166
7.11	Drawing of the Twin City Metropolitan Area	167
7.12	Transect drawing showing the potential difference in transect densities between 2016 and 2050	167
8.1	Diagram by the Center for Rural Design illustrating the innovative potential for creative problem solving	180
8.2	Small girl with calf illustrating the human–animal bond	181
8.3	Children plowing with oxen in Nepal	182
9.1	Design sketches illustrating the diatom as the inspiration for architectural form for the new Bell Museum of Natural History	192
9.2	A traditional Myanmar house in a rural village	195
9.3	Dewey Thorbeck showing school children in a Myanmar village his sketches	195
9.4	Sketch of the pathway up the river bank to Minhia village along the Ayevarwaddy River in Myanmar	196
9.5	Sketch of a sheep farm in Patagonia	197
9.6	Sketch of the Italian rural town of Scanno	197

9.7	Sketch of the Vedema Resort on the Greek island of Santorini	198
9.8	Sketch of the Borgund Stave Kirke near the rural town of Laerdal on Sognefjord in west Norway	198

Acknowledgments

One day my wife Sharon asked me why I am writing this second book about architecture and agriculture. I replied that it's something I just have to do because I want to try to make the world a better place, and do my part to advance rural design and rural architecture to help make rural regions worldwide more economically and environmentally sustainable.

In my first book, *Rural Design: A New Design Discipline,* I discussed rural landscapes, agriculture, and rural places, and the problem-solving process of design and design thinking that rural design can bring to rural issues. That book started with a grant from the Graham Foundation for Advanced Studies in the Fine Arts to write about the architecture of agriculture. In this book, *Architecture and Agriculture: A Rural Design Guide*, I am building on the original premise to discuss in more detail what rural issues are, how rural and urban issues are interconnected, and how the human dimension and human spirit has shaped rural architecture and agriculture into many different forms in cultures worldwide. Living in harmony with the land, as done by so many of these agricultural systems created by indigenous peoples, can help us frame and design a sustainable future – urban and rural.

I want to thank David and Claire Frame, good friends and retired teachers, who were in the Peace Corps in the 1960s in Malawi, East Africa, and recently returned for a visit 48 years after they taught there. As a result of their Peace Corps involvement they see the world with keener insight and have taken wonderful pictures of their travels around the world visiting places that most experienced travelers would not see. I am so grateful that they have shared their insight, pictures, and comments for this book.

Professional architects around the world have supplied photographs and information on their work that is in the book, and they deserve special mention and my heartfelt thanks, including: Peter Stuchbury (Australia), Brad Cloepfil (Oregon), Knut Hjeltnes (Norway), Roberto de Leon (Kentucky), John Lin (China), Francisco Viera De Compos (Portugal), Quingyun Ma (China and California),

Mary Ann Ray and Robert Mangurian (Michigan), and Irena Niedźwiecka-Filipiak (Poland).

Others wrote or provided descriptions about their places and experiences in rural issues and architectural projects, and I am very thankful and appreciative of their writings and comments, including: Dr. Xiaomei Zhao (China), Dr. Kerry Arabena (Australia), Dr. John Troughton (Australia), Andrew Wald (America), Dr. Katherine Swanson (America), Avant Energy (Minnesota), Peter Sonstegaard (Iowa), Ag Reliant (Minnesota), Dr. Terje Kristensen (Norway and Minnesota), Paul and Kathy Imle and the Imle family (Minnesota), and Duncan Taylor and the Taylor family (Kentucky).

Ms. Jiang Haoshu in the Ministry of Culture in China deserves my heartfelt thanks for her strong leadership in organizing and managing the World Green Design Organization (WGDO) and the World Rural Development Committee (WRDC). She invited me to speak about rural design at the WGDO conference in 2013 in China, and again to attend the founding ceremony of the WRDC in Beijing in 2015, for which I was named Vice Director. She also helped get my first book translated and published in China by PHEI, and I very much appreciate her assistance.

I particularly wish to thank Thomas Fisher, the former dean of the College of Design and now director of the Minnesota Design Center at the University of Minnesota. He is a highly acclaimed author and educator who wrote the Foreword to my first book and also for this one. I also want to recognize landscape architect Stephen Roos, my long-time colleague at the Center for Rural Design and a Senior Research Fellow. He has been most instrumental in helping shape the vision and mission of the Center for Rural Design and managing the many rural design projects we have been involved with over the years.

I also greatly appreciate the professional support, creative advice, and assistance of Francesca Ford, Commissioning Editor; Grace Harrison, Editorial Assistant; and the entire team from the Routledge/Taylor Francis Group who worked with me to clarify the intent and scope of my book. I also appreciate the comments from the five anonymous reviewers of my book proposal. Their criticisms were very helpful in finalizing the proposal and developing the manuscript.

As in my first book, I especially want to thank the love of my life, Sharon. She is my wife, best friend, and business colleague, who organizes and manages our life and travels. Without her love, patience, and encouragement this book would not have been written. My book is dedicated to her and the parents of our seven beautiful granddaughters, and to the grandchildren who can accomplish anything they want to pursue in life: Callie, who will soon be going to college, seeking her own way in the world; Julia, who is a very creative and all-around high school student; Bailey, whose heart is in all sports and loves design; Riley, a born leader, swimmer, and gymnast; Remy, a strong hockey player with a lovable and mischievous personality; Addison, with a great smile, who is inquisitive and can tackle anything; and the smart Siena, who is a very creative young artist.

They remind me daily why visioning a better quality of life and sustainable urban and rural future is so important.

Foreword: The Invention of Rural Design

In the book *The Invention of Nature*, Andrea Wulf tells the story of how the 19th-century scientist Alexander von Humboldt helped us see the natural world as an integrated whole. The author of this book, architect Dewey Thorbeck, has helped us see the rural environment in the same way. He has shown, in his previous book *Rural Design: A New Design Discipline* as well as in this work, the many ways in which the city and country remain inseparably linked and equally the product of human design decisions. In these books, though, Thorbeck also reveals several blind spots in how we think about and treat rural areas.

At the scale of individual buildings, he causes us to wonder why we exempt most agricultural buildings from life-safety codes when those structures, no longer the simple wood-framed farm buildings of the past, have often become large, industrial-scale operations. Just as the early life-safety codes arose in the wake of worker injuries and loss of life in urban factories over a century ago, this book raises the question of whether the time has come for these codes to apply to what have become factory equivalents in rural areas. With farming remaining one of the most hazardous forms of work, why shouldn't we design safer facilities? And, with the rise of urban farming, does it make any sense to have buildings standing next to one other, each meeting a different life-safety standard simply because one has an agricultural designation and the other not?

Thorbeck raises other questions at the regional scale. While farms once had a high degree of self-sufficiency, the extent of the rural infrastructure needed to serve remote farmsteads has become a costly burden to install and maintain. This book suggests that renewable resources, such as solar, wind, and biomass, offer a much more sustainable and resilient way forward, reducing infrastructure costs and empowering farmers and the local economies of their region. At the same time, providing digital infrastructure, like broadband internet access, has become critical to rural economies. The idea that Thorbeck describes in this book of a cloud-like balloon floating over each rural community, providing residents very low-cost wireless internet access while also illuminating streets at night and shading public spaces during the day, exemplifies the creative thinking that design can offer.

Indeed, design thinking may represent the most valuable resource that rural design can provide agricultural communities. Thorbeck makes a compelling case for this in one example after another in this book as he describes agricultural buildings that respond to their climate and context, reduce energy consumption and resource dependence, and recall the resonance that farm buildings once had with their purpose and place. To some, the difficult transition happening in rural economies and the struggle within rural communities may make such designs seem irrelevant or unresponsive to the challenges of rural areas, but the opposite is true. As Thorbeck argues, rural design can help agricultural communities regain the tradition of innovation and creativity that has long characterized farm life, using design thinking to invent new modes of living and working more attuned to the 21st century. Plant, animal, and soil science have made tremendous improvements to the production of food, but with these advances in efficiency have come disruptive changes to the livelihoods of farmers and the health of farming communities. Rural design addresses the latter head-on and holistically. While we have designed our rural landscapes for many thousands of years, ever since humans began to cultivate crops and keep animals, rural design has only recently emerged as a field of study and an area of research, largely the result of Dewey Thorbeck's leadership.

He demonstrates, in both his previous book and this one, how we will never adequately address the interrelated challenges facing rural families and communities until we approach them from a much more interdisciplinary perspective and with a much more creative form of problem solving. Rural design offers both. Designers have a long history and great skill at assembling interdisciplinary teams of people depending on the demands of a particular project or problem, and rural design brings that ability to the complex challenges of agricultural communities and landscapes. At the same time, designers bring to a situation an ability to reframe a problem and see it from a different perspective or a larger context in order to arrive at more innovative solutions or better alternatives.

This goes against the popular misperception that designers only care about aesthetics or that they can't meet budgets or schedules. As Thorbeck demonstrates repeatedly in his own design work as well as that of others in this book, good design is anything but that. Design, properly done, results in lower life-cycle costs, better long-term performance, and greater real-world results – pragmatic values that align well with those of agricultural communities and that set rural design, in many ways, apart from the more urban-oriented practices of most designers. Fashion may matter more than functionality to some big-city designers, but in most rural areas, practicality reigns. That does not mean, though, that ugliness or cheapness must as well. Thorbeck shows in this book how the most creative solutions often have an elegance and simplicity that comes from everything having a purpose, and how the most innovative outcomes often have a directness and efficiency that come from completely rethinking a problem.

Just as Alexander von Humboldt's work transformed our understanding of nature, so much so that we never saw the natural world in the same way ever again, so too has Thorbeck's writing about rural design altered our view of agricultural landscapes and communities in ways that make it hard for us to ever see them as separate and unrelated again. The rural areas of the world remain ecosystems as finely tuned as the natural ones first described by von Humboldt, and because these agricultural landscapes arose by design, so too can we improve their health and that of the communities that depend on them through design – through Dewey Thorbeck's invention of rural design.

Thomas Fisher is the Director of the Minnesota
Design Center at the University of Minnesota

Chapter 1

Introduction

I like to have a man's knowledge comprehend more than one class of topics, one row of shelves. I like a man who likes to see a fine barn as well as a good tragedy.
Ralph Waldo Emerson (American essayist and poet, 1803–1882)

Today it is your imagination I am speaking to and in order to provoke your imagination it is imperative that we suspend ourselves from the normal encumbrances that we use to anchor ourselves into our everyday comfort, into relationships, into identity and society. It is your inner self that I seek to engage in this conversation.
Kerry Arabena (Australian Professor of Public Health)

Architecture and agriculture has existed ever since humans first developed skills to grow plants and raise animals for food and fiber. With these skills they became rooted in one place, started to live and work with nature and constructed shelters for themselves and their animals as protection from the elements and for storage. It began a new relationship between humans, animals, and the landscape. No longer having to constantly move around to forage for food, human settlement emerged out of this new way of life and architecture began. It is the architecture of agriculture that is the subject of this book along with its connections to rural design, rural land-uses, and rural landscapes – historically, today, and in the future.

In America a number of historic barns and farmsteads are on the National Register of Historic Places and some are listed as National Landmarks, but when they are it often has more to do with the accomplishments of the farmer than with the architecture. Working buildings in the rural landscape have rarely been discussed by architectural historians other than in vernacular terms referencing historic building types or styles, yet these buildings are an integral aspect of the beautiful agrarian landscapes in America and around the world. Some of the best books on vernacular architecture that go beyond simply showing pictures by describing working buildings and other structures and landscaping constructed by people living in rural ecosystems include: *Barn: The Art of a Working Building* by E. Endersby, A. Greenwood and D. Larkin (1992); *Barns of New York* by C. Falk (2012); and the comprehensive *Vernacular Architecture: Towards a Sustainable Future* by C. Mileto, F. Vegas. L.G. Soriano, and V. Cristini (2014).

What is it about rural landscapes and the farmsteads, farm animals and fields that make them so interesting? Perhaps it is the nostalgic connection to our agrarian past where the making of architecture was directly connected to place, growing food, and the rituals of life – human, animal, and environmental. Rural architecture that has a strong relationship and fit with culture, climate, and place resonates with us because this connection is part of our human heritage. America was settled by immigrants and most were farmers who worked the landscape and melded with other farmers, creating the unique character of small towns and farm buildings in the American rural landscape that we love.

The small rural towns in America that developed along with agriculture were often located along roadways a distance apart (approximately 12–16 miles) so that a farmer could milk his cows in the early morning and travel by horse and buggy to town for supplies and home again for the evening milking. As these towns developed important public buildings like schools and courthouses were designed and constructed to reflect permanence. The most important of these was the county courthouse in the county seat, and they often adopted historical classical architectural styles as the model to portray permanence and the city and county's intentions to be around for a long time. Many rural towns had a city square as the focal point and center of activities, with important buildings surrounding it or in some cases in it.

As my wife and I travel around the world we visit many rural places and have observed the similarity of how rural people have worked the land to provide the necessities of life. The scale and character might be much different in rural America with 400 years of agricultural experience than rural China with 5,000 years, yet each has developed its own unique culture, language, social organizations, and traditions based on their agricultural and economic systems, climate, and landscape. These agricultural systems around the world developed over time with indigenous techniques and practices based on human ingenuity respecting landscape, climate, and place while providing community food security in a way that conserved natural resources and biodiversity for the future.

The intention of this book, however, is to go beyond a picture-book view of the vernacular to begin a discourse about rural buildings and rural landscapes with the same critical eye that urban buildings in the urban landscape are looked at. My hope is that it stimulates readers to think about their own rural heritage and the importance of shaping sustainable rural futures for everyone including their own wellbeing and quality of life even if they live in a city. The book is also intended to help readers realize that urban and rural issues are interconnected, and that healthy and prosperous urban and rural futures require new understandings of our mutual connections and place on the planet.

In his book *The Prodigious Builders* (1977), author Bernard Rudofsky writes about architecture without architects as unorthodox architectural history while lamenting the ignoring of vernacular architecture by architectural historians. He goes on to describe American agriculture as being developed by immigrants who abandoned their cultural roots and became pioneers with no love for the land and the things that grew on it. He says this was

> because the American frontier was a formidable obstacle to be conquered and that it wasn't until the beginning of the 20th century that soil conservation was considered good for farming even as practices like contour plowing to prevent soil erosion had been in force in China for 5,000 years.

To Rudofsky, "What touches the heart is the mark left by the man who cultivates the land, and cultivates it wisely; who builds intelligently; who shapes his surrounding with a profound sense of affection rather than in the pursuit of profit." It is this emotion that is at the soul of architecture and agriculture and the human spirit that I hope is conveyed in this book.

Rudofsky goes on to discuss the 1964 exhibition *Architecture without Architects* at New York's Museum of Modern Art. Vernacular architecture was not well recognized nor considered respectable at that time and he enlisted the support of a number of prominent architects and educators including Josep Lluís Sert, Gio Ponti, Kenzo Tange, and Richard Neutra, who were supportive. Walter Gropius had to be gently persuaded, but the tide turned when Pietro Belluschi, dean of architecture at the Massachusetts Institute of Technology, wrote a letter to the president of the Guggenheim Foundation, where he said: "Somehow for the first time in my long career as an architect I had an exhilarating glimpse of architecture as a manifestation of the human spirit beyond style and fashion and more importantly, beyond the narrows of our Greek–Roman tradition" (Rudofsky 1977).

The *Architecture Without Architects* exhibition traveled around the world over an eleven-year time frame, ending when Rudofsky published *The Prodigious Builders*, which was his second book about vernacular architecture. Since that time no one has written as well about indigenous cultures and the human spirit shaping architecture and communities as he has done.

Rural and agricultural cultural heritage is now being recognized around the world by the United Nations as they declared some of these rural cultural areas as Globally Important Agricultural Heritage Systems (GIAHS). They are defined by the United Nations Food and Agriculture Organization (UN-FAO) as "Remarkable land use systems and landscapes which are rich in globally significant biological diversity evolving from the co-adaptation of a community with its environment and its needs and aspirations for sustainable development" (Koohafkan and Altieri 2011). How these rural cultural heritage sites are going to be authentically preserved is a major rural design issue that needs careful and sensitive analysis. There is much to be learned from the people living on these heritage sites for both new and renovated urban and rural developments in how to live on the land without destroying it. One of the designated GIAHS sites that illustrate this is the Chiloe Islands in Chile that have a unique and interesting culture of raising potatoes that evolved over time with nearly a thousand different varieties before the onset of agricultural modernization. This GIAHS is important for its genetic diversity providing a major social-economic service to the people who live and work in the group of islands (Figure 1.1).

Green design principles and design thinking might help political and governance entities worldwide to cross borders and engage with the diversity of peoples and their cultural, religious, and ethnic differences to make decisions about the land in a way that incorporates citizens into the planning process. If done sustainably it can help shape the urban and rural landscapes for a better future today without diminishing the opportunity for future generations to shape theirs. This means that any planning and design for future sustainable development needs to be accomplished on a bottom-up basis rather than the traditional top-down government approach. That is a rural design challenge that needs to be accomplished for both rural and urban futures.

1.1
The Chiloe Islands in Chile are a Globally Important Agricultural Heritage System representing a land use system and landscape that is rich in globally significant biological diversity.

Author's background

To better understand my point of view about architecture and its connections to agriculture, and the goal of this book, here is a brief outline of my background. I grew up in the small rural town of Bagley in Clearwater County on the edge of the prairie in northwestern Minnesota and have admired barns and their animals ever since I first visited my immigrant Norwegian grandparents' farmsteads. My mother's parents, Olaf and Hilda Hanson, are shown in Figure 1.2 posing in front of their barn in the 1940s. Olaf emigrated from Norway through Canada to northwestern Minnesota in 1893 and settled in the river town of Thief River Falls in 1895. Shortly after he started to utilize his Norwegian boat-building skills, along with his father Olai, to construct steamboats on the Red Lake River, and began a career as a steam boat captain delivering supplies to early settlers along the river and Native Americans on the Red Lake Indian Reservation. He married Hilda Clemenson in 1901 and together they had twelve children including my mother, Emma, born in 1906. When the railroads were constructed the steamboat business declined, and in 1914 they purchased a farm in northern Clearwater County and moved there with six children.

1.2
The author's maternal grandparents, Olaf and Hilda Hanson, in front of their barn in northern Minnesota in the 1940s. The farm and barn were a fascinating place to visit and discover.

My father's mother, Synevva Eri, emigrated from Norway in 1903 and joined an older brother, Nils Eri, on his homestead farm in North Dakota. Several years later she met and married my immigrant German grandfather, George Thorbecke, who died in the great flu epidemic of 1918. After his death she moved with six children, including my father David who was the oldest, from her farm in North Dakota to be near another older brother, David Eri, who had a homestead farm near Gonvick in Clearwater County in Minnesota.

Shortly after arriving in Minnesota she purchased a farm across the highway from her brother and the story goes that she hired a neighboring Norwegian bachelor farmer, Oscar Graftaas, to build her a barn – and he never left because they soon got married! Big Oscar, as we called him, was my step-grandfather who could not read or write, yet the barn he constructed in the 1920s is as straight and true today as it was when he built it. Synevva had two more children with Big Oscar and with her strong and sparkling personality she was an inspiration to all of her seventeen grandchildren. The farmstead with house, barn, and outbuildings is very typical of the cluster of buildings seen in the rural landscape throughout Midwest America (Figure 1.3).

My father drove a gasoline delivery truck to farms in the Gonvick area. One day he made a delivery to the Hanson farm and for the first time saw my mother perched on top of a haystack piling up fresh hay, and the story is that he was immediately smitten and fell in love with her! They married soon after and moved to Bagley, where my father became the owner of a gasoline station and also a grain farm outside of town. From the time I was tall enough to wash windshields I started pumping gasoline and drove a tractor working the grain fields on the farm through high school until I started college.

1.3
Aerial view in 1954 of the farm of the author's paternal grandmother, Synevva Eri, which was published in the local newspaper.

It was on my grandparents' farmsteads that as a boy I first experienced the uniqueness of a barn and its wooden construction and size, its mystery, the power of light as it streamed into the dimness through small windows and cracks in the siding, and the high arching roof structure of the hay loft. Here I first smelled farm animals, learned what they ate, milked cows and cranked a milk separator, helped harness horses, shoveled manure, climbed to the hayloft and jumped into the hay. On those farmsteads I first handled a team of horses, drove a tractor, helped collect hay in the field and pile it up in haystacks, load hay from wagons into the hay loft of the barn, and tinkered with machinery and woodworking tools. It was a place where people, animals, buildings, machinery, and nature all work together – and it was a marvelous place to experience.

I always liked to draw and thought I would become an aeronautical engineer when I started college; however I soon learned that it was more about fluid dynamics than airplane design as I imagined it. I was taking a course in engineering drafting and expressed frustration to my college professor, Burton Fosse, who invited me to visit an architect's office with him. When I saw drawings of proposed buildings on the walls of the office I suddenly realized that people designed buildings. Up to that moment I thought contractors just built them, and was so excited that the next day I enrolled in the architecture program at the University of Minnesota and transferred to the university the next fall. My decision and passion to become an architect came so quickly I sometimes tell people that I am "a born-again architect" and I am forever indebted to Professor Fosse for introducing me to the world of architecture and design.

After graduating with a Bachelor of Architecture degree, and working part time during school with a local architectural firm, I was awarded a scholarship to study at Yale University for a Master of Architecture degree. Later I was fortunate to win the Rome Prize in Architecture and spent two years at the American Academy in Rome. Traveling around Italy with other Fellows I discovered the beautiful Italian hill towns and the wonderful architectural cluster of buildings for people and animals on top of a hill leaving the rich soil in the valleys for growing food. When I traveled around Italy with Charles Stifter, the architect who received the prize the year before I did, he told me I was like a blotter soaking everything up, and he was right.

Those hill towns had an enormous impact on my architectural thinking because they were so different from the rural landscapes and small rural towns I had grown up with on the flat plains of Midwest America. The hill town was a very special place with social, cultural, and economic development, and with an architecture constructed of local stone creating an ensemble that reflected their heritage, culture, climate, and way of life. The houses were closely connected along a narrow street and usually constructed with animals on the ground floor and family living quarters above. There were public squares, markets, churches, banks, schools, and shops providing basic needs along with social, religious, educational, and cultural sustenance integrated into the daily routine of life in the village. The farmers would pack up their donkeys and travel down into the valley

1.4
A sketch from the balcony of a restaurant in the Italian hill town of Montepulciano in Tuscany looking down into the valley below where agriculture still takes place as it has for centuries.

early in the morning, work all day in the fields and then come home before night fall to their homes on top of the hill. The Italian hill town was a place of refuge providing security and social and cultural continuity for the community – a place where architectural and agricultural interests worked and harmonized together.

The medieval hill town of Montepulciano, with its buildings perched on the edge of the bluff, is a good example of a hill town providing wonderful views into the valley below where agriculture still takes place. Figure 1.4 shows a sketch made from a restaurant balcony overlooking the valley in 2011 when my wife and I were exploring hill towns in Tuscany during one of our many trips to Italy.

Returning to the United States after studying in Rome, I started my professional architectural career working with an architectural firm, and later with my own. As a result of my architectural work designing projects involving animals I began to think again about rural landscapes. These project included a new zoo in Minnesota, the first northern climate zoo in the world designed to be open year-round and exhibiting animals in their natural habitat; public interpretive centers for both domestic and wild animals in Minnesota and Missouri; and several animal agriculture research facilities (dairy, swine, poultry, sheep, and beef) at universities in different parts of the country.

In all of my work I try to make a very strong connection between architecture and landscape reflecting climate and place, and in the case of the animal projects the historical connections between humans and animals became paramount. The first project was a public interpretive center called Purina Farms for the Ralston Purina Company on a site at their research complex outside of St. Louis, Missouri. Two existing barns were remodeled along with an outdoor amphitheater and a pet pavilion. The architecture for Purina Farms was based on traditional Missouri farmstead wood construction with shade porches. The other project was a poultry research complex at Penn State University in Pennsylvania where the architecture utilized post-frame wood construction with metal siding for walls and roof reflecting traditional poultry barns in Pennsylvania. They were painted white to minimize solar heat gain and provide a stable temperature for the poultry. The interior exhibit was organized and designed to explain the historical connection and bond between humans and animals (Figure 1.5).

1.5
Interior view of the Purina Farms exhibit highlighting the historical animal and human bond.

Simultaneously I was teaching architectural design in the School of Architecture and Landscape Architecture at the University of Minnesota and had organized a number of studio projects that involved architecture students in the design of animal facilities and multifunctional educational buildings located in small towns in rural Minnesota. The studio projects included presentations to the students by academicians and experts involved in animal agriculture and the buildings constructed for it. The studio projects also included discussions with rural residents who outlined their concerns about the profound changes that were taking place in rural America and the struggles that rural communities were experiencing.

We learned that because of rapidly changing economic conditions many small farmers decided to sell their farms and seek job opportunities in the cities. As a result the economic changes were impacting a profound shift toward fewer farmers on larger farms with many more animals requiring the construction of large livestock buildings. These buildings were often using pre-engineered post-frame buildings with metal siding and roofing, and all looked the same regardless of place. Also, this shift from fewer farmers to larger farms, and people moving from rural to urban areas, was negatively impacting rural economics, small towns, schools, and quality of life.

These collective experiences provided a new insight into the rural dilemma and I came to realize that the design schools and the design professions had fundamentally ignored rural America. As a result I founded in 1997 a new research center at the University of Minnesota called the Center for Rural Design (CRD). The Center is located in both the College of Design and the College of Food, Agricultural, and Natural Resource Sciences, and we began working with rural communities to bring design, for the first time, as a problem-solving process to rural issues the same way that urban design was involved with urban issues.

While researching the impacts on small towns, abandoned historic barns, other agricultural buildings, and new specialized animal buildings constructed for dairy, swine, and poultry (including my own work), I began to realize that the issues impacting rural regions of North America were much broader and more comprehensive than I had realized. Global economics were impacting a wide range of agricultural, social, cultural, economic, health, and environmental interests. Rural areas were experiencing profound demographic shifts with less population, lack of jobs for young people, and limited access to high quality communication, educational and health services. Social conflicts resulting from various ideas about sustainability, food safety, and the size of farms and farming methods contributed to the dilemma.

Many of these issues were discussed in my first book, *Rural Design: A New Design Discipline* (Routledge, 2012), which established the theoretical base for rural design and the importance of looking at connecting rural issues to create synergy and optimal solutions from a global, national, state, region, and local perspective. That book also argued that urban issues and rural issues are interrelated, and that you cannot shape rural landscapes through rural design without also thinking about and shaping urban landscapes through urban design. It is this urban/rural connection and the fact that we are all living on the same planet along with plants and animals and that a sustainable future requires inclusive design.

Architecture and agriculture

Architecture and Agriculture: A Rural Design Guide is a follow-up to my first book, to discuss in more detail the architecture that humans construct for themselves in rural regions around the world for shelter and support of food and fiber production. It is intended to be a design guide for thinking about the meaning, design, and construction of buildings in the agricultural landscape. The book discusses their historical social, economic, and artistic meanings and fit with the rural landscape to help identify ideas for future buildings emphasizing architectural form that follows function, culture, climate, and place.

It is the architecture of those buildings and the human spirit that created them that is the focus along with the premise that architecture in rural areas deserves critical architectural analysis about their appearance, engineering, safety, and fit within the environment which they are constructed the same as urban buildings. The book uses case studies of architectural projects connected to agriculture from around the world to illustrate exemplary contemporary design and construction in rural regions in the 21st century that connect to culture, place, and climate. The case studies will inform readers, scholars, farmers, policy makers, and rural communities about the values of rural architecture with strategies as to how rural design can be utilized to create buildings that are rooted in place, sustainable, enhance quality of life, and fit the character and climate of the agrarian heritage and landscape within which they are located.

Rural change worldwide

Rural regions worldwide are experiencing loss of population, aging infrastructure and inadequate transportation, poor access to high-speed internet, and lack of quality education and healthcare. This is being exacerbated by fewer economic options and environmental degradation from changing land use patterns leading to a decline in quality of life – especially for young people.

Global climate changes will further impact the function and character of the agricultural landscape. These impacts along with food supply, food security, and water resources are international sustainability issues that will bring dramatic changes to rural social, cultural, economic, and environmental landscapes around the world – particularly in responding to the rapidly growing world population that may increase by 2.5 billion people by 2050.

Probably no country has experienced rural change more than China with its government program to shift millions of rural people to urban areas raising

1.6
Sketch of the rural Chinese village of Chuan Di Xia where Beijing families can visit as tourists and for a weekend try to get some idea of what life and their culture was like.

many questions about what happens to rural China. Where is the food security that the country needs and what will happen to the remaining rural villages and rural population? The rural village of Chuan Di Xia, 40 miles outside of Beijing, is being preserved primarily as a tourist destination where urban Chinese families can visit and stay in a restored house for a week and learn about life in the rural village as it once was (Figure 1.6). Tourism may provide some economic stimulus to the rural village; however, there are many more villages with traditional agricultural systems throughout China, Asia, and Africa, and also in America that are struggling to upgrade their lifestyle and find their place in the rapidly changing modern world.

The global challenge is to find a way to preserve local rural traditions that are based on indigenous agricultural models of sustainability while finding a way for them to improve their quality of life. As described by Parviz Koohafkan, president of the World Agricultural Heritage Foundation based in Rome, Italy, in a paper on globally important agricultural heritage systems these agricultural communities promote biodiversity, thrive without agrochemicals, and sustain year-round yields in the midst of socioeconomic change.

As poverty alleviation and food security remain elusive for nearly a billion of the world's population, and with climate change threatening major disruptions with particularly strong impact on the poorest and most marginal, it is clear that humanity will soon need new models of agriculture that is more biodiverse, local, resilient, sustainable, and socially just. The future of civilization on the planet will need an agriculture that is rooted in the ecological rational of traditional farming systems to be sustainable through the 21st century.

(Koohafkan and Altieri 2011)

Rural change in America

Farming methods were brought to America by immigrants and modified by their interaction with other farmers and the landscape, soils, climate, and agricultural economics where they settled. This experience gave form to the unique visual and cultural character of farmsteads, barns, and other working buildings and rural towns in rural landscapes. This continues today in America with new immigrant farmers from all over the world providing fruits and vegetables through farmers' markets, working on farms growing and harvesting food and food products, and providing a labor force for animal agriculture.

The architecture of animal agriculture buildings has changed over the years from wood timber frame and siding barns in the 18th and 19th century, like a barn in Pennsylvania (Figure 1.7) constructed with dignity and symmetry, to a labor-saving round barn in southwestern Minnesota (Figure 1.8), to pre-engineered

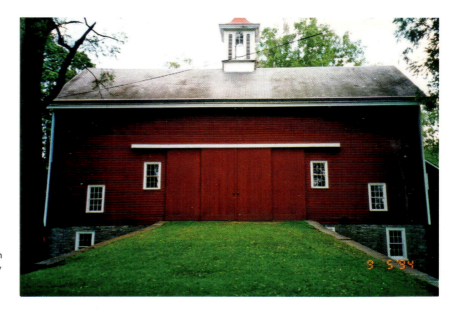

1.7
A historic bank barn in Pennsylvania along the Hudson River constructed with all of the attributes of a quality family and the importance they placed on the barn.

1.8
A round barn near New Prague, Minnesota designed and constructed based on labor-saving ideas.

1.9
A contemporary swine barn in Minnesota using post-frame (pole barn) construction and built in repeating patterns like military barracks.

post-frame wood construction (sometimes called pole barns) with metal siding and roofing like the swine barn in Minnesota shown in Figure 1.9. The post-frame construction system with metal siding and roofing has been common since the 1960s, with the development of chemically treated wood so that it can be placed directly into the ground, and is still the most used construction methodology for new agricultural and rural commercial buildings in America today.

Linking urban design and rural design

Rural design and urban design have many similarities in that both embrace quality of life. Rural design seeks to understand and embody the unique characteristics of open landscapes and systems where buildings and towns are components of the landscape, rather than defining infrastructure and public space – as in urban design. To be most effective, rural design is an interdisciplinary design discipline for resolving rural needs through the lens of spatial arrangement, community engagement, research-based evidence, and the integrated problem-solving process of design.

Design is a powerful tool for integrating knowledge across disciplines, and while not directly engaged in research, designers can translate and apply research knowledge to the design process – helping bridge the gap between science and society. Unfortunately, the issue of applied research through design is not well understood by many funding organizations that support scientific research regarding agriculture and rural environments and the linkages between urban and rural. To them research is discipline oriented and focused on subjects that end up in scientific journals to inform other researchers.

Rural design is an interdisciplinary design discipline that can help rural communities manage change through the lens of spatial arrangement, and in the process provide a link between science and society to improve rural quality of life. Rural design brings design thinking as a means to utilize research knowledge and translate that evidence through the design process. Because it is a new design discipline it brings creativity and innovation to a landscape that has not received much attention in the past, but is now starting to receive a great deal of attention, including urban agriculture. The landscape between urban and rural – the peri-urban landscape as it is now being called – is of particular importance as cities and their surrounding regions cope with all of the issues of urban population increase and future urban development in expanding cities while preserving land for agriculture and growing food.

Agriculture has existed ever since humans settled in one place, but today it is beginning to be looked at as an integral aspect of urban and rural design as one of the factors to shape future development by including food production as a critical component of city development along with transportation corridors; residential, commercial and industrial zoning; and infrastructure issues of power, waste management and water.

To more effectively deal with global environmental issues, food security, and public perceptions of animal agriculture, food producers should reconsider how they locate, house, and manage animal facilities by adopting sustainable design guidelines that bring rural animal facilities into the mainstream of rural commercial building design and construction. This can be accomplished with architectural design that embraces performance guidelines that increase animal productivity, reduce energy consumption, use more durable and environmentally friendly building components, improve rural landscape character, provide more socially acceptable and understandable animal housing systems, improve worker and animal safety and health, and maintain animal biosecurity that are cost competitive over the building's life. The goal is to raise awareness about the cultural importance of designing sustainable rural communities and buildings for animals and production agriculture that reflect the highest standards of design excellence fitting culture, climate and place – whether rural, urban, or peri-urban.

Not long ago in America any trip to the agrarian landscape was enhanced by seeing animals outside in pastures on small diversified farms or in low-intensity migratory livestock systems. While these scenes still exist, most new large farms are specialized and use standardized confinement-type buildings designed and constructed for housing specific livestock because that is the most economical method for animal architecture. These confinement-type buildings result in far fewer animals seen outside on the land, creating the public impression that the animals suffer because they are confined indoors throughout most of their lives. Yet, animal care is the highest priority for the farmer because healthy and more productive animals bring more income to the family.

In the past the small, diversified farm was common and generally functioned well as a sustainable, self-sufficient unit. Since most people lived in rural areas they understood animal farming operations and the scale allowed for each farm to be mostly self-sufficient. Today specialization is the norm, and this shift in farming has strained the public's ability to understand how modern large-scale farming is practiced and their trust in the environmental regulations that govern animal agriculture.

Environmental protection regulations are based on the number of animal units. As the unit count goes up the regulations become more stringent, yet the public is suspicious that environmental concerns are not being properly addressed. This concern along with the public's uneasiness with their perception of "factory" farming and odor issues sometimes creates a social conflict between farmers and non-farmers. Also, the regulations generally are state wide and do not adequately address the unique land characteristics of regions within the state that may have a variety of geological differences.

Research is needed to continue to develop integrated performance metrics for sustainable commercial animal buildings based on production, energy, environmental, economic, animal welfare, workplace environmental health and social criteria that will bring large-scale facilities to the same level required for commercial building design and construction. These metrics will be effective when they optimize animal productivity, reduce energy consumption of fossil fuels and animal feeds, and maintain cost competiveness over the buildings life. To maximize performance the facilities will use more environmentally friendly building components, provide better working conditions for worker health, improve animal health by maintaining biosecurity, and help ensure increased food safety and security for the public.

The global impacts of climate change, population increase, food security, renewable energy, and health encompass both urban and rural regions worldwide – what happens in one part of the world affects us all. I hope the book makes a strong argument for linking rural futures together with urban futures to utilize the problem-solving process of rural design and design thinking as a strategic resource to bring creativity, innovation, and entrepreneurship to find ways that limited land and water resources worldwide can be better shaped and utilized. We all share the same planet and it is critical to find out how it is shaped for human uses today so that we do not eliminate the ability of future generations to shape theirs. The answer will require an understanding of both urban and rural futures, and we should keep in mind that we all live on planet Earth and it is the place we all call home.

Chapter 2

Rural architectural heritage

When mankind first developed the skills to grow plants and raise animals for food and fiber, a revolutionary change in human settlement took place. With the advent of farming an entirely new way of life emerged. In hunting and gathering societies people were always moving around pursuing food, but with farming people stayed in one place and worked with the land. No longer required to constantly relocate to find enough to eat, the early farmers selected a site for growing food, domesticated animals to help them in their work, and designed structures to protect themselves from the elements and others for storage. It began a new human relationship with animals and the landscape.

Recent research indicates that as these early farmers began to live in close quarters with other people and domesticated animals and started eating new foods a social and genetic evolution took place as humans developed the ability to digest milk and metabolize fats. With the rise of agriculture, and as population expanded, people started to migrate to new regions. Research shows that starting about 8,500 years ago early Europeans migrated from the region that overlaps Turkey today (Curry 2013).

As these immigrant farmers began to grow foods and market their products they would gather in places along transportation routes, sea ports, and river crossings to reach out to travelers and other farmers to exchange goods and produce, and socialize. Some of these crossings developed into rural villages, and over time some developed into cities, like Rome, Paris, London, and other urban areas around the world. It was this process of urbanization and the social ritualization of life patterns and rules to live by that formulated the governing bodies within a region.

Frank E. Brown, the eminent classical scholar from Yale University who was responsible for a number of excavations of early Roman sites in the 1930s, writes that to the Romans ritual became the customs, traditions, disciplines, and laws that they lived by. The form of ritual in Roman society is what created their architecture. To Brown, the greatest rituals of the earliest Romans were the cultivation of gods, the life of the family, and the ordering of the community and out of these developed an architectural character for each creating the patterns of cities and hill towns and the adjacent rural landscape throughout Italy (Brown 1961).

The Romans liked order and clarity in how the military operated and this carried forward in how their camps were laid out. The Roman landscape around the camps was also organized using the method of centuriation to measure land (approximately 710 meters square) and the layouts they did for farms and roads in Italy is still being used today. This idea of organizing the land was also utilized in America with the Public Land Survey System started in 1785 to divide the land on north/south and east/west axis into sections one mile square.

Ancient roots and European origins

Little is known about buildings for housing domestic animals during Roman times; however a mosaic from the floor of an early 2nd century AD villa in the Uthina (Oudna) region of Tunisia attests to the strong rural heritage and economic importance of agriculture to ancient African cities where trade in products with the centers on the north side of the Mediterranean Sea was flourishing. The mosaic was installed in the atria of the luxurious home of the Laberii family (Figure 2.1) and provides a rare glimpse of life on a Roman farm that was centered

2.1
A beautifully detailed Roman mosaic from the second-century Liberii farm villa in Tunisia depicting a small barn and a variety of rural scenes of life on the farm.

on horse and cattle breeding, and the production and processing of wine and olive oil and salt-cured products (Rostovtzeff 1957).

The center of the mosaic illustrates a barn with axial symmetry, high entrance door, and interior loft for storage. Scenes around the barn illustrate farming life with a man plowing with oxen, a herd of cattle approaching the barn, a primitive well, a man milking goats, another worker collecting olives, and a group hunting wild boar. The barn, with its central aisle, columnar structure and gable roof, and arched entrance was a simple plan organization and construction system that we call the basilica form.

This form was also adopted and utilized by Roman priests as a ritual space for worship. The central axis for circulation with left and right sides forming symmetrical lines for activities became the ordered structural idea for the temple, and the basilica form became the archetype for many churches and for many public and ritual buildings throughout Western civilization.

The basilica form with its central aisle and columnar structure also transformed later into the 13th-century ecclesiastic Coxwell Barn in England (Figures

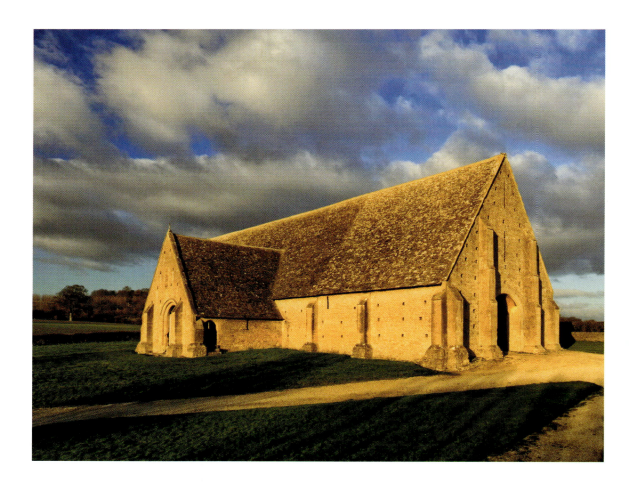

2.2
Exterior view of the Coxwell Barn in England. It is one of the great medieval barns following the Roman basilica organizational form that influenced barn construction all over Europe and in North America.

2.3
Interior of the Coxwell Barn illustrating the structural and axial symmetry of the basilica form use in the construction of Gothic cathedrals throughout Europe.

2.2 and 2.3) located midway between Oxford and Swindon. It also became the basic form for many of the great Gothic cathedrals constructed throughout Europe in the Middle Ages. Farmers by nature are ritualistic and using the basilica paradigm in designing and constructing barns they thought it might provide divine assistance, but also it was a very functional building pattern for managing and housing animals and storing feed.

In much of rural Europe in the 19th century control of the land was highly restrictive. The unavailability of land and the lack of a methodology for new families to become landowners were a major problem. The transfer of land from one generation to the next was traditionally to the eldest son. Even with equitable distribution younger family members had to either marry into a farmstead, or work for someone else, until they could purchase a small parcel. With land in America available at little or no cost it became a beacon for many young Europeans to become a landowner and start a new life.

Farmers carried with them their experience in barn types, construction methods, and farming practices. Upon arrival and homesteading in the new land they had to quickly learn the American ways of doing business, and had to adjust to the types of soil, climate, and economic situation in the area in which they settled. In his book *Peasants to Farmers* (1985), Jon Gjerde quotes an immigrant who wrote back to his family in Norway about settlements in America: "I can truthfully say that the only thing that seems to be the same are the fleas, for their bite is as sharp and penetrating here as elsewhere." Another wrote, "He who hangs on to the old ways when they do not pay will lose out. He must learn anew." In America, a study of barns is also a study of the experience of immigrants and their efforts to shape a new world.

In America there was a lack of hired labor to assist an immigrant farmer in farm work as in Eurpoe, leading to circumstances by which all members of the family, and sometimes their neighbors, had to contribute to farming operations. The lack of labor helped speed the invention and development of implements and machinery as a substitute for human labor. Once a farmer became aware of a new piece of equipment he had to have it, and the need to purchase created an emphasis on cash crops rather than basic farming just to take care of the family. Because of the lack of hired help, large families were essential as children became a source of labor, and farming was diversified to cover all of their needs.

Jon Gjerde's study of early Norwegian settlements in Wisconsin noted that children as young as six years old were driving teams of horses in the field, and I know this is true because my father did the same when he was a child on the family farm in North Dakota. At first, perhaps due to European traditions, women were primarily responsible for the care of animals, while the men were involved in field duties. Later, as rural society stabilized in agricultural methods, women focused more on domestic chores and the care of the house, while men took over the barn duties. Farming remained a family affair, however, even while the family work roles were changing.

The rural environment changed rapidly during the 19th century. Jon Gjerde quotes a journalist from Norway who wrote in 1869 about his amazement of the settlements he observed in America:

> If a person had last seen this region three decades ago everything would assuredly strike him now as a grand illusion, like stories in Oriental fairy tales. The forests have been cleared, the wild prairies have been plowed and transformed into billowing fields of grain, the Indian trails have vanished, the prairie grass has been replaced by cultivated species, luxuriant orchards surround the homes of prosperous farmers, good roads have been laid out, well equipped schools provide education and refinement, factories have been founded, churches with their lofty spires testify to the peoples' respect for religion. . . In sum, the progress is phenomenal, the transformations like a dream.
>
> (Gjerde 1985)

The journalist may have been somewhat carried away in his description about the speed of change, nevertheless, the ethnic heritage and cultural traditions immigrant farmers brought with them, coupled with the evolving way of farming, gave rapid form to the development of American agriculture and rural architecture. By creatively melding their traditions with the farming methods, indigenous soil, climate, vegetation, and geography where they homesteaded, the immigrants created the form of agriculture in America and its architecture. It is this synergistic mixture that gives each region of the country its unique rural character that led to the productive effectiveness of American farming.

Farmsteads

When the second Homestead Act was enacted in 1862 in America, the pattern of farming on individually owned farm units of 80 acres or 160 acres was firmly established throughout most of the country. In the Upper Midwest (Minnesota, Iowa, Wisconsin, North and South Dakota) the vast majority of farmsteads were established in the latter half of the 19th century. It should be noted that the land that was offered to homesteaders was taken from the indigenous people who had lived on it for centuries creating social and economic conflicts in North America that have never been fully resolved. While the indigenous people were isolated in reservations to fend for themselves, the Homestead Act was a solution and a methodology to provide land to immigrant settlers that allowed them to create farmsteads, rural towns, and gathering places for themselves to build a new form of rural American community.

The house, the first building constructed on the farmstead to satisfy the Homestead Act, was thought of as a temporary, utilitarian shelter only. It was the barn, as a shelter for animals, that received the most attention because it was critical to family livelihood and survival. The pride of a successful farmer was the

2.4
Sherping Farmstead in western Minnesota. This enormous barn sitting on a hill is one of the largest in the state. With the small, but ornate symmetrical house below it portrays a successful American farmer in the nineteenth century.

Rural architectural heritage

barn, and it wasn't until later, after the farm family had acquired some wealth and became aware of image drawings and plans for houses from magazine publications, that the house began to co-exist with the barn as a status symbol as seen in the historic Sherping Farmstead near Fergus Falls, Minnesota (Figure 2.4).

Farm buildings

Three types of working building were generally constructed on the farmstead to support farming operations: (1) barns to house animals and store the feed necessary to carry through the winter; (2) granaries to protect and store grain, corn, and other cash crops until they were needed; and (3) sheds to protect and repair and maintain farm equipment. The silo, a vertical storage system that improved the quality and ease of distributing feed, came into use in the 1870s. Once it was united with the barn, it became the standard working unit for dairy cattle operations for the next 100 years, like the large gable barn and silo in northern Illinois, shown in Figure 2.5.

The farmstead, an informal cluster of functional buildings built of local materials and arranged to maximize work efficiency, established the architectural character of the rural landscape. The multi-use barn, as the keystone of the cluster and located downwind of the house, was the largest building on the farm and many variations were constructed to work with local conditions. In the Upper Midwest, the multi-use barn followed the basic basilica plan, in either gable or gambrel roof design. It almost always had a hay loft for the storage of dried grass as feed for horses and dairy cattle through the winter. The hay loft was effective as storage and acted as an insulating blanket in the winter. Feeding

2.5
Typical gable barn in northern Illinois with silos and accessory buildings.

2.6
John Eidem farmstead in rural Hennepin County, Minnesota. It is a former potato farm now functioning as a living history museum for the City of Brooklyn Park.

was easily accommodated by dropping hay through openings in the floor to the animals below.

Modifications of the basic typology were made to relate to the specifics of each farm operation. Where potato crops were the primary source of income, such as in the rural areas north of the Twin Cities in Minnesota, the barn was designed with a drive-through to collect, clean, and bag potatoes for immediate shipment. In this region sheep were fed through the winter and their manure fertilized the potato fields. The Brooklyn Park Historical Farm, constructed by John Eidem in 1894 (Figure 2.6), is a good example of this type of specialized barn and how a family farmstead was organized around a central working courtyard. The barn had no silo since it only housed a few cows for domestic needs and horses for labor to grow and harvest potatoes, yet it also was located on the farmstead as the focal point of the farm.

A definition of the barn, from the 1860 Webster *American Dictionary of the English Language*, describes its many functions:

> BARN, *n. A covered building for securing grain, hay, flax, and other productions of the earth. In the Northern States of America, the farmers generally use barns also for stabling their horses and cattle; so that, among them, a barn is both a cornhouse, or grange, and a stable.*

America developed as an agrarian society and images of the rural landscape, farmsteads, and rural life were widely published by Currier and Ives on their calendars and other publications for both urban and rural audiences. These images have little to do with the kind of farms and life on the farm today, but they still remain as the nostalgic vision of rural architecture and rural life in the mind of most of the urban population.

The trend to fewer, but larger farms started in the 1920s during the agricultural economic depression, which squeezed many small farmers out of business. This trend to a large scale continues today as farming practices and global economic situations create fewer farmers and larger farms. In 1935, America had 6.8 million farms. By 1986, the number had shrunk to 2.21 million farms even though the number of acres farmed had increased. Today most of the farms that still exist are family owned and passed on in the family. It is almost impossible today for someone to become a farmer without inheriting the land because of the large capital investment that is required.

Following the Civil War, when large areas of the country was being opened for settlement, an array of agricultural business and cooperative entities developed that specialized in processing of grain, transportation, and processing and marketing of agricultural products. In the Upper Midwest, with its vast prairies that were plowed and converted to grain and animal farming, rivers provided water power for flour milling, and access to rail and water transportation provided an opportunity for the Upper Midwest to flourish as an agricultural center. For example, Minneapolis and St. Paul grew into a major urban center focusing on agri-business and food production with international companies like Cargill, General Mills, and Pillsbury.

Land-grant universities, established by Congress in the 1860s to bring agricultural knowledge and research to the developing frontier, contributed greatly to the quality of agriculture and method of farming through research and extension programs that disseminated knowledge to farmers. At the University of Minnesota the former dairy research barn (now the Ben Pomeroy Alumni Center for the College of Veterinary Medicine renovated by Miller Dunwiddie Architects) was constructed on the St. Paul campus of the university in 1916 (Figure 2.7). The

2.7
Historic dairy research barn at the University of Minnesota now the Pomeroy Alumni Center for the College of Veterinary Medicine. The facilities design illustrates the importance of agriculture in university research in the early 20th century.

design for this dairy research facility is typical of the importance universities placed on the architecture for agricultural research in the early part of the 20th century.

These noble buildings and the agricultural research conducted at the University of Minnesota, and other land-grant universities, helped create healthier animals, new farm products, and ways to increase production on the same land, and disseminated knowledge to prevent environmental catastrophe from natural phenomena. The innovations of farmers using the land-grant university research and outreach system (including technological inventions to conserve labor, and entrepreneurship in processing and transporting agricultural products) are what helped America become the world's leader in the production of food and fiber.

Historically in America the climate, landscape, soils, topography, availability of arable land, and accessibility of water all influenced how the farmstead and its working agricultural buildings were designed and constructed. The farmsteads reflected the tradition each immigrant brought with them, including each country's functional rituals of farming and their architecture and way of life just as other cultural traditions were manifested in division of labor, clothing styles, music, food, drink, dance, and the social life of the family and community.

English influences in America

Since the United States was originally established as a colony of the United Kingdom, England influenced the character of rural landscapes the most. In New England, the English traditions of farms and the many small towns established to support agriculture are where this influence is seen most clearly. Although the primary method of construction in Europe in the 17th and 18th centuries was masonry, in America the availability of wood and its use in the construction of buildings (using stone mostly for foundations and fences) created the unique visual character we can still experience in the New England countryside.

In England the earliest farmers lived in small villages and moved out into the fields to tend crops and animals similar to many rural towns all over Europe based on medieval traditions. Often the villages incorporated a village green (some with ponds) as the community gathering place. Later in the 18th century, by government decree through "enclosure commissioners" the fields were divided into smaller strip parcels with detached homes and barns as family farmsteads.

The English traditions that shaped America were the result of hundreds of years of development from early Celtic times to Roman Britain to Anglo-Saxon settlement to Tudor and then Georgian England. It was the act of parliament under George II that shaped the English landscape we know today and it became the model for early North America in the New England states, and in the United States English became the official language. After the American Revolution, with its strong emphasis on individual property rights as outlined in the constitution, citizen farmers and the democratic ideal defined the culture of the rural landscape and the rural villages that supported it.

Worldwide there are unique characteristics of the rural landscape within countries with unique climate and cultural dynamics influencing traditional architecture. Yet, all of the rural regions exhibit similarly the same connections between humans, animals, and the environment. Language, social, and cultural differences manifest in the architecture and the landscape of each country. However, when you look deeper, a rural village in China is not much different than a rural village in Norway even though the architecture reflects the uniqueness of their place (Figures 2.8 and 2.9).

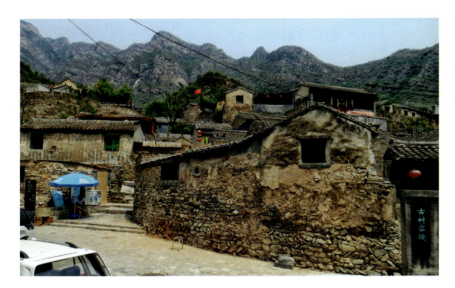

2.8
Rural Chinese village of Chuan Di Xia that now is a weekend tourist destination for residents of urban Beijing. It is located in the mountains west of Beijing.

2.9
Rural Norwegian village of Laerdal with its traditional wooden architecture in the old section of the rural town near Sognefjord in west Norway.

Rural Malawi and Tanzania (East Africa), and Mongolia

David and Claire Frame, retired teachers living in the rural community of Albert Lea in southern Minnesota, worked in the Peace Corps in the 1960s in rural Malawi in East Africa. They recently returned from a visit to the region and I asked them to write about the changes they observed over the past forty-eight years and their thoughts about the future of rural Africa. These are their reflections:

Recently we returned to Malawi after an absence of forty-seven years. We had served in the Peace Corps teaching school in a fairly remote rural area from 1967 through 1968. We noticed many changes had taken place throughout the country since we left and I would like to describe some of changes we observed. Of course our return trip was very short and we did not see but a sampling of the countryside, so it would be a mistake to conclude that the comments we make are as accurate as they might be if we had stayed there longer or had researched the topic more. We will limit most of our observations to rural Malawi (Figure 2.10), as we didn't spend much time in the big cities forty-seven years ago.

One of the first observations we made concerned the population explosion that had taken place in Malawi. This was very evident, especially

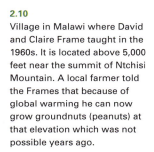

2.10
Village in Malawi where David and Claire Frame taught in the 1960s. It is located above 5,000 feet near the summit of Ntchisi Mountain. A local farmer told the Frames that because of global warming he can now grow groundnuts (peanuts) at that elevation which was not possible years ago.

Rural architectural heritage

in the cities we visited. The population has increased from around 4 million in 1968 to about 17 million today. Towns that were quiet little places when we left are now swarming with people on the streets and building expansion has taken place far from the small city centers that we knew. This population explosion drives so many of the problems the country is experiencing today. There is a lack of schools (although the increase in the number of schools is amazing), more land has to be cultivated to feed all the people, more trees need to be cut down to provide the fuel for cooking, more hospitals need to be built to take care of the sick, and more wastes need to be disposed of without polluting the environment. We have only scratched the surface of the huge problems an increase in population brings.

As we traveled from the southern part of Malawi to the central region, one of the observations we made was the deforestation in the country. When we left Malawi in 1968, we would describe the countryside as being a savanna ecosystem, primarily sparse open deciduous woodland. During the dry season and shortly before the rains came, the trees would be very colorful, similar to how our deciduous trees are in the fall of the year in the USA. We did not see the beautiful color now, due to the lack of trees. Much of the land that was once covered by grasses under the trees is now hand cultivated into ridges prepared by the farmers in anticipation of the planting season which would arrive shortly. Of course the land needed to be cultivated to produce the food needed to feed the growing population, but the trees were needed for fuel to cook the food. When we lived in Ntchisi 48 years ago, we purchased wood for our cooking needs from local women who would go out a short distance from our home and pick up sticks, bundle them up, tie them together, and carry them on their heads to our house. Today we saw very little wood being carried by women. Instead we saw men and younger boys with huge loads of firewood on their bikes, pushing the loads miles to where it could be sold. We also saw huge lorries loaded down with firewood transporting it long distances to be sold and large sacks of homemade charcoal for sale along the roads far from towns that people would buy and transport long distances to be used for cooking.

Over the last 48 years, not only has there been a huge increase in acres farmed, but also in methods of farming and crops grown. When we left Malawi 47 years ago much of the land in production was from a method called slash and burn agriculture. Farmers would go to fields that had not been farmed recently, they would use their machetes to cut down the smaller vegetation, let that vegetation dry and then burn the area off before cultivating their "new land." Now with the increased pressure for more cultivated land this practice has diminished greatly. As a result the land is being degraded faster as farmers are not enriching their soil enough with animal wastes, composted wastes, or commercial fertilizers. Two practices we did see that encouraged us were: (1) many of the ridges in some areas were contoured, which would lessen land degrading by water erosion;

and (2) belts of tall grasses planted also on the contour that would aid in controlling erosion. This was an improvement over the way farming had been done in the past (Figures 2.11 and 2.12).

Maize is the most widely grown crop in Malawi as *nsima* is their most basic food. *Nsima* is made from maize that has been pounded to make flour, soaked to let it ferment, dried in the sun, pounded again, and then mixed

2.11
Farm on a ridge in northern Malawi with farm buildings and steep slopes farmed by making contoured ridges up the hillsides.

2.12
A unique brick dome covered with mud and painted white for corn storage with freestanding structure above to provide protection from rain in the northern district of Malawi.

Rural architectural heritage

2.13
A proud and happy villager selling potatoes in a rural market in the central district of Malawi.

with water and boiled to make a paste-like gruel that might resemble thick mashed potatoes. Sauces are eaten with *nsima* and I feel it is only as good as the sauce prepared with it. Other common crops grown include rice and cassava in the hotter regions, groundnuts, and tobacco, mostly for export. The amount of tobacco acreage has diminished greatly as prices have plummeted. Sweet potatoes are grown more now than when we were there before and they seem to complement maize growing, as they can grow with maize and enrich the soil by nitrogen fixation. Irish potatoes were only grown at high elevations during the 1960s, however, today they are grown more widespread as can be seen by the pails and sacks of potatoes for sale lining the roads or selling in the markets and seeing "fries" listed on the menus in many restaurants (Figure 2.13). There are also some tree crops like bananas, coffee, tea, and macadamia nuts grown, but in limited amounts.

In 1968 David constructed a demonstration chicken house and yard out of local materials (reeds, bamboo, and grasses) so our chickens would be safe and the eggs would not be laid just anywhere. We are not sure if anyone paid any attention to what David was trying to show, however we did see many sets-ups something like it in both rural and urban areas where Malawians were raising their own chickens and getting eggs. At one of our former student's homes we also saw quite a sophisticated hog confinement operation, and this was in the largest city.

Climate change is taking place and will affect agriculture in Malawi. Even though we were visiting in the dry season, we sensed that it was much dryer than during the 1960s. We visited a rainforest on top of a mountain that we used to visit often, and even the underbrush in the rainforest was now dry and brown. A local farmer who had a farm at a high elevation told us, "We never could grow groundnuts [peanuts] at this high an elevation before, but now with global warming it is warm enough to grow them." He then gave us a gift of a big sack of groundnuts. Terrible droughts and floods have occurred in Malawi in recent years which severely affect agriculture, making it hard for the country to feed itself.

The cities now have very modern sections which are like cities all over the world; however, they usually have slum sections where the standard of living is very low. The villages we visited were much like they were years ago. One change that has taken place is in the construction of their homes. When we lived in Malawi years ago, most of the village and small town houses were constructed by making a framework out of branches and reeds and plastering this framework with thick mud dug from a hole, usually adjacent to the new house. Another method used involved a rectangular wood form about 10 inches wide by two feet long and 10 inches high to make the walls. Mud was tamped into the form and the form then was moved around the perimeter of the house; when one layer was done and dried then another layer was done. With either type of construction a thatched roof was attached. Today most of the homes are constructed using locally made clay bricks. Large holes are found near many houses, and the mud or clay used to make bricks that are then sun dried come from these holes. After drying on the ground, the bricks are stacked in piles with passageways underneath where fires are made so the bricks, even though low grade, are of better quality than sun dried bricks. Thatch is still seen on many village houses; however, more of the new houses have corrugated metal roofs.

When we left Malawi in 1968 there was probably less than 100 miles of paved roads in the country. Since then the major roads have been paved, some being fairly new and used very little so they are in good shape. Some of the older paved roads, however, are quite rough and potholed. Also, we were surprised at how bad the unpaved roads were. They seem worse than when we lived there years ago. We suspect the roads are heavily used as there are so many more cars and trucks and they have eroded more every year and Malawi doesn't have the equipment to maintain them.

Both of us thought village life had not changed a great deal since we lived there 48 years ago. Tilling the farm land is still mostly done by hand or with crude plows pulled by oxen. Planting is done by hand, as well as the hoeing, harvesting, shelling, thrashing, storing, and then preparing the food. Water is still carried by hand in many places; laundry is done by hand near the local hand pump or at the edge of a stream. The clothes are dried by hanging them on bushes or laying them on the ground. Women still cook the same food over a wood fire between three stones or bricks. People are still constructing their own homes. Women seem to be saddled with more of the work than the men are and life is physically very hard. Even in the village some dramatic changes have taken place. Cell phones are common, solar energy is becoming widespread, some villages have running water or a local well, and computers are being used. The people in the villages are living in two worlds.

What do we see happening over the next 50 years? We could predict gloom and doom with all of the problems facing a country like Malawi, but instead we will mention some things we hope will happen. The population explosion in Malawi will level off. Global warming will be slowed down. Solar energy will be used in new ways for cooking. A massive reforestation project will be implemented with mostly native trees being planted. Production of food crops are increased by improving seeds, improving soil, and conserving the water that comes in the rainy season. We would like to see the small farms persist that are labor intensive so more people do not migrate to the cities, and we would like to see more tree crops grown to augment the reforestation. If most of these actions take place, Malawi could have a bright future.

After visiting Malawi, the Frames traveled to Tanzania and toured a wildlife refuge where they were able to get a number of wonderful pictures of wild animals and birds in their natural setting. They also had an opportunity to visit the Maasai region where the cultural and pastoral system of rotational grazing that for over an thousand years has maintained a social and environmental balance in a fragile environment. The region has been declared one eight of Globally Important Agricultural Heritage Systems by the UN-FAO that represent landscapes of aesthetic beauty while maintaining agricultural biodiversity, resilient ecosystems, and a valuable cultural heritage. The UN-FAO define these agricultural heritage systems as "Remarkable land use systems and landscapes which are rich in globally significant biological diversity evolving from the co-adaptation of a community with its environment and its needs and aspirations for sustainable development" (Koohafkan and Altieri 2001). Today the Maasai continue to live in scattered rural villages and manage livestock herds raising sheep, goats, camels, and cattle as shown in this typical village that David and Claire visited in 2015 with a corral in the center (Figure 2.14).

A few years before their trip to Africa, the Frames traveled to north central Mongolia where the Nomads move between the grasslands and the forest. During migration they move their whole village from one location to another. They move when they need to find more food for their animals and load up everything, including their gers (tent houses that are sometimes called yurts), and move with their cattle, yaks, and horses to a new location as they have been doing for hundreds of years. Today they also move with a satellite dish and solar collectors to power their lights, cellphones, computers, and television sets (Figures 2.15 and 2.16).

2.14 (opposite)
Maasai village and cattle in rural northern Tanzinia near Kenya toured by David and Claire Frame at the same time they visited Malawi in East Africa.

2.15 (opposite)
Mongolian herdsman moving from one grassland area to another with cattle, yaks, and horses.

Rural architectural heritage

2.16
Mongolian ger (yurt) tent structure for living that is packed up and moved from one site to another.

Ichiu rural village in Japan

Rural villages in Japan, like others around the world, are struggling to redefine themselves in the 21st century. Andrew Wald, a former graduate student in architecture at the University of Michigan, lived and taught in rural Japan before returning to the United States. He currently is working as an architectural researcher at the University of Michigan. His studies focused on Tokushima, a region that is almost completely covered by steep densely forested mountains, and how two villages – Kamikatsu (which has become entrepreneurial to create a community-wide online business) and Kamiyama – have taken advantage of a government program to bring buried high-speed fiber-optic communication networks to rural villages. Here is what he wrote about his experience and knowledge of rural regions in Japan:

> Ichiu Village is an archipelago of tiny settlements tossed among a sea of mountains in the middle of Japan's Shikoku Island (Figure 2.17). Today, fewer than a thousand residents, mostly elderly, live in some forty hamlets

hidden among rugged peaks and dark valleys. I arrived in Ichiu in 2008 to teach at the local junior high, just fifteen students in a building that once held over 200. That school closed in 2010 and the elementary followed in 2015, now, Ichiu has no schools and little hope of attracting new families. Since 1975 Ichiu has lost three-quarters of its population and most of its remaining residents are older than 65, putting it in a category rural sociologist Akira Ohno calls *genkai shūraku*, or "villages on the brink" of collapse. Ichiu's vanishing communities are not alone. A 2006 Japanese government assessment of over 62,000 rural communities found that one in six surveyed was at some risk of vanishing in the near future and that 422 of them would disappear in less than ten years.

Places like Ichiu must choose to reject decline as the inevitable result of demographic and economic shrinkage. For example, the nearby town of Kamikatsu decided to invest everything in local quality of life and the well-being of its remaining residents, fighting the negative effects of shrinkage rather than trying to resist shrinkage itself. Kamikatsu is among Japan's ten most-elderly communities, yet its seniors are far healthier and more independent than elsewhere in the region. The percentage of seniors needing

2.17
Remote rural village of Ichiu in rural Japan where Andrew Wald taught in the local school.

Rural architectural heritage

special care is far below the national average and its per-person medical costs are just half of what Ichiu residents pay. Many credit their health and well-being to the *Irodori Project*, a community-organized online business by which elderly members sell local leaves to urban restaurants and hotels as decorations. Irodori members sell an average $12,000 worth of hand-picked leaves per person each year, generating a degree of financial autonomy. But more important, Irodori provides the challenge and mental stimulation of running a business, promoting physical and outdoor activity, and building on a deep local knowledge of the landscape. These efforts reinforce a sense of stewardship for the local environment (Kamikatsu has also launched a town-wide "zero-waste by 2020" policy); and reconnects physically isolated households to local neighbors and to the outside world. These factors have helped restore a sense of purpose, pride, and connectedness in a once-depressed community. Kamikatsu has shown that a community can grow stronger even as it shrinks.

Kamikatsu's neighbor, the former logging town of Kamiyama. has also drawn praise for its approach to shrinkage without decline. Kamiyama has another of Japan's oldest populations and its numbers have fallen from 21,000 in the 1950s to fewer than 6,000 today. Local nonprofit leader, Shinya Ominami, champions "creative depopulation," stressing preservation of community vibrancy even if it means upending tradition. Since 2011 his organization, Green Valley Inc., has promoted Kamiyama as a rural tech-haven capitalizing on fiber-optic internet service ten times faster than anywhere in Tokyo. Nearly a dozen Tokyo and Osaka-based IT firms have opened satellite offices in old farmhouses and traditional warehouses remodeled by a young architecture firm with local roots (Figures 2.18 and

2.18
Village of Kamiyama with old shops now functioning as high-tech offices and modern transportation.

2.19
Engwa house in Kamiyama now renovated into technology offices for a media company.

2.19). Ominami is aware that Kamiyama is still projected to shrink rapidly and notes that most of the new tech workers never settle in Kamiyama. But, he explains, they bring new energy and ideas to Kamiyama and contribute to the local economy and culture; as a result, more young locals are deciding to stay in the town. Ultimately, Ominami hopes to maintain a state of "sustainable shrinkage" through 2030 by managing a steady but predictable rate of loss. This will provide the community more time to anticipate crises, take stock of its needs and assets, and reinvent itself again if necessary.

The vanishing communities in Ichiu can learn from the examples in Kamikatsu and Kamiyama. In the face of immediate crises and uncertain futures, terminally shrinking communities, like Ichiu, should critically examine every possible option for preserving the common good and creating outcomes beyond decline by:

- Carefully examining the present use-value of their 'obsolete' things, including abandoned homes, businesses, and civic buildings, as well as infrastructure like roads, dams, retaining walls, and other geo-technical works. They are an important part of rural landscapes and their presence, condition, and use can have profound, transformative effects on local psyches. Ichiu should evaluate both conventional and radical ways to erase, preserve, reuse, and reimagine these things.
- Restoring connections to the local environment and strengthen interest in shaping it. For centuries, forestry and farming bound Ichiu residents to local ecosystems. Demographic shifts, climate change, and the decline of the primary sector have endangered these ties, leading to ecological imbalances and poor environmental decision-making.

Forestry was once the livelihood of mountain villages like Ichiu and it should rediscover responsible ways to use its mountains, rivers, forests, and farmlands not just as physical assets, but also as historic, integral parts of their identity.

- Addressing growing mobility challenges. As residents age and become more dispersed, they find it harder to access food and goods, healthcare, cultural and social opportunities. To fight isolation and inaccessibility, Ichiu must reconnect its residents to essential goods and services, to each other, and to the world. "New mobility" solutions should improve access through smarter movement or by reducing the need to move at all. They may include physical mobility, like improved rural transit and enhanced delivery services, or virtual mobility ranging from telemedicine, to on-demand services, to constant-presence technology connecting Ichiu residents with their children and grandchildren in cities.
- Considering the hundreds of former residents who migrated to the cities as part of the extended community and include them in planning the future of Ichiu. Many former residents and their families still return regularly and rural communities continue to hold meaning as *furusato*: imagined, if not lived, hometowns for people all over Japan. Ichiu should be redesigned not only for its permanent communities, but also to reflect the hopes and imaginations of its transient, dispersed communities living elsewhere.
- Planning for Ichiu's physical and cultural legacy after its last permanent residents have all moved on. Many of Ichiu's *genkai shūraku* have already begun to transition from active settlements into uninhabited landscapes defined by both manmade and natural elements. Short- and medium-term designs for Ichiu's residents today should also consider and shape their long-term effects on the regional rural landscape.

Ichiu and other terminally shrinking communities face a multitude of challenges for the present and many difficult questions about their futures. However, places like Kamikatsu and Kamiyama have shown that shrinking can also lead to opportunity. Communities can *grow* through shrinking and, in the process, may invent radical new ideas for what rural life can be. As rural communities in developed regions worldwide begin to feel the impacts of aging and shrinking, these Japanese villages may serve as important models for shrinking without decline. In 1989, when Ichiu had nearly triple its current population, novelist Haruki Murakami asked his readers what happens when a whole town disappears. "Nobody knows," was his answer then. Now, Ichiu and other shrinking rural communities across Japan are about to decide what happens – and they have the chance to show the rest of the world how to do it right.

Dong community in rural China

Dr. Xiaomei Zhao is a lecturer at the Beijing University of Civil Engineering and Architecture who has done extensive research on the rural cultural heritage of the Dong community in rural China. Dong is one of fifty-six cultural groups in China whose culture remains vibrant in terms of agricultural production with the landscape including daily life, social structures and spiritual beliefs, crafts and arts, buildings and spatial organization, and management of natural resources. The Dong community is socially organized by family relationships with leaders who are selected by the villagers to establish local laws to deal with daily affairs and organize public activities and celebrations. The Dong community has a long history of social organization and land management with no written language and as tourists have become attracted to its ethnic festivals and culture the boundary between authentic culture and tourism is often blurred (Figure 2.20).

Her studies focused on the social organization of one community, Zhaoxing, that centers around drum towers located in the center of each of five villages surrounded by other buildings (Figure 2.21). The drum tower is the center of activity for social gatherings in each village of the community and often there are competing events between villages with families focusing on other drum towers,

2.20
Dong community of Dali in a remote region of rural China studied by Xiaomei Zhao.

Rural architectural heritage

2.21
A family dinner at a funeral around the drum tower in Zhaoxing village – one of five in the Dong community.

2.22
Villagers in traditional costumes sing and dance under the drum tower during a festival in Zhacxing village.

with games and dances helping each increase their sense of belonging to their own drum tower (Figure 2.22). Dr. Zhao says that the best way to involve a community into their heritage to preserve it is to let the locals decide and manage it. That is a rural design principle that is as true in rural America as it is in rural China.

The critical issue for rural China is to find a way to preserve their rural cultural heritage while offering rural people the opportunity to embrace the impacts of technology, communication, and education as they choose them while maintaining their traditional way of life. I asked Dr. Zhao about this issue and here is her reply:

> I began my study of the Dong community in 2009 when I participated in the conservation plan of a drum tower in Dong village as a national heritage site. I found the Dong villages a totally new world for me – a different way of living, very kind people, and the wonderful buildings. Even though I had been to many other rural places in China and was always fascinated by vernacular architecture I decided to do my PhD research on the Dong villages.
>
> Like other rural communities, Dong had been changing throughout its history and I consider change as essential in continuity of a society or culture. There are different kinds of change. Some are forced by external impacts while others in a more indirect way and they are difficult to define the difference. In general, people avoid change to stay secure but their opinions may be altered by official propaganda, such as "modernization" and "poverty alleviation." The situation becomes more complicated when the concept of heritage and tourism business gets involved.
>
> Ethnic cultures at large are considered less civilized than Han. It is true that the GDP is much lower in ethnic areas like Gizhou; however, I don't think it is right to take the modern economic index as the only standard to judge. In the case of the Dong villages people are implanted that they are backward, and their facilities and way of living must be modernized. The signs of modernization include the brick buildings, automobiles, and of course money, while traditionally rice, the family, and fame used to be considered more important. Actually I am not against change as long as people reflect independently and not only depending on what they are indoctrinated by the authorities. I believe the new technologies would definitely improve the quality of living, but not necessarily at the price of the loss of traditions.
>
> Ethnic tourism started in the 1980s in the Dong area; however I do not see the local Dongs having much benefit so far. The presence of tourists certainly strengthens the Dong identity as an ethnic minority since their villages are labeled "cultural heritage." However, the tourists stop visiting them as soon as the locals modernize their living according to the propaganda (for example constructing brick or concrete houses) with their slightly increased income from tourism – although most of the revenue goes to the local government. As a result Dong people are confused. Don't they have the right to improve their living and why is their culture not considered authentic even if they are still the Dong? They do not understand what went wrong.
>
> There is another way of tourism exploitation, even worse than the previous one that only consumed the old things, and that is when new buildings are built and old buildings are renovated in the style "imagined"

as ethnic by tourists to meet their tastes which could not be found in a Dong village. Dong people are not considered competent to work in the new businesses and soon are replaced by outsiders. They have to sell their houses to the newcomers and are forced to leave their own villages under economic difficulties. They lose everything. What about the so-called heritage? The drum towers would probably be used as a performance stage to the tourists and no longer be a social center for the villagers – which I wish would never happen.

I think there are certainly possible methods to continue with the rural traditions while improving living conditions; however the current modes of tourism are not appropriate. People need to know there are other options to achieve happiness. The tourists are not supposed to be only consumers, but also to become educated from their heritage experiences with respect for other cultures and the local people as well. This experience of learning may be a better way.

Rural architectural heritage is unique to each rural region around the world and as changes due to population shifts to the city and farming practices are being developed it is important to remember that urban and rural issues have shaped cultures in the past and continue today.

Urban architecture seeks to connect and define the pedestrian experience by shaping public space. Rural architecture, on the other hand, seeks to express the human relationship with the landscape and animals in support of farming operations and social and cultural traditions. When urban and rural come together a new dynamic comes into play and as a result the peri-urban landscape around cities is a region that is gaining attention. Rethinking about how it might be sustainably (economic as well as environmental) developed may be the key to shape both urban and rural futures.

Chapter 3

Rural architecture and rural design

As the expanding world population has become more urban, how the land is used and concerns for future food security have become political issues which are influencing approaches to agriculture and land uses worldwide. For example the perceived need for larger numbers of animals on a farm, in order to be economical, is influencing changes in the way animal husbandry is done. This has led to larger and larger farms in rural areas with fewer people farming. The population shift has put a great deal of strain on small rural towns in figuring out how to survive. In contrast, small specialty farms, focusing on fresh food, have developed near large cities as a lifestyle of choice. These farmers, utilizing sustainable principles, provide food to urban populations. This movement, called community-supported agriculture (CSA), is in keeping with the tradition of small vegetable farms adjacent to an urban area. This is being reestablished as a way for urban people to contract with CSA farmers to obtain fresh food. Community gardens are also being established on vacant public lands in existing urban neighborhoods as part of this movement for fresh food.

As urban areas expand, there is a critical need to find ways to differentiate land-use in the urban/rural interface edge to allow for the many different competing forces for land. What is needed is a way that preserves the best of the land for agriculture, while providing for urban development in a way that utilizes sustainable principles while preserving nature, open space, and agriculture within and among residential, commercial, and industrial development – particularly urban agriculture where urban farmers grow and distribute through farmers' markets and cooperative endeavors, providing fresh vegetables and other commodities to an expanding health conscious urban population.

The St. Paul Farmers' Market is one of the best in America and it has been in operation since 1853. The market offers a wide range of produce and products that are locally grown within a 75 mile radius of the City of St. Paul (Figure 3.1). The Minneapolis Farmers' Market across the Mississippi River, on the other hand, also has a large number of local vendors selling only local food, but it allows

3.1
Local farmers selling products at the St. Paul Farmers' Market in Minnesota.

vendors to sell fruit and produce from outstate areas (like bananas that are not grown in Minnesota). They are both good markets, but St. Paul is very clear in what it is, and it is a delight to visit and see the same farmers year after year. Over time you get to personally know the farmers who sell, and while at the market you often run into friends and neighbors. One farmer I know, who in his other job was a city administrator for a suburban community for many years, has been selling food products in the St. Paul Farmers' Market from his family greenhouses for over 60 years starting out when he was a boy with his father and grandfather.

Rural change

American agriculture is undergoing rapid changes in the way farming has been traditionally done. Specialty farms that focus on dairy, beef, swine, poultry, or cash crops are the norm today. The demand for cheap food is forcing farmers to operate with larger and larger numbers of animals and acquire larger tracts of land in order to grow feed, dispose of waste, and amortize the costs of equipment and buildings. This rapid change has led to the proliferation of prefabricated agricultural buildings for large confinement type farming facilities.

Perhaps the most significant technological change affecting the appearance of farm buildings has been the advent of chemically treated wood in the 1930s, allowing wood to be placed directly into the ground. With the development of vinyl-coated sheet metal, corrugated for stiffness, and used for roofing and siding applied directly to the wood structure, the low cost of this type of construction has radically changed the appearance of contemporary barns. This construction system, called post-frame construction, was patented in 1953 and includes the setting of pressure-treated wood posts that prevents deterioration, to serve as a primary framing for the walls. Roof trusses are then attached, forming a single, continuous unit. Covered with metal panels they are inexpensive buildings for agricultural uses (Figure 3.2).

This kind of construction (sometimes called pole buildings) is generally built by prefabricated building manufacturers using engineering standards modified for rural use. Because they are standardized, they are inexpensive and can be quickly built. Farmers that purchase these systems, however, must be very clear in how they want the building to function and work because they become the designers who need to coordinate all of the construction issues. Without an architect to assist it becomes the responsibility of the individual farmer to coordinate with the building manufacturers and local builders the many site and building design, grading, structural, mechanical and electrical systems, equipment, and feeding and waste handling systems required to make the building work properly for their functional programmatic and economic requirements.

3.2
Typical contemporary post-frame and pre-engineered wood building with metal roof and walls used for animal housing.

Since they follow the same process these pre-engineered post-frame building systems often look the same regardless of where they are located or for what purpose they are built. It is the largeness, sameness, and lack of fit with the land that has created a lot of distrust in how animals that are housed in them are treated. This has led some of the major food vendors in America to change their buying procedures to only purchase from farmers who raise animals in a manner that allows the animals the freedom to move around. Also, these farms with large numbers of animals resulting in large waste handling lagoons and odor problems are creating social conflicts and location issues as a land-use issue that is being forced into the political arena.

In some areas of Minnesota, for example, limited land around rural cities is causing land competition, placing swine growers or dairy farmers who want to expand their facilities in social conflict with new housing developments required for a growing rural population. These housing developments, with many urban retirees who want to live in a rural area but have no background in agriculture, are in social conflict with farmers over odor and manure management (Figure 3.3).

In other parts of the world, like rural China, vast numbers of rural citizens have abandoned their farm life and moved to cities creating age distortion and social change that could lead to food shortage for China's rapidly increasing population. Minnesota is a state with a 150 year history of rural farming and coping with rural change; whereas rural China has a 5,000 year history of farming and living with cultural traditions that have developed out of human, animal, and environmental relationships with the land. Rural design, as a problem-solving process, is a methodology to address these kinds of issues to help find innovative and creative solutions.

3.3
Rural image illustrating the spatial relationship between animal agriculture and residential dwellings and the potential for social conflict over odor when the farmer wants to expand the number of animals on his farm.

Models of farm architecture

The following two farms are very good examples of farm architecture constructed with common building systems and intelligent thinking has worked well, even without an architect. They are projects where the owners have a passion for what they do, knowledge of what needs to be done, and the availability of land on which they could organize, construct, and manage their family farming operations.

The farm maintenance complex for the 7,000-acre Pine Lake Wild Rice Farm, along the Clearwater River in northwestern Minnesota, is an excellent example of transformation of previously low value, often flooded farm land into a landscape of high production value. The Pine Lake Rice Farm has done this by shaping the flat land into fields with ditches and pumping water from the Clearwater River into and out of the fields as necessary for wild rice, potatoes, soybeans, and other crop production with the highest level of environmental concern.

The world-class thoroughbred horse-breeding farm, Taylor Made Farm, near Nicholasville, Kentucky is an excellent example of a family that grew into the racehorse business with knowledge of the race horse business and horsemanship that was passed down from the father to his four sons and incorporated into the design and construction of their horse farm in rural Kentucky. It is a horse farm that is primarily functional exhibiting a high degree of concern for the safety and health of the horse with a remarkable sense of design and fit with the rolling rural Kentucky landscape.

These two farms are included because they were both designed and constructed without architects by families and will be passed down to the next family generation. Both farms exhibit a close connection between landscape and building where form follows function, culture, climate, and place and both were constructed over time with strong environmental control and sustainable principles.

Pine Lake Wild Rice Farm in Minnesota

This family enterprise is one of the largest in Minnesota producing cultivated wild rice, potatoes, and soybeans on approximately 7,000 acres of land that has been carefully shaped and leveled to draw water from the Clearwater River, which bisects the property, into fields and then to drain back into the river before harvesting. It is owned and operated by Paul and Kathy Imle and their son Peter, a graduate of Carleton College and the University of Minnesota with a Master's Degree in Agronomy. They expect that the farm will remain in the family and eventually be owned and operated by one or more of the grandchildren. The farm along the Clearwater River, and the building complex, has a number of specialized buildings, each serving a particular function, along with many tractors and combines and other equipment that need constant maintenance and upkeep. Constructed over time the complex was never thought out at once yet there is a functional organization that ties it all together with an aesthetic of steel buildings and post-frame construction that fits the landscape and climate of the site. The owners, Paul and Kathy Imle, describe the process they went through:

When constructing farm buildings in our area of northwest Minnesota there are basically four choices. Totally steel buildings offer large spans and tend to be used in large commercial applications. Stud wall or stick wood buildings are usually constructed on finished concrete slabs and utilize wood rafters that limit the span somewhat. Pole buildings are largely built on graded sites with gravel floors for machine storage. Quonset buildings can be constructed of wood or steel with concrete floors and are multi-use. All of these types of buildings are typically roofed and sided with steel. We chose stud wall buildings for our shop, potato warehouse, and chemical storage building because they are easily insulated and more efficient to heat. The Quonset Building was on the site before we acquired the property so we adapted it to our use. The remaining buildings are of pole construction for cold storage of machinery. We chose galvanized steel roofs and grey painted steel siding for all of the buildings so that they look like they belong together. All of our buildings were built by neighbors who were experienced in stud wall and pole construction.

The farm building site is located in a grove of trees providing food protection on the north, west, and east sides from wind and weather (Figure 3.4). The site has been graded and drain tile has been installed for good drainage. The nucleus building is the year-round shop which contains the office and headquarters of the operation. The site was selected to allow room for other buildings to be added as needed. The north side of the shop

3.4
Pine Lake Wild Rice Farm shop complex viewed across a ripening wild rice field.

3.5
The Central Building of the Pine Lake Wild Rice Farm where all farm management and maintenance activities take place.

has no doors and few windows due to our severe winters. The shop has a large open area for maintenance and fabrication, access doors are on the south side for ease of entry in the winter along with an office and parts rooms, break and coffee room, and an outdoor deck for shade for lunch breaks outside when weather permits (Figure 3.5).

Nearby the shop is an existing Quonset building used for large machine parts storage and parking service vehicles. To the west of the shop is a pole building for machine storage (potato harvesters and planters, combines, and tractors). To the east of the shop is the potato warehouse building, and the most recent building is for chemical storage. The fuel storage area was recently brought up to code to capture leaks and spills. Security is handled by sensors on all of the shop doors and windows that are connected to phones and law enforcement. We use security cameras around the farm that we move around to provide information on license plate numbers and pictures of trespassers.

Our farm is in compliance with the various rules and regulations administered by the Federal Farm Service Agency, The Federal Natural Resources Conservation Service, and state rules on wetlands and ditch jurisdictions. We also use best management practices for the various crops we raise and have a long history of conservation practices for farming for wildlife and planting trees. All applications of fertilizer and chemicals are tracked by computer and applied using the U.S Global Positioning System (GPS).

The Pine Lake Wild Rice Farm is an example of a building complex using post-framed buildings that are now the dominant farm building technology throughout the United States, and, because of their low price, are the envy of many other parts of the world. What once was a strong tradition of wood farm buildings reflecting unique landscape and cultural heritage has been replaced by standard metal buildings that look the same regardless of where they are built.

Rural architecture and rural design

Although post-framed buildings are based on sound engineering principles, their factory production methodology and indiscriminate use, making no allowances for the differences in site topography and climate, have contributed to the profusion of look-alike metal buildings throughout the rural countryside. The companies that manufacture, sell, and install these structures concentrate only on marketing their product, leaving it up to the owner to determine functional and aesthetic decisions.

The Pine Lake Wild Rice Farm illustrates how it can be done well when the owner has a strong sense of place, a concern for aesthetics and design, and fit with rural landscape and climate, and an ability to articulate what they wanted to all of the builders involved (Figures 3.6, 3.7 and 3.8). The American tradition of family-owned farming is illustrated in the picture of three generations of the Imle family – father Paul, son Peter, and granddaughter Sara, who may someday take over the farm (Figure 3.9).

3.6
The new building for storing and handling chemical activities on the farm.

3.7
Shop buildings with metal roofs and walls and fields beyond illustrating the architectural relationship with the landscape.

3.8
Large tractors and other equipment for planting and maintaining the variety of things grown on the farm, including wild rice, potatoes, and soybeans.

3.9
The three family generations running the Pine Lake Wild Rice Farm – father Paul Imle, son Peter Imle, and granddaughter Sara Imle (who may take over the farm someday). The photograph was taken at the farm on July 14, 2014.

Taylor Made Farm in Kentucky

This horse farm near Lexington, Kentucky is one of the top thoroughbred breeding farms in the world and is owned and operated by the Taylor family who settled in Kentucky in the 1760s. The Taylor Made Farm is today managed by the four sons of Joseph Lannon Taylor – Duncan, Frank, Ben and Mark – who grew up in the horse business when their father was the manager of nearby Gainesway Farm. The Taylor Made Farm was started in 1969 when Joseph Lannon Taylor purchased

3.10 (above)
The breeding center on Taylor Made Farm is located in the center of the 1,200 acre farm and it is the focal point of activities.

3.11 (left)
One of five stud barns on Taylor Made Farm where stallions are housed prior to breeding. Extensive landscaping is an inherent aspect of the farm's architectural and site character.

an existing tobacco farm that was used in a variety of ways until the 1980s when it was started to transform into the horse farm we see today (Figures 3.10 and 3.11).

The first horse barn at Taylor Made Farm was built in 1983 by Joseph Taylor, who was still managing the Gainesway farm until he retired and joined his sons in 1990. However, he was instrumental in guiding the farm's design and construction using his ideas and knowledge that he documented in his 1993 book *Complete Guide to Breeding and Raising Racehorses*. In the book Taylor describes in great detail about finding the right land (he prefers it to be rolling because of good drainage and the opportunity of exercise for the horse) and layout of the farm starting with a drawing of the arrangement of buildings, roads, paddocks, and pastures. He emphasizes the location of the home and that it should be on a high point and positioned to see the horses when enjoying an evening cocktail from the porch.

Most horse barns should have a sign posted on the side, he writes, "warning this building may be hazardous to your horse's health." And he goes on to describe how the barn is not the natural home for the horse and that they evolved as animals to be outside. The barn is necessary for modern horse practices which impose schedules and training on the horse. A properly designed barn allows the breeder to manipulate the horse with the least danger to its health and safety. He says that a horse needs a barn where he can eat a meal in peace without competing with other horses in the pastures and that "four hours a day inside the barn gives the horse time clean up his grain, lie down and take a nap." Since the horse only needs the barn to escape from sub-zero wind chills the barn should be designed and constructed to approximate natural conditions by protecting from winter winds and being cooler in the hot summer.

Describing the steps in building a horse barn, Joseph Taylor defines his thinking about the process:

1. Site selection, grading and drainage – and find a naturally high site to quickly remove water away from the barn during rain storms. Use an engineer to create a topographical map to help determine the optimum location for the barns and drainage system.
2. Floors – design and construct to allow water and urine to drain through it using a base of rock and sand covered with coarse asphalt and pressure-cleaned each year.
3. Construction materials – using the strongest materials available that require the least maintenance. Taylor favors concrete block for the walls because of its durability and flexibility and wood frame for the roof.
4. Ventilation – the most critical design consideration to avoid health problems for the horse requiring a barn shape to take advantage of natural breezes in the summer and close out cold winds in the winter without making the barn too warm. A high pitched roof allows for ventilation and skylights above the stalls, but he cautions against storing hay in a loft area because it can produce dust, molds, and chaff which the horses breathe into their lungs resulting in respiratory problems. He goes on to discuss stall size and design with doors openings aligned on opposite sides of the aisle along with windows into the stall to allow for good ventilation, along with detailed descriptions of hardware and doors with metal mesh for ventilation without protrusions on which a horse can injure itself. Also, that if the horses can put their heads outside over a Dutch door on the outside wall they will feel less confined.
5. Water, feeding, wash racks, right-angle turns, lighting, and storage areas along with fire protection and planning for emergencies, and maintenance issues are also discussed in great detail.

Taylor Made Farm is a delight to visit because one can feel the strong connections between the family that runs it and how they care for the horses and their wellbeing. The horse farm layout and design of the buildings and landscape was done in a way that expresses the family passion for breeding and raising thoroughbred racing horses in a manner that exemplifies the culture of horses and humans working together. Starting as a small boarding operation Taylor Made Farm has evolved in a world-renowned thoroughbred nursery, sales agency and stud farm (Figures 3.12, 3.13 and 3.14)

As described in Taylor's book it was "Joseph Taylor's passion and, wisdom and insatiable thirst for perfecting the art of horsemanship that has been passed down to his family." The Taylor Made Farm is today owned and operated by the four sons of Joseph Taylor shown with their father in Figure 3.15.

In his book Joseph Lannon Taylor emphasizes the principle that "every item of convenience is secondary to the safety of the horses." About his reason for writing the book he says that it "was to bring new people into the horse business, help others do well and remember that success is more than making money." About his life as a horseman he wrote: "The horse is the most noble and generous of God's

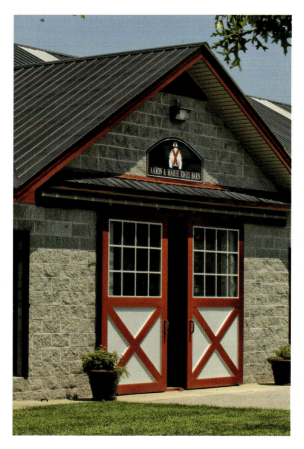

3.12 (left)
One of the horse stables showing typical details of the architectural and construction designed by Joseph Lannon Taylor, the father of the brothers that now operate the Taylor Made Farm.

3.13 (above)
Interior of a Taylor Made Farm horse stable with wooden post-frame construction and high ceilings for ventilation, sky lights, and concrete block for stalls and exterior walls that Joseph Taylor favored for cost, flexibility, and maintenance reasons.

3.14

Typical horse stall at Taylor Made Farm.

3.15

Frank, Ben, Mark, and Duncan with their father, the late Joseph Lannon Taylor.

creation. A good racehorse will give his life trying to finish a race simply because he was asked to do so. Allow yourself to be moved and humbled by this spirit. Treat all of your horses with the respect and kindness due such a gallant animal. Be good to the creatures entrusted to you" (Taylor 1993).

The design and construction of Taylor Made Farm in rural Kentucky, like the Pine Lake Wild Rice Farm in northern Minnesota, was accomplished without the formal involvement of professional architects and landscape architects, yet like farmers throughout history they worked with local builders using their own sense of their place on the planet and their climate to create a farm that is functionally and aesthetically special – one involving animal housing for horse breeding and sales and the other for growing and harvesting wild rice, potatoes, corn and soybeans.

An educational and economic dilemma in barn design and construction

Land-grant universities and agricultural extension services have contributed to the visual sameness and land-use dilemma as a result of research into standardized animal housing systems. University research has promoted ideas for the construction of confinement-type housing for large numbers of animals to increase production at lower cost. From an animal health and production perspective these animal housing ideas incorporate ventilation and control of the environment for better disease control, and veterinarians tell me that the animals don't care if they are outdoors or not as long as they are fed well, have water, and are protected from the harsh weather. As discussed earlier, domesticated animals evolved from a species that were always outdoors and animal rights activists have responded to this issue and are insisting that animals be treated more like they were historically born to live.

University-developed technical improvements in feed handling, waste management, and production, and methods to better manage large numbers of animals under a single operation have reduced human labor and minimized equipment and building costs. This research work has been largely focusing on animal care and health to maximize production, while the larger social issues affecting site location and layout and impacts on community and natural environments have been generally ignored, leaving it up to the individual farmer to wrestle with the building permitting process.

A number of pre-engineered building systems for animal housing are being provided by design/build companies, and they are the typical resource for building information and barn layout that farmers work with on design and construction. Historically, traditional barn builders understood how a barn worked and managed to combine a sense of style with functional layout and methods of animal husbandry, type of construction, and technology of their time. With the advent of industrial building systems this sense of style has been lost and new architectural models are needed today that will help re-establish a proper balance between function, aesthetics, economics, and the landscape. Models are needed that utilize the latest technology, help instill public confidence and agreement about the types of farming, and establish an approach to stewardship of the land in a regional area that allows for economic competitiveness in a global market place, yet remains responsive to community and neighborhood concerns.

To deal with this issue the Center for Rural Design outlined potential improvements to environmental practices on dairy farms in a study for the Minnesota Dairy Association. Financed by the Minnesota State Legislature, it was a study for the dairy industry in Minnesota that: (1) developed an environmental inventory of landscape features and resources, including human features impacting the dairy industry; (2) assessed the priority of importance of the features of the inventory; and (3) analyzed methods to accommodate and integrate the features through the planning and design process.

The study linked four high priority models for dairy farms – surface water, ground water, habitat, and community relations – and then combined them to create a fifth model for an Environmental Quality Assurance Program for existing and new dairy farms. It is clear from its research that the public does not like to have domestic animals spend their entire lives indoors. They want to see animals outside, and having cows outside where the public can see them is a good thing for the animals as well as the public, even though veterinarians tell us that it makes no difference to the animal (Roos et al. 2003).

In order to clarify where the architecture for agriculture might be headed, it might be helpful to understand the different types of farming and barns constructed around the country. In the Upper Midwest the types of farm buildings being constructed are specialized for the types and numbers of animals involved. Due to economic realities the numbers of animals on a single farm have rapidly increased. In 1930, for example, the average farm was diversified with a few dairy cows as well as hogs, cattle, and sheep. By the 1960s the small diversified farm was disappearing and the specialized farm was developing. Dairy farms, to remain competitive, became larger and the average was nearly 60 cows. Today, according to dairy economists, a minimum of 150–200 cows is necessary to be economically feasible and it is not uncommon to find farms with 400–800 cows. In some parts of the country there are a few facilities with as many as 10,000 cows! The economic reality today is toward fewer, but larger farms, and this trend will continue into the near future.

The movement in dairy farms is toward large confinement type cow barns built with the latest technologies in animal management. These barns are usually high ceiling spaces designed to maximize ventilation in the summer and eliminate moisture in the winter. The idea for this type is to shape the barn to utilize natural air currents with minimal reliance on mechanical devices for feeding and manure handling. They use drive-through lanes where feed from outside storage bunkers is distributed from a wagon with the cows eating through a headlock directly into the side of the alley. This type of barn, called free stall, allows free movement of the cows between their bedding stalls and the feeding alley with automatic waterers and milking at regularly scheduled times in separate milking parlors. Manure is usually scraped with small tractors and pushed into manure bunkers. The liquids are siphoned off into lagoons or holding tanks for treatment and then spread over fields.

The milking parlor is the heart of the operations of a dairy farm involving highly sophisticated equipment. The trend is toward low technology building construction with high technology milking equipment. Robots have been developed for milking operations allowing the cows to have free access to milking, but the method has not yet received universal acceptance due to costs and tendency for technical problems. The challenge for dairy farmers in the Midwest is to design and construct an economical and ecologically safe complex of buildings with ventilation that can change with the seasons, operate with minimal labor and equipment for feeding and waste management, provide isolation facilities for animal health, and utilize automated milking parlors.

Beef/sheep barns, on the other hand, are low-tech buildings built for open feed-lot operations, which are either covered or uncovered depending on the climate. With this system, the cattle seek their own comfort inside the shelter or in a wind-sheltered area of the feeding lot. Feed bunkers that are mechanically connected to storage silos are the usual method of feeding. Scraping techniques or slotted, pre-cast concrete floors are used to collect manure which drains into a treatment lagoon similar to a dairy facility.

Feed-lot type facilities require careful consideration of the natural influences of the site for orientation, ventilation, shelter, and wind break. In northern climates windbreaks and shelter are most important; in southern climates shading and cooling are most important. The challenge is to design a facility that recognizes natural forces and utilizes them to stabilize the environment throughout the year with minimal reliance on mechanical devices. Land form to integrate the facility into the landscape, control drainage and odors, and shield manure from public view is a design idea to explore for beef/sheep facilities.

Hog facilities are high technology, very specialized, and almost always designed around the total confinement concept. Pigs are housed in insulated, mechanically ventilated buildings to better control disease, market more pigs per litter, and maximize production. The major reason for the total confinement concept is to stabilize the temperature and distribute the farmer's labor and income more evenly over the year. Various combinations of specialized spaces for breeding, feeding, cleaning, treating, and marketing have led to unique areas for each phase of a pig's life.

The idea for hog facilities is to keep the buildings operating at capacity throughout the year with multiple farrowing operations. Proper ventilation and heat to maintain optimum temperature, control disease, feeding with automatic conveyors, and manure collection through slotted floors characterize the contemporary hog facility. To control odor, most socially responsible large hog producers use manure storage tanks with the least amount of surface exposed to the air, and a pumping system to inject liquid waste with machinery directly into the fields after the corn is harvested.

Since they are high energy users the utilization of heat recovery systems, methane gas production, natural ventilation, and odor control is the area of research that is most needed. Because of their potential to create a strong odor, hog facilities are usually located remote from human habitation. Public concerns about odor, waste handling, and the dangers of environmental damage when large numbers of animals are contained in one area will have a big impact on hog farming in the future. Research by the Department of Agricultural engineering is currently under way at the University of Minnesota to measure and monitor odor and environmental problems.

Poultry facilities are also specialized complexes depending on which program is involved – egg production, pullet or broiler production, broiler feeder, or turkey breeding, growing and finishing. The factors which determine the type of poultry farming is based on the market characteristics of a particular region resulting in a geographical situation. With the development of highly mechanized equipment "assembly line" techniques are now standard for poultry production and management within controlled environments. These facilities are often built near poultry processing plants that are located outside rural towns leading to many odor complaints. University research is focusing on this odor problem to identify odor standards that are acceptable and those that are not to an average person.

The storage of corn and grain are essential parts of the farmstead. They have evolved since colonial times with distinctive characteristics. It was the Native Americans who introduced corn to the immigrants and innovations to provide for its storage and drying led to the corn crib. Many farmsteads also had a small grain storage building to collect and store feed or cash crops on the farm. All of these accessory buildings are directly related to the region and type of farming that was done. The corn crib has changed the most as mechanization, hybrid corn, and commercial fertilizers became prominent, and have evolved from vertical sloped and open slat walls for natural drying of eared corn, to masonry silos and transitional complexes, to large round metal storage bins with mechanical drying of shelled corn. Today, these round metal storage bins are the most pronounced construction seen in the American rural landscape (Figure 3.16).

3.16
Large contemporary metal grain bins for drying and storing corn in Nebraska that are now typical sights along highways throughout the Great Plains region of America.

Machinery is integral to farming and has evolved from wooden plows pulled by oxen in Roman times to a variety of special tractors, combines, and field apparatuses on farms today. Machinery and equipment have always needed to be stored and repaired. Because the farm in America was located remote from town, the farmstead often had a blacksmith and woodworking shop to accomplish repairs as needed. In more recent times with better transportation, the farmer has a much closer relationship with the towns and equipment dealers for repair and service. On large farmsteads today, the large amount of machinery is stored and protected from the elements in a variety of shed or building types depending on the type of farming.

Rural building design guidelines

The following is a list of issues impacting decisions regarding the design and construction of agricultural buildings in the rural landscape that have been developed by the Center for Rural Design. Each issue also has a design guideline connected to it to help make decisions that connect function, culture, climate, and place:

1. The land should determine the kind of agriculture and the character of the buildings constructed on it.
    Design guideline: The characteristics of the landscape with its unique topography, climate, soils, ecology, watershed, and wildlife should be the primary determinant for the kind of agriculture, buildings, and long-term sustainability.
2. What is built should function well and be easily modified and upgraded for new technology and economic development.
    Design guideline: Operational methods, number of animals, labor-saving devices, waste and odor management control systems that impact both short and long-term planning are issues that continually change, and buildings for agriculture should be designed for easy modification and upgrading to meet new standards.
3. The building should pay for itself.
    Design guideline: There should be a fair return on investment, it should be affordable and be managed as a business operation, and become part of the agricultural infrastructure for marketing, transportation, repair and maintenance.
4. The buildings should be sustainable and function in the climate it is in and utilize available bioenergy capabilities in the agricultural landscape.
    Design guideline: Wind, solar, and biomass energy should be harnessed to help cool, heat, and ventilate animal housing and other working buildings. Windbreaks, passive solar heating, and manually adjustable devices to accommodate change from summer to winter should be incorporated to reduce energy requirements.

5. Agricultural buildings must work together as an integrated system.

    Design guideline: An agricultural complex as a grouping of working buildings that should be organized around a central outdoor space (farmyard) to facilitate circulation and service.

6. Agricultural buildings should make a visual statement.

    Design guideline: A good working building in the rural landscape should be considered as good architecture that fits well within its landscape and be maintained with neatness and care, have a positive public image, and be a good neighbor.

Post-frame metal-skinned buildings have the potential to be designed and constructed using these design guidelines. However, models are needed to illustrate the potential and how it can be designed to connect with regional historical culture as well as the future recognizing the diversity of people living and working in the rural landscape. I hope that stories of the Pine Lake Wild Rice Farm in Minnesota and Taylor Made Farm in Kentucky help the reader understand the myriad issues that a farmer has to deal with and how it can be accomplished, even without architects.

I hope the book may help point the way for new design thinking about architecture for agriculture and the rural landscape. What is needed is a new understanding and pride in the architecture constructed for agriculture to help create innovative and exciting rural futures. Futures that welcome urban tourists to explore and appreciate the rural landscape and the buildings constructed for animals and all of the other agricultural needs. Places that preserve the natural environment, enhance innovation and technology, and invite the arts and creative people to rural regions to help create a vibrant and exciting place to live and raise a family.

Chapter 4

Architecture and agriculture case studies

Over the years I have photographed and sketched agricultural buildings in rural landscapes that stand out as icons in the historical role of agriculture, reflecting ancient connections between humans, animals, and landscapes in the development of rural culture. In America the image of an Amish farmer plowing a field near his farmstead in Lancaster, Pennsylvania is a clear reminder of the historic working relationship between humans, horses and machinery on farms all over the country (Figure 4.1).

The great American architect Frank Lloyd Wright had a great interest in agriculture and he designed and constructed buildings to house animals and farming operations, including the Midway barn at his Taliesin complex in Wisconsin and the famous "Romeo and Juliet" windmill in 1916. Several other barns he

4.1
An Amish farmer plowing with three horses in a cornfield adjacent to his farm near Lancaster, Pennsylvania; a scene that was once very common in rural America before tractors.

designed were not built, but he often designed them with a close connection to the landscape with attached living quarters to the barn like the Walter Davidson Little Farms project from 1932. The architectural historian Vincent Scully, Jr. wrote about Wright and his connection to the land: "Wright exhibited a reverence for the landscape which seemed to him to mean that each building should, ideally, be uniquely suited to its special place" (Scully 1960).

Less important rural buildings, not designed by architects, that I have run across on my travels have an architectural language and a close connection to the landscape and agriculture that elevates their functional purpose. They include a beautiful stone house and barn in northern Iowa (Figure 4.2); a vineyard farmstead in Napa Valley, California with careful organization and detail (Figure 4.3); and an elaborate wood-framed horse barn in Nashville, Tennessee (Figure 4.4).

4.2
An attached stone house and barn in northern Iowa built with readily available materials which immigrants from Europe knew how to use. It is typical of how the art and skills of the farmer-influenced farmstead design and construction.

4.3
Historic vineyard farm in Napa Valley, California with wooden house, barn and water tower carefully composed and constructed as functional working units for living, housing animals, and growing and harvesting grapes for the wine industry.

Architecture and agriculture case studies

4.4
A large wooden horse barn in Nashville, Tennessee reflects the important status of the horse on this historic farmstead. Constructed with craftsmanship and decorative detail, it is functionally organized with multiple locations for loading hay, doorways for horse handling, and dramatic cupolas for ventilation.

Storage has always been an issue for farmers, including feed for animals and crops that are harvested and intended to be sold. Corn is one of the easiest grains to store and structures to do so have been a feature of American farmsteads since colonial times. It is a simple utilitarian building constructed to store and preserve corn until later, when cash is needed or the price is right, to sell to the market, like this oval corn crib constructed with clay tile in northern Iowa (Figure 4.5). Today, however, it is a building type mostly constructed on farms with corrugated galvanized steel in round containers that loom large on rural landscapes. They are often constructed in a multiple series of identical bins for drying and storing grain.

4.5
A typical corn crib from northern Iowa commonly constructed on farms throughout the Midwest from the late 19th century. This one was constructed with clay tile and had a drive-through unloading lane

Sometimes a new agricultural production facility that seems to fit into its rural landscape jumps out as I travel along a rural highway. A case in point is the Wensman Seed Company production plant along Highway 10 in northwestern Minnesota that is owned by Ag Reliant Genetics. It is a contemporary industrial design that is all white with a variety of functional forms that fits well into the green summer landscape or white winter snow. Even without architects the corporation that built the facility seemed to have an innate sense of organization and aesthetics in how to tie all its parts together rather comfortably in the rural landscape. The management worked with a design/build contractor and coordinated the design and construction by themselves as the interface with seed manufacturing system suppliers and mechanical and electrical contractors. They describe their decision about why it looks the way it does as "white is a nice clean color and we have tried to maintain a very professional look on housing our value added philosophy." It is a contemporary agricultural building that feels quite at home on the open prairie of northwestern Minnesota (Figure 4.6).

In recent years the most pronounced connection between architecture and agriculture has been in the development of wineries around the globe and the architecture they construct to help market their products. These buildings have owners with a very strong commercial interest in expressing the landscape within which they operate by constructing visitor centers that become tourist attractions to sample and purchase wine and learn about their art of wine-making. Some of these wineries have visitor facilities designed by famous international architects like Frank Gehry, Zaha Hadid, and Foster + Partners, yet the buildings they have designed and constructed seem to me to be simply imports of their architectural

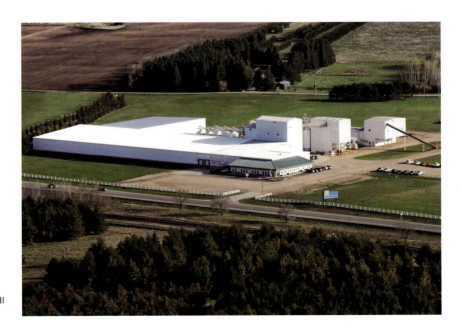

4.6
Wensman Seed Company plant in northern Minnesota along Highway 10. Designed by its owners, working with a design/build construction process provides a good example of architecture without architects that fits well into its prairie landscape.

Architecture and agriculture case studies

styles rather than something new to fit with the unique agricultural landscape or rural culture within which they are located.

Several new winery visitor centers that do have a strong relationship with the landscape, climate, and culture of place are beautiful buildings designed by excellent architects. These wineries plus several other agricultural buildings from around the world are included as case studies for the clear statement they make about their connections between architecture and agriculture.

Sokol Blosser Winery, Dayton, Oregon, USA

ARCHITECT: BRAD CLOEPFIL, ALLIED WORKS

Allied Works is an interdisciplinary architecture and design practice founded by Brad Cloepfil in 1994 with offices in New York City and Portland, Oregon. Their work has been defined by a "deep concern for the landscape, human experience and craft, as well as the preservation and enhancement of the public realm." The Sokol Blosser Winery is based on traditional agricultural buildings in the region (Figures 4.7 and 4.8), and the following is the architect's statement regarding how the winery building and site fit together in a rural setting:

4.7
Sokol Blosser Winery in Oregon showing the main entrance to the visitor center with wood being used in a variety of ways to define spaces and functions.

4.8
Sokol Blossser Winery deck terraces and view to valley with dramatic use of wood siding and paneling to allow light and shape views.

The Dundee Hills are characterized by rolling grasslands, oaks and Douglas fir. The winery sits on a knoll with panoramic views of the Willamette Valley below. This prospect is enhanced by the geometric rows of vines that follow the contours of the earth giving rhythm and measure to the landscape.

The design began by marking the land, cutting a series of gardens, terraces, and paths in the face of the hill. On an upper terrace the building lifts from the earth, carrying a green roof with it. The new, nearly 6,000-square-foot tasting room emerges as a solid mass of wood sliced open and cared out in response to natural light, serene views and the rituals of wine tasting. It is a "transparent solid" – a building that catches and holds space as one passes through it. The building shifts and bends perception as it foreshortens vistas and distorts depth, all in service of intensifying the specificity of the visitor's experience.

The elemental form and materiality draw inspiration from the earliest agricultural buildings in Oregon. Built of hemlock, fir and cedar, they have a close connection to the land and were constructed with an economy and sense of grace. The floors, walls and ceiling of the interior are clad in

Architecture and agriculture case studies

roughhewn cedar, and the exterior is a striated and random series of cedar boards. The faceted surfaces create a unified body of wood that hold the visitor to the hillside while connecting to the landscape beyond.

The significance of this project is how it has created a visitor portal into one of the earliest wineries in Oregon, developed by the Sokol Blosser family that has been producing grapes on the 120-acre estate since 1978. The new building provides spaces for sampling wine products, but also views to the beautiful Yamhill County countryside.

Designed to be net-zero in energy with a future site solar array to provide 100 percent of the power for the new building, the contemporary building design and site are integrated for functional and aesthetic purposes as an exemplary architectural showplace of the rural estate. The Sokol Blosser Winery is now under the management of sister and brother co-presidents, Alison Sokol Blosser and Alex Sokol Blosser. It is an exemplary place that one wants to visit, admire the architecture, and enjoy a glass of Oregon wine overlooking the beautiful vineyards (Figures 4.9, 4.10 and 4.11).

4.9
Sokol Blosser Winery seating terrace showing wood construction throughout. It is a nice place to sit and sip wine and enjoy the rural landscape.

4.10
Sokol Blosser Winery interior view to tree enhancing indoor/outdoor visual connections that enhance the relationship of the building to the vineyard landscape.

4.11
Sokol Blosser Winery open space between two parts of the visitor center with contrasting stains highlighting entrances into the complex.

Architecture and agriculture case studies

Deepwater Woolshed near Wagga Wagga, Australia

ARCHITECT: PETER STUCHBURY

This beautiful agricultural building in a rural area of New South Wales, Australia was designed by Peter Stuchbury (recently awarded the Australian Architects Gold Medal) for the owner of the sheep farm, Michael Darling, and farm manager Andrew King. It is a beautiful building that responds to place, culture, and climate as well as function illustrating a new kind of architectural thinking for agricultural buildings in the 21st century (Figures 4.12 and 4.13). The architect describes the project as follows:

> The Bulls Run property, 50 kilometers northwest of Wagga Wagga in regional New South Wales, is a project that rethinks woolshed design. The program initiated an optimal work environment for shearers, while meeting the highest quality standards for wool preparation and sheep handling. Orientation and siting of the woolshed were integrally considered such to

4.12
Deepwater Woolshed in New South Wales, Australia, framed between rolling grassland and a series of individual trees in the rural sheep country of Australia.

4.13
End view of the Deepwater Woolshed illustrating simple use of materials to shape space in response to culture, function, climate, and place.

benefit all logical outcomes. Managing major temperature changes, particularly extreme heat, was a major design objective.

Roof overhangs are increased so that the walls of the building are shaded and to provide for undercover sheep storage and access. The roof material is a self-spanning structural profile, permitting a simplified portal frame system. Strip skylights within the roof provide for required natural lighting levels. Reticulated irrigation sprays water over the roof, cooling it in summer. On the south-western side large suspended screens protect from prevailing winds. In addition, water drips over the screens and breezes pass through, cooling the temperature within the shed. Heat is caught off both sheep and shearers, and redirected away from the workers.

The entire structure is bolted together with linings, claddings, and floors screw fixed making the entire shed completely demountable eliminating the possibility for future waste should relocation or recycling become required. The concern for a quality work environment is ground breaking and its use of knowledge, materials and techniques sets new quality standards for an Australian icon.

Architecture and agriculture case studies

Sheep handling in sheds is a frustrating task. Yards, gates, directional flow and personnel requirements have all been addressed in the back of house yard design. The emphasis remains with forward movement. Below the shed, people-friendly and large count-out pens reduce the demand on turnaround attendance for sheep handlers. Long throw sheep chutes reduce the potential for accidents and allow the sheep to exit easily into count-out pens. Sheep movement in, under, and around the shed is required to be a minimum effort so anti-glare and shade devices are employed to reduce the potential for baulking by sheep.

The foundation of spatial decisions at Deepwater Woolshed were directed by an accurate sheep flow design coupled with the most convenient shearing board and wool handling area. If those issues were ignored the shed's success is lessened. Other design decisions sprung from strategies to provide a more intimate shearers' recreational zone, and isolated areas of noise (machinery shed), chemicals (a separate building) and dust. Spaces were designed for ease of human and animal movement coupled with adaptable structure and appropriate durability.

4.14
Deepwater Woolshed interior with sheep, illustrating the careful organization and layout of space and day lighting for both human and animal safety and welfare.

Architecture and agriculture case studies

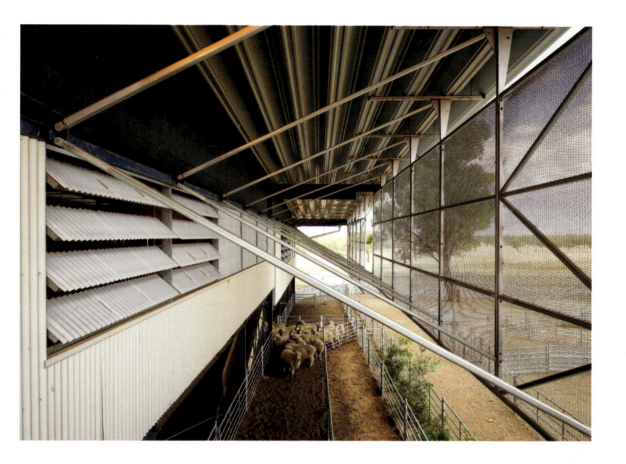

4.15
Deepwater Woolshed detail of roof overhangs to protect from the sun, windows for light, and louvers to control ventilation without depending on electricity.

The Deepwater Woolshed project responds architecturally to the sheep-shearing operations typical of the sheep industry worldwide, but in this case it also responds to the uniqueness of its climate, culture, and landscape to find an economical and sustainable, yet expressive, architectural form. It is a project that demonstrates the innovative synergism that can emerge when a creative architect works closely with farm management to provide a building that meets their needs in a very creative and economical way. It is an excellent example of a contemporary agricultural building in the 21st century that uses materials and technology to resolve functional and climatic issues while expressing place in a unique and beautiful way (Figures 4.14 and 4.15).

Dalaker/Galta Farm House on Rennesoy Island, western Norway

ARCHITECT: KNUT HJELTNES

This farm house is constructed on the foundation of a former pig sty on a sheep farm on Rennesoy Island, outside Stavanger, in western Norway (Figure 4.16). It is an interesting and beautiful insertion of a contemporary building design into a traditional rural context. It was a unique design challenge that inspired the architect, Knut Hjeltnes, to design the rural house for his client, Turi Dalaker, who is a doctor and local politician, and her husband, Tom Galta, who is a photographer. Hjeltnes describes the house and its design as follows:

> The Dalaker/Galta house is very much thought of as part of its agricultural landscape because my client is taking over the farm from her parents. The architectural relationship of the insertion of the new house is twofold in the agricultural setting and the design of the house itself. The new house is pulled away from the existing farm buildings because the old buildings make up a complete entity ("et tun" in Norwegian) and it would be difficult to place a new building into this "perfect" entity. The selected site was a no-brainer – it was close to the old farmstead and a beautiful location with an existing foundation (old pigsty) – especially since a new house by default would have a different scale.
>
> Another factor is the benefit of having 100 yards between the two houses, not so much when her parents are still living there, but more so in the future when the old house might be rented out. The third factor influencing the design is the sheer beauty of the site itself with the existing old stone walls, large maple trees and moss-covered stones, and it was

4.16
Dalaker/Galta House on Rennesoy Island on the west coast of Norway with the new house in foreground and historic barn and house in the background. The image illustrates the rugged landscape and stone walls to divide fields in rural Norway.

economically attractive to use the former pigsty as part of the construction. The last and most important factor is that removing the new house from the old farm is the liberation this gives to the design of the house – we could design the new house with more freedom. Since the budget was very low we selected an outer cladding of fiber reinforced concrete panels that are prefabricated, inexpensive, age well, are maintenance free, and have an association to smaller industrial buildings randomly scattered around the island (Figures 4.17, 4.18, and 4.19).

The house itself is formed with considerable attention to life on the farm following traditional rural houses. The old pigsty foundation (the ground floor) is dedicated to storage and laundry. This is where the "dirty" daily entrance is where you leave and arrive from the sheep stable at the old farmstead or from the fields. The upper floor is the "clean and urban" part of the house. The kitchen is the same size as the living room with no formal dining room similar to traditional farm houses. The kitchen is where most of the daily life takes place.

4.17
Dalaker/Galta house on the foundation of a former pig sty with sheep grazing.

4.18
Dalaker/Galta house and the adjacent rocky landscape that inspired its form.

Architecture and agriculture case studies

4.19
Dalaker/Galta corner detail showing integration of the house with the rugged Norwegian countryside.

Since the new house was built a wing has been constructed that contains two bedrooms for the children and a common living room for them. The underside of the new addition provides covered car parking. In the future the new addition will transform into a photography studio for Tom Galta.

As an architect with strong Norwegian heritage I have been to Norway a number of times and I can feel the sensitivity Hjeltness achieved in his design and the relationship between the historic farm and his modern house. In Norway, as it is around the world, rural change is happening very quickly and one methodology the government of Norway has done to preserve rural character and promote rural economic sustainability is to construct tourism routes with beautiful visitor centers inserted into spectacular rural natural landscapes to promote tourism. One of these tourism centers is the Glacier Museum designed by the late great Norwegian architect Sverre Fehn (Figure 4.20).

4.20
The Glacier Museum in Norway designed by the late great Norwegian architect Sverre Fehn. It is one of a number of rural visitor centers and other facilities constructed by the Norwegian government to enhance rural tourism.

Since most of the economic activity in Norway is urban that is where most of the architects work, and Knut Hjeltnes says that there were some very nice agricultural projects back in the 1960s because of growth in the rural economy, but not much since. Hjeltnes is one of the very few architects that have recently designed a contemporary rural project with connections to agriculture in Norway.

Mason Lane Farm Operations Center, Goshen, Kentucky, USA

ARCHITECT: DE LEON & PRIMMER ARCHITECTURE WORKSHOP

The Mason Lane Operations Center in rural Kentucky consists of two adjacent barns – Barn A for storage and work areas and Barn B for storage of hay and equipment – along with a refueling and storage station that supports a 2,000 acre property used for agriculture, recreation, wild life habitat, and conservation purposes. The farm is owned by Eleanor Bingham Miller and the architects worked closely with her to develop the architecture that utilize typical pre-engineered wood frame construction in an extraordinary way (Figures 4.21 and 4.22). The architects describe their design approach and the project as follows:

Architecture and agriculture case studies

4.21
Mason Lane Farm in rural Kentucky showing Barn A on the left that is a conventional pre-engineered post-frame building with corrugated metal panels on the roof and walls for year-round use; corrugated metal corn crib, and Barn B that is an open-storage building for hay and equipment.

4.22
Mason Lane Farm, interior of Barn A with pre-engineered wood roof trusses.

Rooted in the simplicity of regional farm structures and local building traditions, the project employs sustainable strategies that are decidedly "low-tech," favoring conventional construction methods and ordinary materials over specialized systems. In particular, the project implements strategies that take advantage of the cross-synergies between site and building design, focusing on a holistic approach where both components work as a single integrated system. For reasons of both economy and ease of maintenance, the farm complex utilizes simple, passive strategies that are specifically based on an understanding of the regional climate and the nuances of the landscape. The project has been received a Leadership in Energy and Environmental Design (LEED) Silver Level Certification.

The project location was determined by several pre-existing site strengths: (1) its central location within the entire farm property, (2) proximity to existing utility lines and road infrastructure, (3) adjacency to a tree windbreak line, (4) existing visual screening from the highway through natural topography and vegetation, (5) a pre-cleared and graveled area previously used for farm debris storage, and (6) its proximity to the onsite farm manager's house – only 800 feet away. Consolidating the various programmatic elements into two large barn buildings and a grain silo (in order to minimize building footprints), the majority of the project site is allocated to the circulation and access requirements of large-scale farm equipment. The remainder of the pre-existing cleared area was restored with native planting.

Because facility water usage is minimal and site landscaping is limited to native and regionally adapted plants that do not require irrigation, site-wide stormwater strategies focus on returning run-off to replenish local aquifers. Taking advantage of the existing topography, the porous, drivable gravel surfaces are pitched to channel stormwater into two "rain gardens" planted with native vegetation that provide additional wildlife habitat. Excess run-off is collected within these basins and allowed to percolate back into the groundwater table. In order to minimize maintenance, building roof gutters are eliminated and replaced with "site gutters," a system of drivable, shallow concrete channel swales located and aligned below each roof eave, which directs stormwater to the collection basins. In this manner, the site and buildings work together as a large-scale integrated drainage system. Other than the footprint of the barn buildings, the entire site is pervious. Additionally, the high solar reflectance index (SRI) values of both the gravel surfacing and building roofs reject solar heat and offset the "heat island effect."

Working within the pre-existing cleared area of the site, the two buildings (Barn A and Barn B) are arranged to frame an outdoor work courtyard, visually screening farm equipment from the north and south. This configuration allows for the consolidation of outdoor lighting requirements to an internalized site zone and away from the farm complex property perimeter. Since the farm also serves as an astronomical observation site for local university students, rural "dark sky" conditions are preserved through controlled design of illumination levels within the project site and the complete elimination of light power densities beyond the project boundary.

Barn A, with fully enclosed storage and work areas, utilizes a conventional prefabricated wood truss frame clad with corrugated metal panels. The design strategy is reductive and is intended to eliminate the use of finish materials. By emphasizing the layering of construction, building elements that are typically hidden (such as building substrates, fastening screws and alignment lines) are incorporated as design features and reinterpreted as "finish" materials. Specific to the function of the two conditioned work areas within the barn, insulated concrete floor slabs are embedded with warming coils heated by an external wood-fired boiler (fueled by wood debris from the farm). During winter months, comfortable work area temperatures are maintained – even with the garage doors fully open – from the ambient heat of the heated concrete slab. Natural light, ventilation and views are provided to all interior spaces through full-height operable windows which are working in concert with a whole-house fan to draw air through the building. During the few summer months when local humidity is extreme, a non-CFC-based refrigerant AC unit operates on an as-needed basis to condition the farm manager's office.

Barn B, a large covered shed used to store both hay and equipment, is clad in a lattice grid of locally harvested bamboo sourced only 35 miles from the project site. Considered a fast-growing invasive "weed," the bamboo is a material nod to the square-bale hay that is stacked at each end of the barn, while also providing a breathable skin that allows the hay to dry through natural ventilation. Additionally, the bamboo skin provides an important structural resiliency in relation to the mobile farm equipment. Because bamboo is a large-scale "grass" with fused growth nodes located along its length, the plant material can absorb accidental bumps with farm equipment – incurring only localized splinter damage that springs back into shape without compromising the integrity of the entire stalk. The bamboo stalks are tethered together in three assembly layers through galvanized rebar wire ties that are tightened by hand-twisting with an awl. This simple assembly process allows for adjustment of the building lattice skin as the bamboo stalks dry. The wire tie loop ends are left exposed and extended as a secondary wall texture visible at close range. Since Barn B is a covered open-air structure vulnerable to wind-uplift forces, the concrete drainage channels below its roof eaves also function as a counterweight through an interlocking detail with the column concrete footings below grade.

A particular focus on recycled and locally/regionally sourced materials informed the choice of construction systems and finishes. The building materials are comprised of the prefabricated wood trusses, pressure-treated wood framing, high fly-ash concrete slab on grade with insulation/drainage board containing 40 percent recycled content, concrete piers, prefinished corrugated metal panels (siding and roof) with 49 percent recycled content, locally harvested bamboo, galvanized wire ties, insulated glazing (fixed and operable windows), and wire-glass (Figures 4.23, 4.24 and 4.25).

4.23
Mason Lane Farm, end view of Barn B showing bamboo screen.

4.24
Mason Lane Farm, interior of Barn B with hay storage.

Architecture and agriculture case studies

4.25
Mason Lane Farm with Barn B from adjacent hay field.

Although the project is grounded primarily on passive heating and cooling strategies, several conventional mechanical approaches are used during extreme climate conditions like humid summer months. They include the following: Inslab hot-water coils heated with a wood-fired boiler (renewable, onsite energy source from agriculture waste wood) with propane fuel back-up, whole-house ventilation fan, inverter-controlled ductless split system AC unit (non-CFC-based refrigerant), florescent light fixtures on IR sensors and timers with manual override, low-flow toilet and low-volume water fixtures integrated to an adjacent septic field.

The Mason Lane Farm Operations Center, despite its beautiful design and construction, is an example of how guidelines and building codes that are primarily developed for urban buildings are difficult to interpret for agricultural buildings. For example LEED (which is the methodology most often used today to determine the sustainability aspects of a building design with four different levels of performance) and the architects describe the challenge:

> As a project type, the agricultural facility does not fit easily within LEED performance criteria – no precedents exist as a baseline case. The programmatic necessity of building new structures on prime farmland in order to facilitate agricultural production is counter intuitive to LEED site design guidelines. Specific functional needs, like providing adequate area safety lighting for operating farm equipment within a rural environment, present

new challenges when applying design criteria such as maintaining "dark sky" conditions. As such, the reinterpretation of LEED criteria within the agricultural context necessitated a rethinking of the regional farm vernacular – presenting new opportunities for the implementation of conventional building materials and systems, as well as the use of locally available but unconventional materials in new applications.

(LEEDv4 2016)

This is why it is important to develop new Sustainability Performance Metrics that architects, engineers, and owners can use to measure their building design proposals – urban or rural – as to their potentials to become net-zero carbon facilities. Anything less than LEED Platinum (the highest level) is substandard in terms of sustainability and the LEED criteria does not work well in rural settings. That is why sustainability needs to be thought of systemically and holistically as a society and cultural issue linking urban and rural.

House for All Seasons, Shija village, northwestern China

ARCHITECT: JOHN LIN

John Lin is an architect and assistant professor in the Department of Architecture at the University of Hong Kong. He also is a leading practicing architect in China, and with a grant from the Luke Him Sau Charitable Trust and support from the Shaanxi Women's Federation and the University of Hong Kong he developed a prototype design for a house in rural China, based on traditional village house vernacular that is a contemporary prototype. By combining ideas from other regions of China as well as traditional and innovative technologies, such as integrating rammed earth, biogas, rainwater storage, and reed bed cleansing systems, he based his sustainable design around the traditional domestic courtyard where much of rural life takes place.

He says of development in rural areas that when new houses are being considered the decision makers abandon traditional styles in favor of standardized housing types that do not reflect the culture or character of the landscape in which they are located. He says that this is the result of a shift in rural China away from economic self-reliance as more and more rural people migrate toward urban centers. When new housing is constructed the builders bring in labor and materials from outside with little or no involvement by citizens in the village. He describes his work and the context of the project:

> Over the past 30 years the mass migration of rural villagers has not only enabled the growth of Chinese cities but has had an equally dramatic effect on their rural homeland. The rural is undergoing dramatic economic, social and physical changes that will only accelerate as China prepares to further

urbanize half of its remaining 700 million rural citizens over the next 30 years. These changes are being accompanied by a transformation in the vernacular architecture of China: a wholesale shift from regionally specific building types to generic, concrete, brick and tiled buildings constructed by the government. Within this scenario of potentially extreme changes to the social and built landscape the architect is wholly absent. Indeed, the most relevant question for the profession is: what can an architect do in a context where architecture is deemed unnecessary?

Traditionally, villages in China allocate individually owned land for farming as well as maintaining other collectively owned plots. Land for building houses was sub-divided from within a limited common area typically surrounding the ancestral home. Newly married male heirs, entitled to their own plot of land and their own house, add their structures to the agglomeration, so that villages have typically grown in a disorderly fashion. Shija village is located in the northern province of Shaanxi near the city of Xian. Our project there looks at the idea of the vernacular village house and attempts to propose a contemporary prototype. By combining vernacular ideas from other regions of China as well as traditional and new technologies, the design is a prototype for a modern Chinese mud brick courtyard house (Figures 4.26 and 4.27). Currently the process of rural development increasingly favors the destruction and abandonment of the traditional in favor of the new. Shija village houses attempt to bridge between the two extremes and preserve the intelligence of local materials and techniques. However, the project is not simply a traditional courtyard house. It is a

4.26
Shija village in rural China showing traditional courtyard houses with blue roof coverings.

4.27
House for All Seasons as a contemporary prototype based on historic traditional rural houses in China.

result of investigation into the modern village vernacular and represents an architectural attempt to consciously evolve vernacular construction in China.

There are two worlds of Chinese architecture. One is the heroic urban architecture with an "anything goes" audacity claiming an international identity for contemporary China. The other is construction that occurs without architects with a generic mentality that seeks to construct, by the most efficient means, as much and as quickly as possible. As China manufacturers more and more of the world's building supplies, we might take note of the need for generic mass production and a radically efficient framework while incorporating self-expression into the process. In China today, the new construction is a collision of urban forms against a rural backdrop. As a result the architect must find a balance between individual and collective ambition and find a way to design in a place without architecture by bringing order to the disorderly or bringing diversity to the monotonous.

All of the traditional houses in the region of Shija are constructed of mud brick and occupy a site roughly 10 meters by 30 meters. The design of the House for All Seasons uses this framework and an understanding of the courtyard as an important component of the home. The house includes four distinct courtyards throughout the house to integrate the main functional rooms of the kitchen, bathroom, living room, and bedrooms. As part of the increased self-sufficiency objective, the house's multifunctional roof provides for human activities and collection of rain water (Figures 4.28, 4.29 and 4.30).

The House for All Seasons is a sustainable prototype for rural China, but it also has become a gathering place for local women's handicraft bridging the

Architecture and agriculture case studies

4.28
Prototype House for All Seasons from above showing courtyards where most family social gatherings take place.

4.29
House for All Seasons with courtyard number one.

individual and collective identity of the village. With its construction the House for All Seasons has developed a new industry for the village, based on traditional straw weaving, initiating a new phase for the local economy. Time will tell, but this project is a very strong architectural attempt to evolve rural house dynamics in China (Figure 4.31).

4.30
House for All Seasons with courtyard number two.

4.31
House for All Seasons showing three stages of construction: Concrete structure showing courtyards (top), brick infill to provide privacy walls (middle), and exterior screen wall of brick with openings (bottom).

Quinta do Vallado Winery, Douro Valley, Portugal

ARCHITECT: FRANCISCO VIEIRA DE COMPOS

My wife and I had a chance to visit the Quinta do Vallado Winery in 2014, and we were immediately struck by its beautiful and simple contemporary design, tightly integrated into agricultural terraces that step up the side of the steep landscape for growing wine along the Douro River in Portugal (Figure 4.32 and 4.33). The utilization of thin stone slices as the exterior finish of floors, walls, and roofs is simple and profound, providing a dramatic integration with the landscape. Victoria King (2012) described the project and the architect's intention to be very precise and very simple in material and form. The design idea was a melding of the production requirements to make wine with an integration of the buildings into the beautiful terraced landscape along the Douro River valley for growing grapes. She says that "seduction of the visitor was always part of the game" and I can attest that the building complex is indeed seductive. The design was further challenged by the need to integrate several existing buildings into the design concept.

The Douro River valley has a number of vineyards and wineries located along its banks that are places to visit. It is a beautiful rural river valley and a place with a very high destination for tourism, including several river cruises. However we saw the valley from an automobile and it is a beautiful landscape that is easy to tour with many interesting places to stop and stay with many wineries to visit. Portuguese wines and ports are excellent and well worth the trip to visit this unique agricultural landscape.

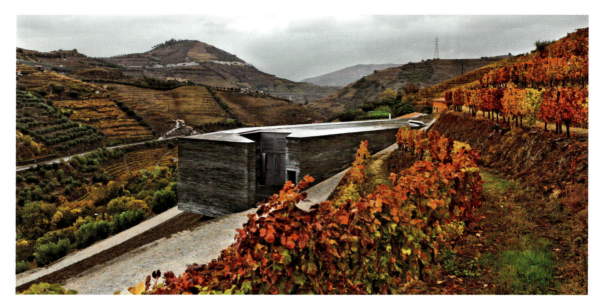

4.32
Quinta do Vallado Winery along the Douro River Valley in Portugal showing hillside terraces for growing grapes and insertion of the visitor center into the terraces.

4.33
Entrance terrace to the Quinta do Vallado Winery with all exposed construction made of marble bricks with rolling hills and Douro River in background.

The Quinta do Vallado Winery, completed in 2012, is certainly one of the best examples of contemporary architecture that I saw in the Douro River valley and one that is more sensitive to its place than visitor centers elsewhere designed by internationally famous architects. It is an excellent example of sustainable architecture that connects with the culture of the Douro Valley and Portugal and fits the unique landscape and climate of its site with architectural form derived to serve functional as well as aesthetic and marketing needs (Figures 4.34, 4.35, 4.36, and 4.37).

4.34
Entrance to the Quinta do Vallado Visitor Center.

Architecture and agriculture case studies

4.35
Interior of the Visitor Center with a wine bottle display on the left and simple wooden benches and tables for wine tasting. Stairs in the background lead to the Aging Cave and on to the Production Room.

4.36
Interior of the Production Room of the Quinta do Vallado Winery.

4.37
Aging Cave at the Quinta do Vallado Winery.

Jade Valley Winery and Resort, rural China

ARCHITECT: QINGYUN MA

Qingyun Ma is an architect born in Xian, China, and now the dean of the School of Architecture at Southern California University. He is also the design principal of MADA, an architectural firm he founded specializing in sustainable design that is globally focused and grounded in the practicality of Chinese contemporary architecture. The firm tries to integrate culture, education, fashion, exhibition, and visual strategy into its projects. As a result he has been awarded a number of honors with exhibits in Russia, Vietnam, and Cannes. As a native of Jade Valley he established the Jade Valley Winery and Resort (Figure 4.38) in 2000 with the goal of making Jade Valley not only the home of the "Lanatian Man" and "Lanatian Jade" but also the home of Lanatian Wine. He describes the winery in three parts:

> The Well House, also known as The Father's House, is designed especially for my father. The construction started in 1993 and has taken 11 years to complete. Set in a very unique and exceptional site at a confluence of the Qinling Mountain, Bahe River, and Bailuyuan Plateau, it was built to combine modern comfort and local heritage into a tranquil seclusion. The

Architecture and agriculture case studies

4.38
Jade Valley Resort and Winery in the rolling hills of rural China based on vernacular rural Chinese dwellings.

source of building materials are the rocks which were pulled down from the mountains by the river over time. The water and the stone correlate in the sense that the stone's size, color, and level of perturbation are all shaped by running water. The Well House is a collision between rough, organic materials with a highly regulated spare form. This order gives the Well House an ephemeral quality encased in distinctly modern formalism.

The Well House was inspired by traditional Guan Zhong folk houses, but further adapts itself to the native surroundings encouraging new ways of living. Entering the Well Hall, one finds an instant peace of the mind with the open sky as though it could be reached by hands as an exceptional experience of Taoism. The Wine Dorm was transformed from an old office building into a hotel as a best countryside destination for visitors with an iconic 8 meters tall glass façade (Figure 4.39, 4.40, and 4.41).

4.39
Jade Valley Resort and Winery with the Well House designed for the father of the architect.

4.40
Jade Valley Resort and Winery with the entrance to the Well House.

4.41
Jade Valley Resort and Winery resort adjacent to the winery.

The Jade Valley Winery and Resort, and the House for All Seasons, are two projects in rural China where two distinguished architects have went out of their way to find a contemporary architectural idea based in traditional Chinese rural living patterns.

Architecture and agriculture case studies

Fabric-roofed dairy barn, Minnesota, USA

ARCHITECT: CENTER FOR RURAL DESIGN

An example of a future commercial animal housing facility is a design proposal for a sustainable, net-zero-energy, 2,500-cow dairy barn in America developed by the Center for Rural Design at the University of Minnesota in consultation with the Department of Agricultural Engineering. The design proposes to use fabric as the roof and wall material in a series of adjacent and connected animal spaces.

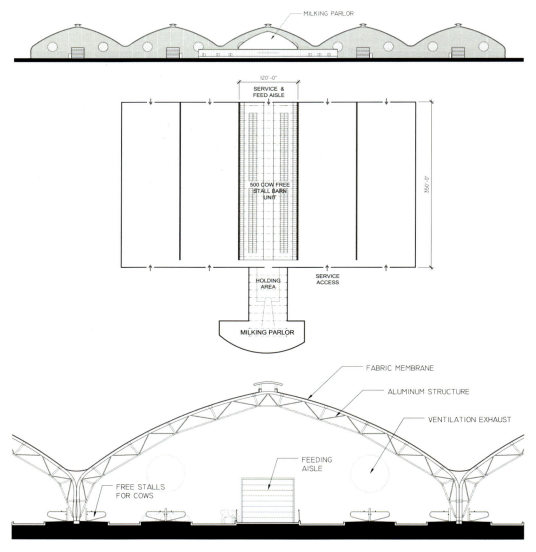

ELEVATION, FLOOR PLAN & SECTION OF 2,500 COW DAIRY BARN UTILIZING FABRIC STRUCTURE

It functions with a single rotary milking parlor for 50 cows that operates 24 hours each day. Manure is intended to be processed through anaerobic digesters to create methane gas to generate electricity for ventilating the barn, lighting and milking operations while eliminating odors. Extra unused power is sold into the electric grid. Solid waste is separated in the manure handling process and recycled as bedding. Liquid waste is injected (to reduce odor) into fields as fertilizer. The design proposal follows the International Building Code with regard to worker safety and health even though agricultural buildings are currently exempt (Figure 4.42).

Fabric architecture is an established building technology that is utilized for a broad range of building types around the world ranging from airports to convention centers. For animal facilities it has several benefits not found in contemporary farm buildings for dairy, in that it is relatively inexpensive and environmentally friendly, using basalt continuous filament fabric and recycled aluminum for the structure. It can be easily modified to meet new dairy technologies and code requirements, can function with a variety of milking technologies including robotic, and when the facility reaches the end of its life cycle it can be dismantled and recycled.

The design proposal was developed to provide an example of how a new dairy facility could respond to an earlier Center for Rural Design study that outlined improvements to environmental practices on dairy farms. Financed by the Minnesota State Legislature, it was a study for the dairy industry in Minnesota that: (1) developed an environmental inventory of landscape features and resources, including human features impacting the dairy industry; (2) assessed the priority of importance of the features of the inventory; and (3) analyzed methods to accommodate and integrate the features through the planning and design process. The study linked four high priority models for dairy farms – surface water, ground water, habitat and community relations – and then combined them to create a fifth model for an Environmental Quality Assurance Program for existing and new dairy farms.

The fabric-covered dairy proposal responds well to the program's guidelines, and along with shaping the landscape to connect with the architecture and having dry cows outside where the public can see them it would be an exemplary dairy facility. Because of its odor eliminating process through anaerobic digesters it could be integrated into the peri-urban landscape along with other green houses and vegetable farms providing food for urban centers.

The manure digester system (depending on the cost of fossil fuels) has a number of other positive impacts including reducing the release of methane gas into the environment, creating fertilizer that farmers can use or sell, eliminating the need for manure lagoons and the danger of water pollution. The manure digester is expensive to install and maintain, but if fossil fuel prices are high enough the system will pay for itself, particularly if the electricity generated can be sold to utility companies. One of the digester manufacturing companies claims that the electricity from a typical 1,000-cow dairy farm can provide power to about 250 homes.

4.42 (opposite)
Fabric-covered dairy barn for 2,500 cows with a fabric roof supported by aluminum trusses for a new dairy complex following guidelines prepared by the Center for Rural Design in the Environmental Quality Protection Program for dairy farmers in Minnesota. It illustrates the potential of new structural and sustainability technology adapted to a building for animal agriculture.

Architecture and agriculture case studies

St. Paul Farmers' Market, Minnesota, USA

ARCHITECT: THORBECK ARCHITECTS

The St. Paul Farmers' Market was established in 1853 in downtown St. Paul, Minnesota as an indoor public market that was an important public building and public meeting place (Figure 4.43).

Later as the urban population increased, requiring more distribution of food products, it was demolished and a new market constructed as a series of covering shed roofs for farmers to bring products in to the city by vehicles and then transferred to other vehicles for distribution throughout the city. The current facility was constructed on a different site in 1982 in the historic Lower Town neighborhood, yet it followed the shed roof model even though it now functions as a series of marketing stalls under the roof sheds for farmers to sell directly to urban consumers who come to shop. The St. Paul Farmers' Market is unique in that it restricts growers who sell to be within a 75-mile radius. Regardless of its functional problems the market brings in over 400,000 visitors a year and provides food products to new housing developments in the historic Lower Town neighborhood.

The concept design for reworking the existing and an adjacent site for the St. Paul Growers Association envisioned a year-round indoor market along with

4.43
The first Public Market constructed in St. Paul, Minnesota in 1853 as an important public building for exchange and marketing of local rural farmer's food production to urban customers.

rotating the four aisles of the existing market 90 degrees to provide a level marketing platform for each aisle (the current market has the aisles on a 5 percent slope without adequate cover). The design proposal expanded the number of stalls, accommodates health requirements for refrigeration and hand-washing, and reduces the 7–10 year waiting time to get a space in the market. The market currently has 30 percent of the farmers as Hmong and Vietnamese with the others as families that have sold at the market for many years. Some think that without the recent immigrant farmers and the food products they grow and sell the market might not exist today.

The design concept upholds the charm of the outdoor market which is crowded, intimate, and filled with hubbub atmosphere (Figures 4.44, 4.45, and 4.46). The indoor market provides space for 25 vendor stalls of varying sizes on

4.44
Sketch of the exterior of the proposed redesign of the existing St. Paul Farmers' Market.

4.45
Sketch of the covered selling aisle with farmers' trucks and selling booths.

Architecture and agriculture case studies

4.46
Sketch of the exterior of the indoor Farmers' Market adjacent to the outdoor market.

4.47
Sketch of the interior of the indoor market for year-round selling of produce and processed foods by members of the St. Paul Growers Association.

the first floor with administrative offices, classrooms, commercial kitchen, and tenant spaces on the second floor (Figure 4.47).

Rural design and rural architecture

Before the 1960s any trip to the countryside by town people was enhanced by seeing animals in the landscape. Today, farmers have been constructing standardized confinement-type buildings because they are the most economical method for livestock and poultry farming resulting in far fewer numbers of animals outside on the land. This lack of visibility has created the public impression that the animals suffer because they are often confined indoors throughout their lives. Yet, animal care is the highest priority on the farm because healthy and more productive animals bring more income to the farmer. This is becoming more of an issue as non-farming families and urban people retiring and moving to the countryside construct homes setting up situations where a farmstead and residential development can create social conflict.

This radical shift in farming practices over the past 50 plus years has strained the public's ability to understand how modern farming is accomplished and their trust in the environmental regulations that govern animal and crop agriculture. Environmental protection regulations are based on the number of animal units and as the unit count goes up the regulations become more stringent, yet the public is suspicious that environmental concerns are not being properly addressed. This concern along with the public's uneasiness with their perception of "factory" farming and odor issues sometimes creates a conflict between farmers and non-farmers in rural areas over the future of animal agriculture. Also, the regulations generally are state wide and do not adequately address the unique land characteristics of regions within the state that may have a variety of geological differences.

Integrated performance metrics, similar to those being developed by the Center for Sustainable Building Research at the University of Minnesota, are needed to guide the design and construction of sustainable commercial animal buildings (Figure 4.48). These performance metrics link the environment and human health together with site metrics and building metrics and endpoint indictors that can be measured. Using production, energy, environmental, economic, animal welfare, and workplace environmental health and social criteria they could bring large-scale animal housing facilities to the same level that are required for commercial and industrial building design and construction. These metrics will become effective when they optimize animal productivity, reduce energy consumption of fossil fuels and animal feeds, reduce insurance costs, and maintain cost competiveness over building life. To maximize performance, the facilities will use more environmentally friendly building components, provide better working conditions for worker health, improve animal health by maintaining biosecurity, and help ensure increased food safety and security.

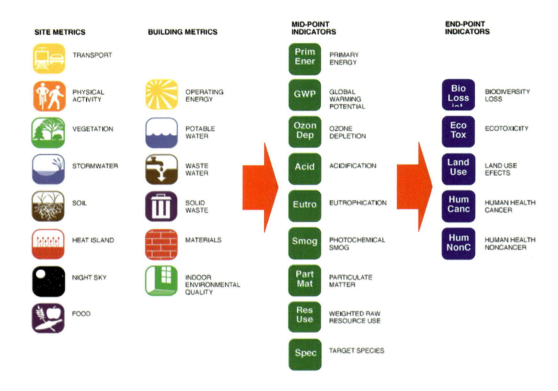

4.48

Diagram prepared by the Center for Sustainable Building Research at the University of Minnesota illustrating interrelated performance metrics for environmental and human health to guide the design of sustainable buildings and communities.

There are not many leading architects who are designing farm buildings in rural landscapes around the world. The projects that I have included are the only completed agricultural building projects that I have been able to locate for my book that had a very good architect involved in their programming, design, and construction from the beginning. These have all been designed by architects with a strong sense of rural understanding and connection to climate and place. As case studies they illustrate how exciting it can be to have the opportunity to design buildings in the rural landscape. It is important for future rural buildings that good architects recognize the value of the rural landscape and the buildings constructed within them and begin to seek out opportunities to explore architectural concepts that link these facilities to their climate and place in a profound and sustainable way.

There is nothing inherently wrong with pre-engineered building systems for agricultural buildings, but when they are constructed indiscriminately around the globe for agricultural purposes without any architectural idea of fit with climate or place, they leave a monotonous blot on the landscape. Because of their utilization anywhere in any climate, sustainability is not part of the pre-engineered vocabulary. Rural citizens constructing commercial buildings and farmers who are constructing agricultural buildings must utilize design thinking in the layout and construction so that their place is enhanced through sustainable designs that reflect rural culture and regional sense of pride. By embracing design they can enhance local economic sustainability, rural tourism, and their own quality of rural life.

Chapter 5

Worker and animal safety and health

In other chapters I have described some of the changes in American agriculture that have been taking place over the past 50–60 years that have led to fewer farmers and bigger farms, resulting in specific and unique requirements for animal agriculture that has specialized buildings for poultry operations, dairy farms, swine facilities, and horses. Because of the larger size and the way these buildings look some people refer to these buildings as "factory farms" (even though they are mostly owned by an individual family), in contrast to the small diversified family farm of the past where relatively small groups of animals – horses, cows, swine, and poultry – were cared for by the individual family alone.

In response to this concern there is a growing trend for small "organic" farms near urban cities that specialize in growing food and flowers for restaurants and farmers' markets. In some cases they operate as a community-supported agriculture (CSA) farm growing food for customers who subscribe for annual deliveries. Nevertheless, the size of the farm has nothing to do with worker and animal safety and health. They all need to pay attention to the issue of worker safety because of the potential for injury from handling animals, equipment usage, or farming operations.

The large specialized buildings for animal agriculture are often constructed in clusters on a farm with each building having a different purpose – like on a dairy farm where some buildings are for milking cows (free stall or tie stall), others for heifers and dry cows, and others for newborn and weaned calves. Central to the dairy complex would be a central feed center, manure management area, milking parlor and milk house, and an office/locker/toilet area for workers. Similarly poultry and swine farmers also have a variety of buildings each specific to the role that the animal is playing in the animal housing system.

The Midwest Plan Service is an entity of the United States Department of Agriculture and it provides plans for typical animal agricultural buildings to farmers in a wide range of animal housing. Figure 5.1 shows the first of eighteen pages for a swine growing and finishing building that is 28 feet $\times$ 80 feet in size with a single-slope roof and modified open-front building to house about 240 pigs. The plan provides detailed floor plans, cross sections and specifications (Figure 5.2), along with cautionary notes warning the purchaser that

> additional professional services will be required, including but not limited to: assurance of compliance with codes and regulations, review of specifications for materials and equipment, supervision of site selection, bid letting and construction, and provision for utilities, waste management, roads or other access. Furthermore, any deviation from the given specification may result in structural failure, property damage, and personal injury including loss of life.
>
> (Midwest Plan Service brochure)

MWPS-72603
Swine Growing - Finishing Building

28' x 80' monoslope, modified open-front building to house about 240 pigs. Three plans are included. Plan A shows a 10' wide by 8' deep manure pit under slats. Plan B shows a 10' wide flush gutter under slats. Plan C shows a 5' wide open flush gutter. Natural ventilation.

CAUTION!

Additional professional services will be required to tailor this plan to your situation, including but not limited to: assurance of compliance with codes and regulations; review of specifications for materials and equipment; supervision of site selection, bid letting and construction; and provision for utilities, waste management, roads or other access. **Furthermore, any deviation from the given specifications may result in structural failure, property damage, and personal injury including loss of life.**

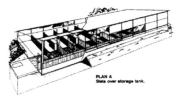
PLAN A
Slats over storage tank.

PLAN B
Slats over flush gutter or scraper.

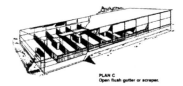
PLAN C
Open flush gutter or scraper.

5.1
Midwest Plan Service provides drawings and plans for a Swine Finishing building. This is page one of a brochure.

Worker and animal safety and health

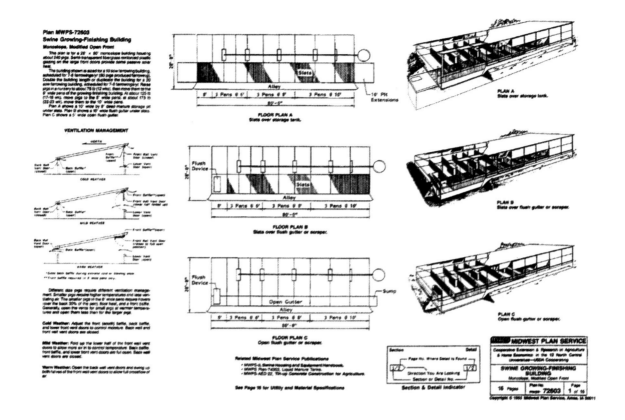

5.2
Midwest Plan Service provides typical plans and sections for animal housing offered as a service to farmers. This is page 2 of the brochure showing different plan arrangements for swine.

This cautionary note fundamentally leaves it up to the farmer to deal with all of the issues of size, site layout, design coordination, construction, operation, and management of the facility. Since the International Building Code exempts agricultural buildings, farmers do what they have to do and hope for the best. Worker and animal safety is not discussed in the Midwest Plan Service plans, but ventilation is incorporated for cold, mild, and warm weather situations.

Human occupancy overlaps with animal housing in farm operations to distribute feed, clean barns, and remove manure (even though mechanized systems may be utilized for both feed distribution and manure handling). Larger facilities have more animals, more manure, and more odor – and how odor and manure disposal are environmentally managed are the areas of greatest public concern. These large-scale agricultural building complexes often utilize pre-engineered wood or steel building systems and even though they are structurally designed by professional engineers, it is usually the farmer who is responsible for coordinating and managing the building process, including life safety issues, mechanical and electrical engineering, and in some cases agricultural engineers for assistance in determining the best layout and management system to maximize results. Since the farmer is often coordinating all of the issues and making decisions with the best of intentions, it can result in a rather chancy design, particularly on large-scale projects, when the farmer has to coordinate and manage the overall planning, design, and construction process as well as training hired farm workers to operate the facility. Even if the structure is properly designed by a structural engineer it may not be constructed properly with adequate roof and foundation tie-downs, and as a result there have been a number of recent Upper Midwest building collapses from snow load and wind.

Farm worker hazards

In America farm workers, on both animal and crop farms, are often recent immigrants with cultural and language differences that make it difficult to be sure that the workers understand the farm operations. Some of the hazards for workers involved in animal agriculture, as outlined by Jonathan Chaplin of the Department of Bioproducts & Biosystems Engineering at the University of Minnesota, include:

- Handling animals – potential for slips and falls from water, urine, manure; close contact with animals and getting stepped on; cuts and abrasions and potential of infectious disease; and noise.
- Injectable medications – preparing and handling needles; and occasional bites from the animal.
- Manure, urine and waste storage – toxic gases; flammable and explosive nature; by-product of livestock respiration and manure decomposition.
- Animal operations – lifting and caring; spreading liquid manure; slips and falls around machinery.
- Machinery maintenance – power tools and electricity; hydraulic systems and accidents from unblocked header; icy, muddy, and manure-covered surfaces while operating machinery; tipping of machinery and being crushed.
- Storage facilities – dust; incomplete combustion inside closed garage; noise; and handling chemicals.

While the hazards are different for workers planting and harvesting in fields or small organic farms, they still exist because issues of dust, machinery operations, machinery maintenance, lifting, slips and falls, noise, and storage of chemicals can all contribute to worker or animal injury.

As discussed earlier the most common building construction type for new agricultural buildings in North America is post-frame wood or steel frame with metal siding and roofing. Throughout history farmers have needed to continuously seek out labor and construction savings to deal with changing regional economic circumstances. Today it is even more critical as farmers compete in a global marketplace. As these agricultural buildings have become more complex and larger with humans involved inside the building (sometimes 24 hours a day seven days a week), the building codes do not adequately deal with all of the human and environmental safety, health, and welfare issues, particularly when these buildings are located near rural towns with many non-farm residents or near environmentally sensitive landscapes, leading to social and regulatory problems caused by odors.

Building code issues

Most agricultural buildings in the U.S. are exempted by the International Building Code (IBC) and these buildings are defined in Appendix C, Group U – Agricultural Buildings. Without a building code standard that covers the safety, health, and welfare of agricultural workers and animals, agricultural buildings are often designed and constructed with little oversight except for the attention to it by the farmer and the professional standards of the people involved.

Over the past twenty years the scale of animal facilities has led to the development of hybrid farming operations often with multiple buildings – some for storage, some for repair, and some for food processing and food storage. These larger facilities also may have semi-trucks hauling harvest products that involve turning and moving with increased hazards. The farm may also include food processing with special machinery for cleaning and removing dirt and other elements before the food product is shipped to a processing center. Even small vegetable farms have machinery for field operations covering planting and harvesting, and loading and transportation to farmers' markets or grocery stores.

The IBC is used in the design and construction of commercial buildings throughout the U.S. with the intent to provide consistency between states and

> Establish the minimum requirements to safeguard the public health, safety, and general welfare through structural strength, means of egress facilities, stability, sanitation, adequate light and ventilation, energy conservation, and safety to life, and property from fire and other hazards attributed to the built environment and to provide safety to fire fighters and emergency responders during emergency operations.
>
> (IBC 2006)

Since the IBC for the most part exempts agricultural buildings from the building code, there is considerable confusion in the interpretation of what an agricultural building is and what parts of the code apply. For example (from IBC 2006):

- The definition for an agricultural building is: A structure designed and constructed to house farm implements, hay, grain, poultry, livestock, or other horticultural projects. This structure shall not be a place of human habitation or a place of employment where agricultural products are processed, treated, or packaged, nor shall it be a place used by the public.

- Utility and Miscellaneous Group U lists: agricultural buildings, aircraft hangers (accessory to a one or two-family dwelling), barns, carports, fences more than 6 feet high, grain silo (accessory to a residential occupancy), greenhouses, livestock shelters, private garages, retaining walls, sheds, stables, tanks, towers.
- Section 507 has an exception for requiring an automatic sprinkler system in one-story buildings in areas occupied for indoor participant sports, such as tennis, skating, swimming, and equestrian (horse) activities.
- Table 1003.2.2.2 ("Maximum Floor Area Allowances per Occupant") has a gross floor area of 300 square feet per occupant for agricultural buildings (which is the same occupancy for storage areas in commercial buildings).
- Appendix C, Group U – Agricultural Buildings is a one-page list of requirements that are not mandatory unless specifically referenced in the adopting ordinance by the state, county or township. It lists: livestock shelters or buildings, including shade structures and milking barns, poultry buildings or shelters, barns, storage of equipment and machinery used exclusively for agriculture, horticultural structures including detached production greenhouses and crop protection shelters, grain silos, and stables. It also allows unlimited area if a building is surrounded and adjoined by public ways or yards not less than 60 feet in width. Under code definitions a yard is identified as an open space, other than a court, unobstructed from the ground to the sky.
- Human occupancy areas (like a milking parlor in a dairy barn) are not considered differently than animal housing areas for a Type U building, except when the agricultural building is part of an educational use. Then it becomes a Type B (business) above the 12th grade or Type E (education) building up to and through the 12th grade (animal research facilities at universities generally cost a great deal more than similar buildings on a farm because they need to be designed and constructed to meet the higher standards).

The health and safety of workers and animals is not served well when there are no code requirements for agricultural buildings. The public is not served well when pre-engineered building systems are utilized and constructed in the same way regardless of where they are located by ignoring the climate, culture, and sense of place within which they are located. The question is can a new level of standards for commercial agricultural buildings be developed that will not appreciably increase the cost of food production?

I am unfamiliar with building code regulations in other countries around the world, but I suspect they are very similar in ignoring agricultural buildings and have simply left it up to the farmer's knowledge and understanding about animal agriculture and the design and construction of buildings. However, as in North America, when an animal agricultural facility is a research building connected to a university it becomes more like other commercial buildings. A handsome sheep research center in the Abruzzi region of Italy suggests that this is so (Figure 5.3).

5.3
Sheep research center in the Abruzzi region of Italy as seen from the highway. It appears to be a high-quality facility with an architecture that reflects the Italian place and climate.

Evidence-based design guidelines

New building types in the agricultural and rural landscape – like ethanol plants, anaerobic digesters, photovoltaic solar collectors, wind generators, seed plants, and food processing facilities – are all emerging agricultural building types in the rural landscape. Their building code issues will need to be clarified as to their impacts on safety, health, and welfare of farm workers and the public. The International Building Code has a Factory Group F for these types of buildings if they do not involve high-hazard operations. If so they will need to be considered High-Hazard Group H. Nevertheless, the issue of agricultural buildings in the rapidly changing urban, peri-urban, and rural landscapes needs to be clarified.

Other than size the basic design, construction, and management of animal production facilities have changed little in the past 50 years in the United States. Inexpensive fossil fuel and feed, plentiful water, immigrant labor, and limited concern regarding air and water emissions has resulted in few incentives to critically evaluate, modify, or significantly change the design and construction of animal building systems – particularly dairy, beef, swine, and poultry production systems – and their impact on the safety and health of agricultural workers and their families.

Also, many of the agricultural workers in animal facilities in the Upper Midwest are immigrant families and without this labor force animal production would be severely impacted. In large commercial animal facilities, workers are working with animals 24 hours a day, 7 days a week with little or no standards to guide the design, construction, and operation of these buildings. The working relationships between humans and animals is inherently risky. Animal handling can be dangerous and many workers have been injured – even those with experience and training. Often workers are required to administer injectable drugs in the care of ill animals because many facilities do not have easy access to veterinarians. This situation has created instances of accidental self-injection.

While animal agricultural buildings may not seem significant when compared to other commercial buildings constructed in the U.S., the safety and health of agricultural workers is in jeopardy by working in facilities that are fragmented in their design and construction leading to building and site systems that often do not integrate well. The potential impact on the safety of the U.S. food supply must also be considered when looking at the role of commercial animal agriculture in food production and how these facilities fit and work within the larger social, cultural, and economic impact on rural communities. The bird flu epidemic that hit many Midwest turkey, chicken, and egg producers in the summer of 2015 attests to the big economic impact that animal agriculture has on the economy.

In response to the changes and global food economics, the scale of animal agriculture in America has evolved from small diversified farms into specialized large barns with large numbers of animals involving many workers who manage operations 24 hours a day seven days a week running the complex. For example the Riverview Dairy in central Minnesota, with 7,500 cows (including 5,000 cows in one large barn with a rotary milking parlor), has 50 people working in the building 24 hours a day (Figure 5.4). The owners of Riverview Dairy were very

5.4
Aerial view of Riverview Dairy farm in west central Minnesota with 5,000 cows in a single building on the right and 2,500 cows in a barn on the left, and two manure lagoons in the center. Each barn has its own milking parlor.

5.5
Interior view of animal stalls and feeding lane in the larger 5,000 cow Riverview Dairy barn.

5.6
Rotary milking parlor holding 84 cows in the larger Riverview Dairy barn which operates 24 hours a day, every day with 50 employees working to take care of the cows at all times.

concerned about the health and safety of the workers and animals who would be housed or work in the building and did the best they could (Figures 5.5 and 5.6). However, the current system for responsibility for their concerns is convoluted and cumbersome, involving regulatory rules that each look at only one part of the project rather than as a whole, similar to most other commercial building types.

A good example of the current regulatory system process is a large poultry operations facility in northern Iowa that was designed and constructed with great care by the owners following OSHA regulations and building codes in effect. The Sunrise Farm project is owned and operated by the Sonstegard family. They worked with poultry experts at the University of Minnesota to develop the basic concept for production and processing and went through a number of presentations to governing entities to get permits to build the facility. Constructed in several stages over time, the facility is organized like the letter "H" with a number of individual poultry egg layer barns connected by enclosed conveyors for transporting eggs to the central process facility and feed mill. The Sonstegard family worked closely with local building officials and OSHA inspectors to develop the plans along with engineers for structural, mechanical, and electrical issues as well as industrial engineers for determining production and processing technical systems. No architect or landscape architect was involved so the owners were responsible for project management, landscape layout, manure handling, and aesthetic decisions regarding how the plant looked and fit into the site. They had to coordinating all of the different skills and expertise required for a modern egg laying and processing facility including financial and cost control issues.

Since the poultry barns were classified as agricultural the code review for the poultry barns was very minimal, whereas the processing and feeding center in the middle went through a number of detailed reviews more typical of any industrial manufacturing building. However, because of the issue of manure management and the potential of environmental damage from large-scale animal facilities these projects have to work through environmental assessments that address underground soils, water, odor, and manure handling methods.

An additional problem with large-scale animal facilities is finding a site that the general public will accept. Concerns about the scale and appearance of large facilities with many animals often leads to negative thoughts about the project before the farmer has a chance to present the plans to the regulatory agencies. Issues of odor, landscape fit, relationships with nearby non-farm residential properties, and social questions about the economic impacts of the facility must all be considered by the regulatory agencies before it can be considered a good project for the community. These issues all weigh into the review process that involve public hearings where residents can speak for and against the project.

Because of the difficulties in obtaining permits, owners often seek out sites that are isolated from residential development near scenic landscapes and small towns. This methodology often encourages other animal facilities to locate in the same area so you end up with another possibility of disease transmission from one facility to another with great economic impact. Related to this is the tendency for swine farmers to find sites near nature reserves as they seek isolation which can lead to disease transmission from wildlife to domestic animals.

Research possibilities

The Center for Rural Design, along with Larry Jacoblson, Kevin Janni, and Jonathan Chaplin from the Department of Bioproducts & Biosytems Engineering at the University of Minnesota, proposed a project to the National Institute for

Occupational Safety and Health (NIOSH) to study and draft a proposed revision of the IBC covering agricultural buildings as part of the *Design Guidelines for Worker and Animal Health and Safety in Animal Production Building Systems*. Although not funded, the project envisioned that evidence-based design guidelines may help future animal buildings become integrated animal building systems. The design guidelines would cover all of the system components in an animal housing facility including the building shell, environmental control system, feeding and watering system, animal care and waste management, and the integration of these buildings into the rural landscape to enhance ecosystem health.

This project would have worked with individuals involved (including farmers and workers) in the current industry to identify the risks inherent in an animal agriculture facility for dairy, swine, beef, and poultry to provide design guidelines that will move animal production facilities in the U.S. toward a higher professional level to improve animal welfare and the workplace environment, enhance worker safety and health, and adjust to new environmental, social, and cultural awareness in rural regions.

Design is an effective link between science and society by using design thinking and the problem-solving process of evidence-based design to justify recommendations. Although this project would have focused on the design, construction, and operation of animal production facilities in the Upper Midwest, the research that it identified would help enhance worker safety and welfare while increasing the security of food supply throughout the U.S. – particularly if in the long run the IBC Group U – Agricultural Buildings is revised to bring these buildings into the mainstream of commercial construction.

Design guidelines are needed for commercial animal agriculture that can be disseminated through publications and a website to provide the information necessary to producer groups, building system manufacturers, insurance groups, and individual farmers to:

- help safeguard worker and animal safety and health in animal facilities for dairy, swine, beef, and poultry with design guidelines covering animal facilities in general and specific guidelines for each animal group and the various stages of production unique to that group, including odor control and manure management;
- enhance animal productivity with better understanding of safer animal handling;
- be cost competitive over building life by providing flexibility for modifications and lower operating and insurance costs;
- use more durable and environmentally friendly building components where building form follows function, climate and place;
- improve rural landscape character and fit providing more neighborly and socially acceptable and understandable housing systems;
- outline biosecurity for each animal group for food safety and human and animal health; and

- integrate applicable worker cultural, social, and housing issues into the design guidelines for animal agriculture facilities.

A result of changing demographics in rural regions is that many non-farmers and retirees are now living in agricultural areas, setting the stage for conflict when an existing farmer wishes to expand his animal production facilities, raising public concerns about odor and environmental protection. County comprehensive plans and zoning regulations often do not consider the values of people living in rural townships and towns where expansion of animal agriculture is involved. A farmer can meet all state and county regulations for a new or expanded facility, but the township may not agree. This multi-governmental situation makes it difficult for farmers to plan their futures.

The results of the research project could have helped resolved regulations between state, county, and township governances by bringing evidence-based, comprehensive integrated *Design Guidelines* for sustainable commercial animal buildings that could have a substantial impact over time by providing knowledge to the industry about worker safety and health and how to design and build facilities that accomplish that objective while protecting the environment and not unreasonably impact the cost of production.

Sustainable animal housing

Another research proposal by the University of Minnesota Center for Rural Design along with the Center for Sustainable Building Research and Department of Bioproducts & Biosystems Engineering was to the North Central Sustainable Agricultural Research and Education program of the U.S. Department of Agriculture. The proposal was based on the development of Integrated Performance Metrics for Sustainable Animal Production Buildings. The idea was to partner with industry stakeholders to provide a roadmap for the United States animal agriculture industry that would help transform how it locates, houses, and manages agricultural animal production to effectively deal with local, state, national, and global issues. If funded, the project would have been the first to examine this area of research as described in the proposal:

> Little attention has been paid to the animal buildings that are constructed in rural areas and their important role in maintaining a sustainable healthy food system. Each year, producers and their neighbors become more informed and aware of limited environmental resources, multi-purpose community planning, how the economics of different sectors of a community are inter-related, and the importance of certain animal diseases to public health. The challenge is the lack of available science-based information that can be used in decision making to create more sustainable animal agriculture facilities. Science-based performance metrics based on

production, energy, environmental, economic, animal welfare, workplace environmental health and social criteria will bring animal facilities into the mainstream of commercial/industrial building design and construction.

Sustainable healthy food systems are becoming increasingly more important to the United States consumer and producer. The development of integrated performance design metrics for sustainable commercial animal buildings that incorporate emerging societal concerns in the areas of the environment, society and culture, economy and health into their modeling has the potential to transform the animal production workplace and the social environment in which animal production facilities operate. These science-based metrics will be a key tool for industry professionals and producers, processors, regulators, neighbors and other stakeholders to use to evaluate the location, design, building and management of animal production facilities.

The output of this project will be science-based, comprehensive integrated performance design metrics for sustainable commercial animal buildings that will lead to optimized animal productivity reducing energy consumption of fossil fuels and animal feeds, maintaining cost competitiveness over building life, using more durable and environmentally friendly building components, improving the character of the rural landscape, providing more socially acceptable animal housing, improving working conditions (ergonomics) and worker's health, increasing animal health, maintaining animal biosecurity, and providing for increased food safety and security. These metrics will move agricultural animal buildings toward a higher professional level that is standard in other commercial buildings.

The hope of this project was to create a set of refined design performance metrics for animal agricultural facilities that would assist the industry in creating new or renovating old facilities that meet or exceed sustainability standards for other sectors of the commercial building industry. Unfortunately the proposal was not funded.

Urban agriculture and building code

For several years I have been working with Dr. John Troughton, a highly respected and honored Australian consultant on business, technology, and communication issues. We have been exploring the potential of a second international conference on rural design in Australia (the first was at the University of Minnesota in 2010) with sustainable rural resiliency and linking rural and urban issues together as the focus. Dr. Troughton has also been involved in promoting a global view of the biosphere within which all activities must be fitted – including climate change and water resources. He has defined rural design as the harmonizing of the natural (rural) as it was or is, with how it could be through the creation and interrogation of the designed world by creative and innovative designers to meet human expectations. Human and natural systems in rural areas are dynamic and engaged in continuous cycles of mutual influence and response.

(Troughton 2014)

He goes on to say that "The rural design future belongs to the creators, empathisers, pattern recognisers, meaning makers . . . designers coupled with the practitioners, the action executors from farmers to miners."

It is through creativity and innovation that animal agriculture and other agricultural buildings, currently exempt from the building code, can become similar to other mainstream commercial buildings. But more importantly, they can become the models for integrating buildings and landscapes in rural areas while recognizing the important linkages that rural areas have with urban. As defined by Dr. Troughton,

architectural design focuses on designing individual buildings while urban design is the process of designing and shaping cities, towns and villages and making urban areas functional, attractive, and sustainable to humans. Rural design is the process of designing and shaping all non-urban spaces, and the objects (buildings and tools) and services within them, to make them functional, attractive, and sustainable for both nature and humans.

(Troughton 2014)

As previously discussed, worker and animal safety and health is of paramount importance in the design and construction of future buildings for agriculture when they become buildings that compare with other commercial buildings in size and scope. Having adequate exits for human and animal occupancy, fire alarm and fire protection systems, along with proper planning and design, these facilities can be designed and constructed without excessive additional cost. Also, many of the agricultural workers in animal facilities in the Upper Midwest are immigrant families and without this labor force animal production would be severely limited. In large commercial animal facilities, workers are sometimes working with animals 24 hours a day, 7 days a week with minimal standards to guide the design, construction, and operation of these buildings. Because of language difficulties it is often uncertain as to how well worker training is understood by the people who do the work.

Disease transmission between animals and between domestic animals and wildlife is another emerging issue for food safety in the location and site design of animal production facilities. Likewise, manure handling can create social conflicts, and almost every action in feeding and caring for animals requires the utilization of equipment. The location of powerlines, driveways and movement patterns of machines, and any equipment utilized must be considered an integral aspect of design guidelines to enhance the safety and health of workers and emergency personnel – as typically required for mainstream commercial buildings. As a result, worker and animal safety and welfare is a design issue that has not yet been fully addressed in the design of animal agricultural facilities or in the building codes.

Linking human, animal, and environmental wellness

Wellness is an area of great opportunity for thinking about designing and shaping the future of urban, peri-urban, and rural landscapes. It should be included along with climate change, renewable energy, food security, and water resources as fundamental to human habitation on the planet. It is of critical importance that designing for urban and rural futures be linked together because human, animal, and environmental wellness is an integrated issue.

Wellness is emphasized rather than health because health is associated with taking care of things when they are ill, whereas wellness is really about keeping things healthy. It is much more cost effective to maintain wellness than it is to take care of things when they are sick – human, animal, and environmental – and this is a global design issue. Human health is generally connected to medical schools and to the medical profession; whereas animal health is connected to schools of veterinary medicine; and environmental health is usually connected to ecology and environmental studies. Can wellness be addressed when the health disciplines are so varied?

There is not much clarity as to how they interrelate except by observation and discussion with experts. For example, swine growers have been moving their facilities further and further away from human habitation and in some case are building facilities adjacent to wildlife preserves to avoid social problems with human habitation. This proximity can lead to disease transmission between domestic animals and wild animals and birds. Bird flu can have a devastating impact on poultry farmers when many individual poultry farms are operating in close proximity to each other. Biosecurity has become paramount on commercial swine and poultry farms resulting in total confinement housing for the animals that also raises public concerns for animal welfare.

In April 2016 there was an international conference on One Medicine One Science at the University of Minnesota called iCOMOS. One of the sessions, Science Informing Public Policy and Economics of Health, discussed the need for water of quality and quantity to sustain health that is becoming increasingly difficult to have as populations grow, human land use expands, and water patterns shift due to climate change. The conference organizers went on to say:

> the problem facing policymakers is compounded by the fact that human, animal, and environmental health must be considered in making water policy but each are measured by different standards. Economic and social values vary across the globe and tend to compound rather than simplify

issues at the local level up to global levels. This means that data to adequately inform policy is often hard to come by and putting one use of water above and out of balance with all the other uses has already led to unintended and undesirable consequences.

The conference discussed the linkages between human and animal health and how they both are impacted by environment. Air quality will be one of the topics looking at the science behind major air-related diseases. Water quality is fundamental to life on the planet and the role of science in the formulation of local and global health policies is critical in protecting human health; however science is often compartmentalized and misses crucial interactions. Science needs to be integrated and articulated to provide enlightened public policies for sustaining human, animal, and environmental health (iCOMOS 2016).

Design is a problem-solving process and a methodology to help bring science to society through evidence-based design. The iCOMOS conference was notable for its intentions, but there was no discussion about how design can improve the link between science and society. One of the sessions on the Future of One Medicine One Science is attempting to address this issue, but only from a science perspective. The session program says:

> There is an urgent need for increasing our ability to apply computational tools to mine big agro-ecosystems data through an interdisciplinary team of agricultural, medical and social scientists in order to improve efficiency of food production systems and provide science-based policy inputs, with the ultimate objective of improving health and well-being of local and global communities. The session will promote discussions on the development and implementation of research, outreach, and educational programs at local and global scales, fostering collaboration across disciplines, cultures, and countries, with the ultimate objective of promoting food production, safety and security and animal human and environmental health.

In order to try and get some discussion into the conference about design and its ability to connect science to society I submitted a proposal abstract and was selected to present a poster at the conference. The following is the abstract that I submitted with the title "Rural design as a link between science and society."

> Gaps in our knowledge about complex biomedical and environmental problems limit our ability to develop durable solutions in the spirit of One Medicine One Health . . . Compartmentalized science often misses crucial interactions and science often is not effectively involved into public policy debate . . . If science is crucial to create public policies for sustaining human, animal, and environmental health the science needs to be integrated and articulated so that it is impartial, useful and accepted.

Evidence-based rural design is a problem-solving process that can improve the linkage between science and society. It is a process that recognizes that human and natural systems are inextricably coupled in continuous cycles of mutual influence and response. It is a methodology for holistically crossing borders and connecting issues to nurture new design thinking and collaborative problem solving to create a better and prosperous future for humans, animals, and environments – locally and globally.

Rural design can be instrumental in seeking ways that teams of scientists (agricultural, medical, and social) can better bring scientific evidence to a societal problem and in turn raise new issues that science needs to resolve. It is a process to nurture collaboration and cooperation among rural communities to shape the landscape to provide and integrated system of humans, animals, and environments that meets the needs of people in the present without compromising for the future.

Related to human, animal and environmental wellness is the issue of food supply and food safety for a rapidly increasing world population. Dr. Katherine M.J. Swanson is a world-renowned food microbiologist involved with issues of food safety management and quality with a special focus on microbiological and allergen controls. Because of her global work I asked her to write a brief outline about the future of global food safety and its connections to both urban and rural futures as well as issues of climate change, food supply, and water, and this is her reply:

Food, water and shelter are essential for life, and the well-being of any society depends on how these needs are met. The nutritional needs of a society cannot be met if the food is not safe to eat, thus food safety has always been integrated with food availability. Our world relies on a global food supply and a rapidly increasing global population makes building food safety into the food supply even more important. Some regions have an abundant food supply, growing their own and importing food to add variety to their diets. Other regions cannot sustain their population on food grown locally and thus rely on imported food to nourish their people. The developing world may use food exports to build their economies. Conversely, in the developed world "food deserts" can exist in urban neighborhoods and rural towns without ready access to fresh, healthy and affordable food.

Food safety is both a rural and an urban issue. Good agricultural practices are essential for production of produce that is intended to be consumed with minimal or no processing or cooking to destroy pathogens. Site selection is important to avoid unintended chemical contaminants that may be present in certain soils. This applies to both rural and urban environments. Potential contaminants depend on prior land use and may include pesticides, herbicides, nitrate, metals, petroleum products, asbestos, lead paint, PCBs, pathogens and others.

Both animal- and plant-based food contribute to foodborne illness. Domesticated and wild animals can harbor pathogens in their intestinal tract. These pathogens can contaminate food through direct transfer in close proximity, water runoff (grazing on hills above land where vegetables are grown), flooding, contaminated irrigation water and wind. These pathogens may also transfer to raw meat in the processing facility. People can also harbor pathogens in their intestinal tract. Norovirus, the leading cause of foodborne illness, comes from the human intestinal tract.

While many perceive that foodborne illness rates are increasing, the U.S. Centers for Disease Control reported a 20 percent reduction in the incidence foodborne illness for 2013 compared to 1996–1998. However, one pathogen group, *Vibrio*, demonstrated a 173 percent increase in illness in this time period. *Vibrio* occurs naturally in marine waters and estuaries. Illness is usually associated with exposure to seawater or consumption of raw or undercooked seafood, especially raw oysters. Most outbreaks occur in summer months, and warmer water temperatures can increase the number of *Vibrio* present. *Vibrio* is now being isolated in Canadian waters, which used to be a rare event, illustrating potential environmental effects on food safety issues.

Just as architecture and construction industries have building, electrical, plumbing and other codes to facilitate safe design and construction, food safety codes are also available. The Codex Alimentarius Commission maintains standards for food in international trade, and individual countries adopt regulations relevant to their population. U.S. Food and Drug Administration and the U.S. Department of Agriculture administer regulations for food in interstate commerce. State and local authorities adapt or adopt standards or guidelines for their jurisdiction. For example, plan review is frequently required for food service or retail facilities, during which food safety consideration are addressed by state or local regulators.

Food safety regulations and guidelines are based on a framework that first identifies hazards that are likely to cause illness if not controlled, and then identifies controls required to prevent or eliminate the hazard or reduce it to an acceptable level. The merging of urban and rural environments from an architectural and design perspective may benefit from considering these questions: What can go wrong? And how can we prevent it to stop food safety and other problems from emerging?

(Private correspondence, January 28, 2016)

Dr. Swanson has outlined a challenge for architects, landscape architects, and planners to think more broadly about their projects to find ways that their designs can be responsive to the questions she has raised. Building codes address the safety, health, and welfare of the people who inhabit buildings, but are mostly silent on issues outside of the building. The comprehensive building code that is used throughout the United States, the International Building Code (IBC), establishes "minimum regulations for buildings systems using prescriptive and performance-related provisions." The IBC is also intended to be a forum for discussing issues safeguarding the public health and safety in all communities, large and small, urban and rural (IBC 2006).

I hope this book helps in addressing climate change, renewable energy, food security, and water resoursces in the discussion of human, animal, and environmental wellness to determine regulations to help shape the build environment. Architects and designers are in the unique position to help determine how to manage the development and interface between urban and rural futures and be creative and innovative in shaping the environment with another 2.5 billion people on the planet by the year 2050.

Chapter 6

Rural sustainability and green design

In the summer of 2013 I had the opportunity to participate in two international forums on green design involving sustainability and discussions about urbanism and rural development worldwide. From the discussions it seems as though there is no clear idea of what green design is. Everyone talks about green design sustainability and agrees that it is critically important, but no one is sure how it should be done, who should be responsible, or how to measure its effectiveness.

Richard Heinberg, of the Post Carbon Institute, has written extensively about the need to move away from fossil fuels, and in a publication of the Institute he asks the question: "What is sustainability?" In the article he cautions about the use of the word "sustainable" because it has been carelessly used, but goes on to say: "Nevertheless, the concept is indispensable and should be the cornerstone for all long-range planning." He states that many indigenous peoples have practiced sustainability for centuries and that the term was first used in Europe in 1713 by the German forester and scientist Hans Carl von Carlowitz. However, it gained widespread use after the 1987 Brundtland Report from the United Nations' World Commission on Environment and Development, which defined sustainable development as development that "meets the needs of the present generation without compromising the ability of future generations to meet their own needs." That is the definition that I am following for this book and in my own research and architectural work.

Heinberg has developed five axioms that he describes as self-evident truths to help understand sustainability:

One – Any society that continues to use critical resources unsustainably will collapse.
Two – Population growth and/or growth in the rates of consumption of resources cannot be sustained.
Three – To be sustainable, the use of renewable resources must proceed at a rate that is less than or equal to the rate of natural replenishment.

Four — To be sustainable the use of nonrenewable resources must proceed at a rate that is declining, and the rate of decline must be greater than or equal to the rate of depletion. The rate of depletion is defined as the amount being extracted and used during a specified time interval (usually a year) as a percentage of the amount left to extract.

Five — Sustainability requires that substances introduced into the environment from human activities are minimized and rendered harmless to biosphere functions. In cases where pollution from the extraction and consumption of nonrenewable resources has proceeded at expanding rates for some time and threatens the viability of ecosystems, reduction in the rates of extraction and consumption of those resources may need to occur at a rate greater that the rate of depletion.

These axioms may be self-evident, as Heinberg says, but they do enhance the argument that the purpose of the axioms is not to describe conditions that would lead to a good or just society, merely to a society able to be maintained over time. In urban planning and architectural design circles, the tripartite understanding of sustainability is (1) environmental, (2) economic, and (3) social equity (Heinberg 2010).

Green design is emerging as the means to bring design thinking into the discussion to attain sustainability, yet most green design thinking has focused on urbanism leaving rural resiliency dangling as a separate issue. That is a mistake because urban and rural issues must be connected. While this book focuses on rural sustainability with a rural point of view it is hoped that both points of view will be consolidated to enhance sustainability for both urban and rural ecosystems – and particularly in the peri-urban landscape.

The American Institute of Architects (AIA) has developed the 2030 Commitment as a national framework to improve and standardize reporting to evaluate design decisions for a building's energy performance. This commitment focuses on individual buildings, whereas green design suggests that a building is part of a unique climate and landscape so that issues of climate change, food security, water resources, wellness, and renewable energy must also be included in a building design and construction project.

The World Green Design Forum 2013 was held in Yangzhou and Beijing, China in May of that year. It was organized by the World Green Design Organization (WGDO) created by China and members of the European Union with the intent of conserving resources and protecting the environment in the design, manufacturing, usage, and disposal of products. This was the third WGDO summit, and the first in China, with attendees that included a wide range of government officials, designers, investors, manufacturers, representatives from high-tech zones, economic development zones, industrial parks, and the press. The WGDO focuses on advancing and promoting harmonious development between humans and nature through green design with the following principles:

- Design provides guidance to advanced industries.
- Green is the leading factor for the survival of future human civilization.
- Green design stands for the necessary and critically important development objective of affecting advanced forces of worldwide production and consumption.

I was invited to make a presentation on rural design at the 2013 Forum where I discussed how rural areas around the world can utilize design thinking and the problem-solving process of design to resolve rural issues. While most of the presentations and discussion at the Forum were urban oriented, I was left with the distinct impression that powerful political forces are under way in China and the European Union as governments work to define policies for green design that can help shape urbanization and the future of cities as well as the rural countryside. Even though most people in the future will live in cities, there seems to be a growing concern in China and around the globe for rural development that is sustainable while providing a better quality of life for rural citizens.

The Oslo Architectural Triennale 2013 was held in Oslo, Norway in September 2013 with the theme Behind the Green Door – Architecture and the Desire for Sustainability. Held every three years it is the largest architectural event in the Nordic countries and the organizers selected ROTOR (a Belgian design firm) to curate the conference and outline several exhibits about green design asking questions about sustainability such as: "How do we deal with this difficult, worn and torn, almost limitless concept once again? Do people care anymore? And moreover: can we give up on it?"

The Triennale embraces the idea that architecture influences everyone and can engage with everyone, and that high quality professional, artistic, and academic programs must interact with the actual concerns of communities and its citizens. There were several simultaneous exhibits at different venues involving sustainability and its impact over the past decades on architecture. The exhibits were asking if these old ideas might be more relevant and important today.

The conference focused on The Future of Comfort and how architecture can be an important instrument for creating new and sustainable lifestyles, on different scales and in different parts of the world, asking the question: "Does sustainable living involve a reduction in our current quality of life?" The most compelling presentation linking urban and rural design was by Carolyn Steel, an architect with the University of Cambridge and a leading thinker on food and cities. She discussed food systems as a primary condition for shaping our cities and our lives emphasizing the Global Footprint Network which says:

> The Earth provides all that we need to live and thrive. So what will it take for humanity to live within the means of one planet? Individuals and institutions worldwide must begin to recognize ecological limits. We must begin to make ecological limits central to our decision-making and use human ingenuity to find new ways to live, within the Earth's bounds.
> (Global Network Foundation, www.footprintnetwork.org)

The Global Footprint Network argues that it is critical that urban and rural issues be considered simultaneously and green design is a way to make meaningful sustainability connections between urban and rural development and the man-made and natural environments. Designers need to embrace the idea of One Healthy Planet integrating human, animal, and environmental wellness into their design and business practices while engaging citizens and working on projects in both urban and rural communities.

The ROTOR book that was a follow-up to the conference, *Behind the Green Door: A Critical Look at Sustainable Architecture through 600 Objects* (2014), provides a very interesting and critical overview of 600 hundred ideas expressing sustainable principles as an historic overview for sustainable architecture from the 1950s on. The projects have a wide range of character and meaning ranging from the master plan for Masdar City on the outskirts of Abu Dhabi with 45,000 inhabitants that would be one of the largest sustainable projects in the world if constructed as planed; to the Passive House Standard that in Norway will be compulsory for all residential development from 2015 onwards. It also includes the Whole Earth Catalog that was published from 1968 to 1972 with designs for alternative waste disposal systems and waterless toilets, and a celebration of local food systems.

Lionel Devilieger, the book's editor, describes their intention to

> argue strongly in favor of moving the debate about sustainability to the political sphere, served by science and not the other way around. Out of the labs, and into the democratic assembly halls. The public should be allowed to become knowledgeable again and to regain its competence to judge. It should be confronted again with the pros and cons, with the accusations that the opposing camps throw at each other.

I think the ROTOR book raises a number of questions about sustainable building design and the need for a clear definition of what is sustainable, what sustainable means, and how we achieve it.

The Leadership in Energy and Environmental Design (LEED) program has in America been the method to certify buildings at various levels of sustainability and it has been very effective in raising the bar and making architects and developers think about sustainability. The concern about the LEED program and its four levels of compliance raises the question as to whether a building that is sustainable can be only partially sustainable. If sustainability were to be net-zero carbon and net-zero energy as the criteria it either is or it is not. The LEED platinum level is the only level that approaches net-zero energy, however the program has started the process of designing with sustainability as a goal and that is a good thing. But where do we go from there?

In early October 2013 the Design Futures Council (DFC), an independent and interdisciplinary network of design, product, and construction leaders, organized a Leadership Summit on Sustainable Design in Minnesota. The Nantucket Principles that the DFC embraces outlines the urgency to meet the challenges of a rapidly and radically urbanizing world population that is putting the Earth's ecosystems at risk. The principles end with:

> Compelling evidence tells us there is a direct link between the sudden rise of preventable diseases and qualities of our built environment. We believe that the design professions must take new and energetic steps to lead the sustainable transformation of the human habitat and to bring wise solutions that improve the relationship between humans and the environment and to create systems that are truly sustainable.

The DFC manifesto supports the notion of green design as a problem-solving process where evidence-based design can assist designers in engaging with citizens, governments, and business leaders to provide visionary, sustainable, and integrated urban and rural designs for the good of humanity, for the good of animals, and for the good of the environment (Design Futures Council 2013).

United Nations and sustainable development

In October 2015, at the United Nations Sustainable Development Summit, world leaders adopted a set of seventeen Sustainable Development Goals to end poverty, fight inequality, and tackle climate change by the year 2030. The goal that addresses urbanism is Goal 11 which seeks to "make cities and human settlements inclusive, safe, resilient and sustainable." The UN Secretary-General, Mr. Ban Ki-moon, stated that

> cities are hubs for ideas, commerce, culture, science, productivity, social development and much more. At their best, cities have enabled people to advance socially and economically, however, many challenges exist to maintaining cities in a way that continues to create jobs and prosperity while not straining land and resources.
> (United Nations Sustainable Development Summit 2015, www.sustainabledevelopment.un.org/post2015/summit)

The Executive Director of UN-Habitat, Dr. Joan Clos, discussed the rapid urbanization that is taking place worldwide particularly in developing countries, and she goes on to say:

> Without appropriate legislation, good planning, and adequate financing cities can fail their populations. The problem that we face nowadays is that most of the new urbanization is spontaneous and unplanned. Therefore, instead of positive outcomes, it often yields negative externalities such as congestion, sprawl and segregation. Good urbanization does not come by chance. It comes from design.
> (UN-Habitat 2015)

The seventeen Sustainable Development Goals (each with specific targets to be reached by 2030) that were adopted by the United Nations in 2015 are:

Goal 1 – End poverty in all its forms everywhere.
Goal 2 – End hunger, achieve food security and improved nutrition and promote sustainable agriculture.
Goal 3 – Ensure healthy lives and promote well-being for all at all ages.
Goal 4 – Ensure inclusive and equitable quality education and promote lifelong learning opportunities for all.
Goal 5 – Achieve gender equality and empower all women and girls.
Goal 6 – Ensure availability and sustainable management of water and sanitation for all.
Goal 7 – Ensure access to affordable, reliable, sustainable and modern energy for all.
Goal 8 – Promote sustained, inclusive and sustainable economic growth, full and productive employment and decent work for all.
Goal 9 – Build resilient infrastructure, promote inclusive and sustainable industrialization and foster innovation.
Goal 10 – Reduce inequality within and among countries.
Goal 11 – Make cities and human settlements inclusive, safe, resilient and sustainable.
Goal 12 – Ensure sustainable consumption and production patterns.
Goal 13 – Take urgent action to combat climate change and its impacts.
Goal 14 – Conserve and sustainably use the oceans, seas, and marine resources for sustainable development.
Goal 15 – Protect, restore and promote sustainable use of terrestrial ecosystems, sustainably manage forests, combat desertification, and halt and reverse land degradation and halt biodiversity loss.
Goal 16 – Promote peaceful and inclusive societies for sustainable development, providing access to justice for all and build effective, accountable and inclusive institutions at all levels.
Goal 17 – Strengthen the means of implementation and revitalize the global partnership for sustainable development.

These seventeen Sustainable Development Goals require that everyone do their part: governments, the private sector, civil society, and all people in order for the goals to be reached by 2030. Although the goals seem to focus primarily on urban development however they also apply to rural development. An exciting new initiative emerging from the World Green Design Organization (WGDO) (a partnership between China and the Europe) along with the United Nations is to promote green design worldwide. While the emphasis of the WGDO has been on urban development, it has now established a World Rural Development Committee (WRDC) to "improve the comprehensive level of rural sustainability of the world" (WGDO 2015).

I was invited to Beijing for the WRDC inaugural ceremony in October 2015 and appointed as the Vice Director of the World Rural Development Committee. The following is the Declaration establishing the committee and its vision:

We are people from all over the world who have a passion for rural heritage and culture. In a time of rapid rural change due to climate change, urbanization, and concerns for food security, water resources, and rural sustainability we are gathering in Beijing to initiate the founding of WGDO-WRDC (World Rural Development Committee under the framework of World Green Design Organization).

The purpose of the WRDC is to upgrade the academic standard and international cooperation in policy and practice of rural design worldwide. This will be accomplished by advocating good rural design that is people-centered, culture-driven, green and recyclable, urban-rural coordinated and sustainable development. Also, it will endeavor to inherit fine rural culture, protect world cultural diversity and environmental resource, and promote development of an ecological based civilization.

WRDC is committed to providing guidance and solutions for all countries (developing countries in particular) on the comprehensive and sustainable development of environments, productions, livelihoods, cultures and technologies in rural areas. It will encouraging the rediscovery and dissemination of traditional wisdom derived from agricultural culture, and promote sustainable development of rural areas in China and other countries.

WRDC will be a platform to exchange rural design experiences, such as exploring traditional wisdom of each country and legacy inheritance and discussing related theories and practices. In the spirit of being cross-border, transparent, practical, and forward-looking, WRDC will actively review and disseminate advanced design conceptions and practices in mankind's development that are consistent with the five elements of "ecology, production, livelihood, history, and future." It will promote concepts to reduce irreversible damage to and waste of resources of agricultural production, environmental protection, cultural inheritance, and sustainable development in both urban and rural areas caused by one-sided thinking and irrational behaviors. This is being done to make sure that excellent rural design conceptions will take root in rural developments worldwide. By doing so, WRDC will make its own contribution to the development of human civilization and bring benefits to people around the world.

Rural areas are the cradle for human civilizations all over the world. Agriculture is the base and security source for survival and development of humans worldwide. It is where the hope for a green and ecological society lies. With urbanization, people have become more aware of issues, such as nature oriented urban environments and ecological resources and have come to a new stage where rural value is recognized and exemplary rural designs are needed. *Globally Important Agricultural Heritage Systems* proposed by UN-FAO, *UN-Habitat Award* by United Nations Human Settlements Programme, *World Cultural and Natural Heritage* and *Intangible Cultural Heritage of Humanity* by UNESCO, and *Millennium Development Goals* by UN have all demonstrated the value of rural cultural heritage and sustainable design in its modernization transformation.

Sadly, the brand value of the unique, comprehensive and forward-looking strategic area of rural design has not been universally acknowledged by design schools and the design professions the same as they have for urban design.

The World Green Design Organization was jointly established by China and Europe as an international organization dedicated to the promotion of green design and rural design and development worldwide. The focus of the World Rural Development Committee is on *grand rural design*, which brings the problem-solving process of design to help realize the comprehensive development of rural culture, economy and society. It includes all rural sustainability-oriented design activities that use human intelligence and knowledge to transform nature and themselves, which includes both traditional design inherited from history and modern innovative design. It will involve a number of design areas, such as environment and ecology; symbiosis of animals, plants and human beings; production technologies and products; circular economy and production and consumption system; residential buildings and daily commodities; cultural brand and knowledge dissemination system; community management and talent development mechanism; technology applications; and all steps of the design process from design thinking, to design development, to design implementation.

We believe, we will be able to provide food security, a healthier life, a better world and a more sustainable and greener tomorrow for our future generations by studying, thinking, discussing and advocating exemplary rural design, improving the development experience, stepping up communication and experience sharing, and providing vast rural areas with public and community-based designs for sustainable development. We are looking forward to working with people of all walks of life towards a goal that is worth pursuing for a better world now and into the future.

(WRDC 2015)

The person in China most responsible for organizing and managing both the WGDO and WRDC, and arranging for me to attend the ceremony in Beijing, is Ms. Jiang Haoshu of the Ministry of Culture in China. She is a dynamic and energetic woman who gets things done, exemplifying one of the principles of rural design which is "empowering women to become community leaders is more likely to provide effective resolution of the complexity of rural issues." Ms. Jiang Haoshu proves that principle with a great passion for green design, rural design, and rural cultural heritage and through her strong leadership with the WGDO and WRDC she is influencing the world.

What the WRDC will accomplish for rural areas around the world is unknown at this time, yet it is the first international effort to promote rural design as a new design discipline that brings design thinking and the problem-solving process of design to rural issues. I hope that this effort can find a way to improve the future of rural agricultural landscapes that have been designated as world heritage sites and to find a way that rural heritage and rural futures can be linked in a way that preserves rural cultural traditions while adapting to 21st-century technology and create opportunities for rural people in a rapidly changing world.

At the inaugural ceremony, Parvis Koohafkan, the founder and president of the World Agricultural Heritage Foundation located in Rome, spoke eloquently about their mission to promote and preserve sustainable agriculture and rural developments through policy and technical assistance, networking, research, training, and education for safeguarding and dynamic conservation of the world's agricultural heritage systems and sites. Their goal is to support counties and the United Nations Food and Agricultural Organization in building a major international platform to identify, recognize, and safeguard "Globally Important Agricultural Heritage Systems" (GIAHS) around the world.

These GIAHS are defined by the UN FAO (2002) as "remarkable land use systems and landscapes which are rich in globally significant biological diversity evolving from the co-adaptation of a community with its environment and its needs and aspirations for sustainable development." Examples of GIAHS are described as:

1. Mountain rice terrace agroecosystems
2. Multiple cropping/polyculture farming systems
3. Understory farming systems
4. Nomadic and semi-nomadic pastoral systems
5. Ancient irrigation, soil and water management systems
6. Complex multi-layered home gardens
7. Below sea level systems
8. Tribal agricultural heritage systems
9. High-value crop and spice systems
10. Hunter-gathering systems.

Rural agricultural systems that reflect GIAHS criteria include:

- The Chiloe Agriculture System on Chiloe Islands in Chile. It is a group of islands in southern Chile with native forms of agriculture practiced for hundreds of years based on the cultivation of numerous local varieties of potatoes.
- The Andean Agriculture System in the Cuzco-Puno corridor in Peru. It is a terraced system for planting (like at Machu Picchu) that was developed by the Incas to provide tillable land, control erosion, and protect crops during freezing nights.

- The Ifugao Rice Terraces in the Philippines. The terraces are a 2,000-year-old organic paddy farming system that has a strong culture–nature connection with water management and engineering systems for growing rice that were developed over time.
- The Rice-Fish Culture in Qingtian County, China. It is an integrated farming system of fish ponds and rice patties that perform essential ecological functions.
- The Hani Rice Terraces in China have been operated by the Hani people for over 1,300 years. It is a landscape of forests, villages, terraces, and rivers that fertilize terraces using waste and sewage from the village along with hydropower and water-purification for the people.
- The Wannian Traditional Rice Culture in China. They are using experiences developed over hundreds of years in rice seedling preparation and transplanting, field management, harvesting, storage, and processing.
- The Oasis of the Maghreb in Tunisia. These are green islands in the desert with a sophisticated irrigation system supporting villages and providing income through sale of dates.
- The Maasai Pastorial System in Kenya and Tanzania. This is an old pastoral system and culture with rotational grazing that continues to strike a social and environmental balance in a fragile environment.

These GIAHS sites represent agricultural systems that simultaneously exhibit remarkable features of local and global significance. Climate change, however, is having a negative impact on these systems since the great majority of farmers in developing nations are subsistence farmers who work small plots of land, often in marginal land areas with harsh environments. Yet these GIAHS have much to offer the world in the 21st century as to how to live on the land without destroying it. We need to figure out how to utilize the knowledge of these systems to adjust to climate change without relying on excessive external ideas and technologies that are inappropriate and unsustainable resulting in the loss of the system forever. The GIAHS recognize the changes that are taking place in agriculture and many of the sites have not been calculated as economic resources with value that extends far beyond the food they produce. The challenge is to find new ways of giving value to the GIAHS assets by finding broader markets for consumers of products with cultural identity and promoting appropriate ecotourism so that local farmers can sustain their traditions (Koohafkan and Altieri 2011).

Examples of innovative technology for rural areas

The following are three examples of innovative projects in rural regions that illustrate the opportunity for nurturing entrepreneurship and innovation in rural communities while promoting sustainability and improving rural quality of life. The first is a proposal for a rural village in China to bring high-speed internet access to its residents; the second is a constructed bioenergy project in rural Minnesota to create electricity for a rural city using agricultural waste; and the third is a project by the Institute of Landscape Architecture at the Wrocław University of Environmental and Life Sciences in Poland that is a study of the cultural landscape of a rural region focusing on wind farms.

High-speed internet access in rural China

This is a research project looking at rural villages in rural China by Mary Ann Ray and Robert Mangurian at the University of Michigan. Their BASEBeijing study, *Toward a More Sustainable Rural China*, is the result of several years (since 2007) of analysis and design in the village of Shang Shui Guo (Upper Water Valley) village in the Pearl River Valley Township, Greater Beijing Municipal Region – a forty-minute drive north of the Great Wall. They describe their intentions for the study as follows:

> Today, one in every ten people on earth lives in a rural Chinese village. And yet, the Chinese rural village is the most endangered human habitat on the face of the earth. The discipline of architecture has largely been focused and fascinated by the city and by urbanism. This project turns its attention toward the environment of the rural village in an attempt, through design, to make it a more viable and sustainable habitat option for the 21st century. If the rural village does not survive, the influx of rural residents to urban areas will mean that in the next 15 to 20 years the equivalent of all of the American cities will need to be built to accommodate them. And this would lead to a "whiz bang quick city" scenario of poorly planned or unplanned cities.
>
> The projects and design proposals that are in the report address sustainability for human habitats in two ways. Some of the projects learn from the highly sustainable aspects of the rural Chinese environment already in place and propose exporting them in new forms for contemporary urban life, while other projects propose new sustainable objects and spaces that are meant to bring the rural village forward and make it equally viable, if not more viable than urban settings, as a 21st century human environment.

One of the results of this project working with the rural village was to design an inflatable translucent balloon that could float over the village as a modern visual symbol of the community while providing free wireless internet access to village residents (Figure 6.1). The Team describes the project as follows:

> CLOUD: Village Online is a forty-foot-long illuminated translucent balloon that provides one rural village with wireless internet (Figure 6.2). Rural residents around the world are deprived of online access and of the benefits it provides toward successful entrepreneurism, education, access to

6.1
CLOUD concept for bringing high-speed internet service to the remote Chinese village of Shang Shui Guo.

the wider world and to their family members working in the cities, and entertainment. CLOUD moves information, thereby reducing the need for the transportation and migrations of people while increasing their economic mobility. The balloon assembly is a series of translucent triangular cells of rip-stop nylon filled with standard latex weather balloons that will give it lift. It is intended to be cloud-like, but to also appear like a very contemporary technological thing, giving the village the feeling that it is a part of the 21st century. At night, it glows and illuminates the dark villages (Figure 6.3). During the day, its shadow shades the public places in the village.

The project has been put forth to gain government attention by providing an inexpensive real solution that can be implemented to provide internet to rural areas. CLOUD provides a solution that does not require excessive and expensive physical infrastructure. CLOUD has been successful in tests undertaken in the U.S., in June 2015, and later after government approval it will be tested and installed in Shang Shui Guo village in China.

We will be presenting the project to government officials and propose implementing it at the scale of the Pearl River Valley Township and then to broader areas of rural China. Today, one of every ten humans on Earth lives in a rural Chinese village, and CLOUD has the possibility of directly and significantly affecting their lives.

This is a very interesting project and an excellent example of what dedicated designers, who bring design thinking to remote rural regions, can accomplish through university design research on a global scale. Mary Ann Ray and Robert

6.2
CLOUD concept over the village at twilight.

Rural sustainability and green design

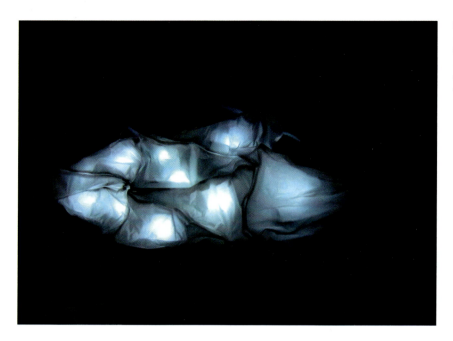

6.3
CLOUD concept over the village at night. The CLOUD becomes a focal point for communication as well as a visual beacon for the village.

Mangurian have been doing similar work for over 15 years. The Team they assembled for the CLOUD project includes engineers from the University of Michigan and representatives from the School of Information at the University of Michigan and Tsinghua University in China.

Energy from agricultural waste in Minnesota

The Hometown BioEnergy facility near Le Sueur, Minnesota was developed by the Minnesota Municipal Power Association (MMPA) to meet state-mandated renewable energy standards. MMPA worked with Avant Energy, Inc., an innovative Minnesota energy management company, that planned, developed, and constructed the facility in 2013. Avant Energy also manages its operation and the facility is now producing energy from vegetable-processing waste from canning facilities and livestock manure in an anaerobic digestion process to produce biogas that run the generators to produce power. The by-products of this process include liquid fertilizer that is sold back to local farmers and the use of undigested biomass that is dried to create a solid fuel that can be sold to other biomass and coal-fired facilities to fuel their boilers.

This type of renewable energy is not familiar in rural America or in Minnesota so Avant Energy had to work closely with and educate the community about the project. Landscape architect Jeff McMenimen and me as the architect were involved in some early design efforts when the biomass facility was proposed to be located along a major highway at the entrance to the community. Since the location was very prominent and had the potential to become the catalyst for a larger industrial park for the city the design had to not only respond to the functional needs of the bioenergy facility but also present a strong image to the community. The site plan and site elevation shown in Figures 6.4 and 6.5 were developed by McMenimen and me for that site.

Later, because of budget impacts and locational issues, the site shifted to a former gravel pit on the outskirts of the community, Avant Energy focused on an engineering approach to the development and we were no longer involved, however many of the architectural ideas were retained. Since agriculture is one of Minnesota's largest industries the utilization of agricultural waste to create energy is a natural fit. Since utilities have been mandated to meet renewable energy standards the flexibility of biogas energy production in responding to energy demand provides advantages over solar and wind resources. The Minnesota Power Association, a joint venture of eleven rural Minnesota cities, is a direct response to this mandate. Avant Energy manages the energy systems for the Minnesota Power Association and, because of the way the facility was designed and engineered, they can adjust power production to take advantage of fluctuations in prices and sell when there is a high demand and reduce output when the demand is low.

6.4
Early site plan drawing of the Hometown BioEnergy facility along a major highway at the north entrance to the City of Le Sueur, Minnesota.

Rural sustainability and green design

The Hometown BioEnergy anaerobic digester on the south edge of the Le Sueur community (the town is the home of the Green Giant Co. with canneries processing sweet corn and peas providing waste material) is the largest system of its type in the United States (Figures 6.6 and 6.7). The facility has two 1.6 million gallon digesters and three large domes for storing the gas that is used to run the generators to produce electricity. Since most of the power is used by the adjacent town of Le Sueur (population 4,000) the facility does not need to connect to large electric transmission lines.

6.5
Elevation drawing of the proposed Hometown BioEnergy facility from the highway side.

6.6
Photograph of the front entry side of the Hometown BioEnergy facility as constructed in an abandoned gravel pit on the south side of Le Sueur.

6.7
Photograph of the back side of the Hometown BioEnergy facility in winter.

Avant Energy worked very hard to involve the community into the design process (an important principle of rural design) to integrate with the agricultural landscape. Odor was a concern, but that is handled by biofilters to eliminate the volatile organic compounds that cause them. Since its opening in 2013 it has been well received by the community and the project was honored as one of the top five renewable energy plants in America in 2014. Hometown BioEnergy with its utilization of agricultural waste was the only honored facility that was not solar, wind, or hydropower.

This project illustrates the kind of connected thinking that sustainability issues require. It is clear that any reduction of global carbon emissions cannot be accomplished by architects alone designing net-zero energy buildings with solar collectors – although it is part of the solution. The real impact is on providing power from renewable resources at local and regional levels that is led by utility companies. The Hometown BioEnergy facility is that kind of endeavor and becomes a model for other community utilities to look at opportunities in their region to create power from renewable and available resources – wind, solar, hydro, and biomass. One should think of these opportunities as an agricultural resource to be harvested.

Rural landscapes and architecture in Poland

Irena Niedźwiecka-Filipiak is head of the Institute of Landscape Architecture at the Wrocław University of Environmental and Life Sciences. For over 20 years she has worked with academic teams conducting research into rural transformations in Poland. Her research work includes a wide range of historic-landscape studies and area development plans. She has introduced the term of "rural landscape distinguishing marks" specifying their form of use for future area development as well as the creation of the Network of the Most Interesting Villages in Poland. She has also carried out landscape analyses regarding optimal locations for wind farms and is currently conducting research into the possibilities of a systemic approach to green area management within urban vicinities.

She is actively participating in the Rural Renewal Program in Poland collaborating with local communities. In 2015, with a grant from the Kosciuszko Foundation, she was a visiting scholar at the Center for Rural Design at the University of Minnesota and for my book I asked her to describe her research work in Poland:

> Rural areas in Poland account for 93.1 percent of the country area and home to 39.4 percent of the country inhabitants. Their futures are dependent on today's decisions and the approach to problem solving. The main problem in Poland is not conducting resource inventory but the ability to grasp and understand the processes occurring here and specifying actions that could have a positive effect on shaping and managing these areas. Providing for the actual needs of their inhabitants while ensuring the preservation of

regional diversity, it also involves maintaining the character of these rural areas distinct from the urbanized city landscape. Villages used to be the farmers' dwelling and working environment, but currently only a small number of rural dwellers live off the land, the remaining have a source of income other than agriculture.

The legally binding documentation for investors is local area development plans, and they account for approximately 30 percent of the area of Poland. Additionally, most of them are rather scattered around the country as they are created for specific investments and do not cover a whole larger area. Moreover they are frequently oriented towards residential development only not taking into consideration the falling demographic figures (depopulation and society aging) or appropriate public space allowances including recreational zones for rural inhabitants. On the other hand we are witnessing now a growing pressure from building investments in suburban areas as well as those ones which are attractive for tourism or industrial ones. Mindless succumbing to this phenomenon frequently results in fragmentation of open spaces and creation of areas which are saturated with building structures but devoid of greenery.

The Project for Green Infrastructure for the City of Wrocław Functional Area is an example of our work and approach to a rural design area. It was carried out in 2014 by the study-design studio at the Wrocław University of Environmental and Life Sciences. The work was commissioned by the Regional Development Institute (IRT) and conducted by the team within the framework of the project "The Study of the Functional Cohesion in the Wrocław Functional Area" that was co-financed by the European Union from the operational program Technical Aid 2007–2013.

The inventories and analyses conducted within its framework as well as the team's own research and analyses formed the basis for seeking solutions. The study itself encompasses the metropolitan area of Wrocław comprising three urban municipalities (including the Wrocław municipality), ten urban–rural municipalities and sixteen rural ones. It covers an area of approximately 4100 square kilometers (290 for the City of Wrocław and approximately 3,800 for the surrounding areas outside the city borders). The region has approximately one million inhabitants (631,400 in Wrocław and 372,300 in the rural areas outside the city). Besides Wrocław there are currently twelve other locations with municipal rights (town privileges).

The aim of the project was to determine a layout for green infrastructure that would substantially contribute to the structural tissue of the area. It was designed to ensure protection of environmentally valuable areas from building investment, and, most importantly, limit and prevent fragmentation of green and open spaces as well as preserve the environmental resources in the vicinity of settlement zones. Consequently, the initial guidelines for land management in this respect were drawn up.

6.8
Location of the study area in Poland including the Wrocław Functional Area and the Municipality of Paczkow.

The Wrocław Functional Area is located in the southwest part of Poland (Figure 6.8). Its prevailing area is of plain character. The area relief structure is of longitudinal type, which is determined by the nature of its individual geographic regions and the direction of its main river the Oder which, along with the rivers Widawa and Oława, flow centrally through it.

In the search for the most optimal solution the authors analyzed the existing structures of high greenery and surface waters taking into consideration their protection forms. Subsequently, they synthesized the data on maps superimposing the boundaries of the protection areas and ecological corridors and then with simplified patterns comprising the high greenery clumps and surface water areas. The main elements of the proposed structure were eventually determined by means of superposition. It forms the axis of the system comprising the valley of the rivers Oder, Widawa, and Oława along with the forest complexes and Landscape Park of the Jerzyca Valley. It has a shape of a sand-clock with a distinct narrowing in the Wrocław urbanized zone. The spanning structures are three green rings of a varied rank, whose function is to connect possibly most of the scattered and fragmented elements (Figure 6.9).

Because of the present conditions the continuity of two of them has been disrupted with an aim, however, to regain it in the future. Based

on the remaining rivers and existing green elements additional wedge-like structures were designed, whose aim would be to reinforce the whole future system. Basing on the studies carried for individual municipalities the authors determined principal functions for separate elements of the proposed green infrastructure (Figure 6.10) as well as for the spaces created between them, which in the project are referred to as units. The system has connections with the greenery system inside the city.

The first Ring will act as a filter and clear borderline between the city built-up zone and rural areas. It is meant to combine parks and areas with high greenery. All the rings perform a leading ecological function but Rings Two and Three have additional tourist recreational functions of a

6.9
Proposed layout for the green infrastructure in the Wrocław Functional Area with green rings. The main axis of the system is in the form of a sand-clock with a narrowing in the Wrocław urbanized zone, the wedges based on the Oder River and its influxes, and the spaces between the main systemic elements.

6.10
Simplified map of the green infrastructure in the Wrocław Functional Area.

single day character for Wrocław inhabitants, and Ring Three of a several day excursion character.

One of the features here can be ecological agriculture with healthy food manufacturing and local produce sale as an attractive element. This ring creates a connection with the supraglacial ecological hubs. The spaces in between the main elements of the structure have been called units with land planned for open spaces, agricultural production, maximally concentrated built-up areas, and business activity inside them. The implementation and execution of this concept must be preceded by detailed studies and preparations carried out in collaboration with representatives of the local authorities, business people, and most importantly all the interested local communities.

(Private correspondence, November 21, 2015)

Irena Niedźwiecka-Filipiak also focuses, in her research work, on the third dimension of landscape, as exemplified by another study conducted by her: The Study of the Cultural Landscape of the Paczkow Municipality, which determined locations for wind farms within the area of Paczkow Municipality. She describes this study:

The Paczkow Municipality is attractively situated in the Sudety Foothills region and the valley of Otmuchow. It is an undulating terrain surrounded by hills with the vicinity of the artificial water reservoirs Lake of Otmuchow and Lake of Paczkow. The town of Paczkow itself is frequently referred to as Polish Carcassonne thanks to its perfectly preserved city walls, historic layout of the streets and valuable monuments. The study is of particular value and interest as besides traditional analyses of cultural and natural heritage values it also takes into account the analyses of the visual values

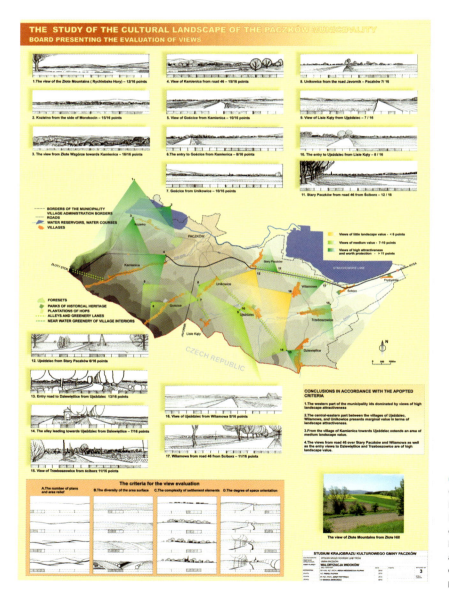

6.11
One of the presentation boards of the cultural landscape study of the City of Paczkow regarding the location of wind farms with analysis and evaluation of views in a series of perspective sketches.

Rural sustainability and green design

of the local open landscape. The study proposes a view assessment method with four assessment criteria: number of investment plans and area relief; land cover diversification; complexity of the settlement elements; and the degree of the area specificity.

It was found that crop diversity has an effect on the diversity of the area surface structure and enriches the colors, which enhances the attractiveness of the views. Also the area undulation, landscape depth, visible relations between settlements and high greenery and alleys of trees accentuating the roads are all diversifying elements contributing to the enhancement of the area's scenic and visual values. Based on this analysis and the evaluation of natural and cultural resources within the municipality the locations situated in the eastern part of the area were indicated as eligible places for wind farm installations. It should be noted that the local authorities have put forward installation of sixty-four wind turbines over the virtually entire area of the municipality, without consideration of scenic and visual values, which would definitely thwart the prospects for tourism development in the region (Figure 6.11).

From her involvement with the Center for Rural Design I can attest to the excellent work that she and her colleagues are doing in Poland. Her efforts to find the design connections to link urban and rural Poland together using green infrastructure, tourism, and cultural heritage concepts to shape the rural landscape are exemplary. The first project will be published in a landscape architecture magazine in Poland and the reader can refer to it for more information on their approach (Niedźwiecka-Filipiak et al. 2015).

Rural futures

These innovative technology projects are all different in their intent to improve rural environments and are all located in different parts of the world, yet they ask the same question: What is the future for rural regions? As in many other regions of America and worldwide, the people living in rural Minnesota are wondering what their rural character will be like in twenty or fifty years. Where will people live and work with the expected rapid increase in population that will impact both urban and rural areas? For example, Minnesota is estimated to have a population increase of one million people by 2050, and where these people will live and work is an important question that is currently not being addressed by the state government.

These are questions, however, that the Center for Rural Design at the University of Minnesota has been discussing with rural communities throughout Minnesota and within the university to find ways to empower rural citizens to shape their futures while considering the following important observations and questions:

- The population will increase significantly in both urban and rural regions due to immigration with a more diversified and aging demography.
- The rural landscape of each region of the state was developed with a particular economy in mind. As new opportunities and needs emerge, what knowledge base can aid the state to recognize the landscape's potential for economies of the future? Where will people want to live?
- For the economies of the future, how can rural design and a regional approach support the critical mass of people (families, young people, and elderly) needed to maintain anchoring institutions such as schools, hospitals, businesses, and churches?
- What will enable transportation (road, rail, and river) needs to be seriously considered as infrastructure – in visioning and supporting economies of the future?
- How can education be best delivered to enhance economic prosperity? How can local school districts and higher education be better connected?
- What is the relationship of small rural towns to regional centers, and what are the relationships of regional centers in Minnesota to the large Twin Cities metropolitan region?
- What are the land-based assets of each region that can be utilized to ensure a healthy future?
- Minnesota is blessed to have four distinct biomes that run diagonally through the state and what are the aspects of the unique geological and landscape character of the state's regions that need to be preserved and enhanced?
- What are the opportunities for entrepreneurship and capital funding to support and enhance environmental protection, economic development, and improving quality of life while allowing future generations the opportunity to find theirs?

Rural design is a manifestation of design thinking that it is part of the transition from the rural economy to the industrial economy to the design economy. The design economy has been expressed as a concept that nurtures the democratic ideal and free flow of information; and its practice can help create a social and business environment where innovation and entrepreneurship will flourish. In support of the design economy Tom Fisher, former dean of the College of Design at the University of Minnesota and now director of the Metropolitan Design Center, writes "What design really does is help us think in innovative, out-of-the-box ways, seeing the world as not just the result of logical, rational decision- making, but also as an emotional and deeply cultural response to reality that has lot to do with the look and feel of things" (Fisher 2013).

Rural design as a problem-solving process can create models so that rural regions can understand their assets and utilize technology so that the production of goods and services through regional cooperation and collaboration contributes to sustainable rural economic development, environmental improvement, and a better quality of life.

Richard Florida calls people who like to function with new ideas and concepts the "creative class." In an essay he states that more and more businesses are starting to understand the importance diversity has in hiring and retaining creative employees, yet most civic leaders fail to understand the same relationship. Places that succeed in attracting and retaining creative people are more likely to prosper. Those places generally have greater diversity of people and higher levels of environmental quality. They are places that accept newcomers and immigrants quickly into all sorts of social and economic situations. Florida goes on to argue that creative people value diversity in all of its manifestations, enjoy a mix of influences with different kinds of music, and try different kinds of food. They want to meet and socialize with a wide range of people. Also, creative people value outdoor recreation very highly and are drawn to places and communities where many outdoor activities are available. Openness to migration is particularly important for smaller cities and rural regions, and to attract and welcome creative people they have to develop the kind of social opportunities creative people value (Florida 2002).

The importance of social capital cannot be underestimated and is often described as two types: external bridging that connects people from different groups; and internal bonding within a homogeneous group. It is essential that both types of social capital be involved in developing the kind of community so crucial to the problem-solving process of rural design thinking in addressing and resolving rural needs. When human diversity and academic knowledge are joined through design thinking and the design process great and exciting things can happen.

Rural development has often been seen as an "external" phenomenon whereby rural regions engage experts to suggest changes and provide guidance to a specific program. For example, if a rural city wants to establish an industrial park to promote new businesses and jobs, it often hires urban consultants who have designed other urban industrial parks to develop a plan. Even when the community is involved in the planning process, the recommended plan often reflects the urban thinking and skills of the consultants rather than the unique land assets of the region and the values citizens place on it. Externally driven plans may have good ideas, but often lack the community support necessary to become successful.

On the other hand, rural development that is "internally" driven is much more likely to gain community support and achieve consensus on a strategy, but may not be so successful in implementation. For example if a regional industrial park is a goal for economic development, a rural region might form a non-profit entity or government authority to coordinate and manage efforts to entice a company to locate and construct a building in the park. Often this role becomes part of the local Chamber of Commerce, and while the intention is good, and may have strong local support, the real opportunities and innovative options for entrepreneurship and business expansion may have been overlooked by local businesses.

Rural development can be best achieved when it embraces and fosters systemic and holistic thinking. In the example of a regional industrial park for economic development, the community-based rural design approach would first survey and determine regional land assets, find connections between economic development, education, financing, tourism, and quality of life; and then, through community workshops, define the values the community places on them. By using the community-based process of rural design, planners and consultants can work with citizens to outline options, provide alternatives, and create a vision for the regional industrial park as an integral part of the social, economic, environmental, political, and cultural fabric of the community. As a result of a vision based on regional assets the name "industrial park" might be reconsidered by the community, and become branded as a "center for innovation" to embrace entrepreneurship, market technological creativity, and promote human diversity as a way to effectively compete in the global economy.

In the end, rural futures are integrally connected with urban futures and this may be one of the great challenges of our time. Thomas Forster and Arthur Gets Escudero discussed this issue in an article *City Regions as Landscape for People, Food, and Nature* where they say urban and rural do not need to be opposing forces. They go on to say: "The dichotomy between urban and rural has been used to support a model of development that is no longer as relevant. It serves present purposes better to think of an urban-rural continuum in all regions, with mutually reinforcing and reciprocal relationships, and flow of resources, people, and information" (Foster and Gets Escudero 2014).

Challenge for higher education

The University of Minnesota recently invited faculty to submit ideas for what it called the Grand Challenge to foster a vision for how the University of Minnesota, as a land-grant institution, is especially well positioned to marshal exceptional strengths and to lead in finding solutions to global issues. I submitted this idea for linking urban and rural futures in a summary:

> In a time of rapid change this challenge is for the University of Minnesota to become a global leader in linking rural and urban futures. Urbanization worldwide has been accelerating as people move from rural areas to urban areas for economic advancement, creating urban development that sprawls into the countryside, eliminating much of the best farmland surrounding cities. By 2050 there may be another 2.5 billion people on the planet. Where will these people live and work, and how will the land be shaped to accommodate needs today without compromising future generations' ability to respond to theirs?
>
> Design and design thinking is a strong University resource to bring multi-disciplinary science, creativity, innovation, and entrepreneurship together to find ways that limited rural and urban land and water resources can be better shaped and utilized to resolve critical issues of climate change,

food security, renewable energy, and human, animal, and environmental wellness.

The results of this Grand Challenge process are yet to be determined by the University of Minnesota, but based on a reading of the 130 faculty proposals there is room for encouragement as it appears that resiliency, food production, and food security are becoming more understandable by both urban and rural people to meet a largely urban population, but in a way that helps integrate discussion and problem solving for both urban and rural regions.

Design that reflects climate, culture, and place is a mindset that both urban and rural architects, planners, landscape architects, systems managers, and policymakers can embrace to improve social, economic, and environmental wellness – urban and rural – while reducing carbon and reliance on fossil fuels. It also may become the opportunity for institutions of higher learning to recognize that rural design is a new design discipline that should be taught and discussed at the same level of importance as urban design.

Time will tell what the University of Minnesota decides, but time is running out as to how to shape the world locally and globally to deal with issues today that preserves and enhances the environment in a way that will allow future generations the opportunity to manage and preserve theirs.

Chapter 7

In-between landscapes

The landscape in-between urban and rural is called the peri-urban landscape. They are zones of transition from rural to urban land uses and located between the outer limits of urban development and the rural environment. It is where urban and rural issues meet, and peri-urban is a relatively new designation trying to define the complexity of natural, agricultural, and urban ecosystems impacted by the demands of both urban and rural areas. The boundaries are porous and transitory as urban expansion extends into agricultural landscapes. The peri-urban zone has existed ever since communities and cities were first established to accommodate the collective needs of people and the dynamics of urban living. These communities were located and developed into cities because they had secure water and energy supplies and fertile lands for food production. As they grew they generally sprawled into available adjacent lands without thinking about the consequences, and in recent times this process has accelerated around the world as rural people have immigrated to urban areas.

For cities to be livable and sustainable into the future there is a need to maintain their natural resource and agricultural base in their peri-urban area, raising the question of how the peri-urban landscape should be shaped in response to growing concerns about water, food and environmental security to meet increases in urban populations. There can be no specific answer since all peri-urban landscapes are different. What can be developed are guidelines that will help people living in these areas better understand the dilemma, challenges and choices they have. This is a great opportunity for designers (architects, landscape architects, and planners) to start to explore and develop ideas that can stimulate discussions about the potentials and possibilities for the future. Urban agriculture may be one of the key components of this exploration to help shape ideas.

Since we have been living with a dichotomy between urban and rural sectors, where the issues have been looked at separately by governments and institutions (including the design professions) the gap between urban and rural has rarely been bridged. There are many people living and working in the peri-urban landscape but usually they have different and competing interests, practices, and perceptions depending on their orientation. There is a clear need for different policy solutions for peri-urban areas than to those developed for urban and rural areas – yet they all have to work from the same understanding of the land and its sustainable characteristics for growing food, providing education, health services, recreation, water resources, transportation, and construction of the buildings required for human living and working.

There is an expanding awareness worldwide that by looking at urban issues separate from rural issues neither can be adequately resolved. They must be linked and looked at as integrated systems. The first international conference on this subject was the Peri-Urban 2014 conference on peri-urban landscapes held at the University of Western Sydney, Australia. The conference organizers felt that water, food, ecosystem services, and livability issues will increasingly head the agenda in many countries as they strive to secure safe, potable water and provide adequate water supplies for agriculture, environmental protection, and recreational sites. The purpose of the conference was to provide policy makers with solid, evidence-based knowledge that will enable appropriate and beneficial outcomes for the people they represent.

The organizers described the conference as a discussion about the competition for natural resources in changing peri-urban landscapes:

> Peri-urban areas are zones of transition from rural to urban land uses located between the outer limits of urban and regional centers and the rural environment. There are growing concerns about water and food security to meet increases in population in urban areas. For cities to be livable and sustainable into the future there is a need to maintain the natural resource base and the ecosystems services in the peri-urban areas surrounding cities.
>
> Development of peri-urban areas involves the conversion of rural lands to residential uses, closer subdivision of land, fragmentation and a changing mix of urban and rural activities and functions. Changes within these areas can have significant impacts upon agricultural uses and productivity, environmental amenity and natural habitat, supply and quality of water and energy consumption. These changes affect the peri-urban areas themselves and the associated urban and rural environments.
>
> In the past, cities and towns have been established in areas that had secure water and energy supplies and fertile lands for food production. The burgeoning population growth and expansion of urban centers worldwide has placed increasing pressure on potable water supplies, energy and food supplies and the ecosystems services on which the community and the livability of the community depend.
>
> (Peri-Urban 2014)

The themes of the conference were selected to focus on the critical natural resource, socio-economic, legal, policy, and institutional issues that are impacted

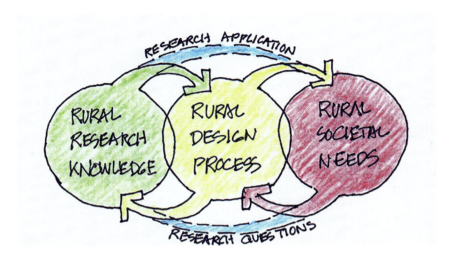

7.1
Diagram of the Center for Rural Design showing the connection that the rural design process can make between rural science and rural society. The diagram illustrates the basis for evidence-based design that is at the core of rural design as a new design discipline.

by the inevitable drift of cities into peri-urban areas. Evidence-based research was an integral aspect of the discussion because academic research may not be the same as those required for policy development within government agencies. Evidence-based design, however, is a way to bring research knowledge to society and in turn bring back to the academy research questions that need answers. Figure 7.1 illustrates the role of design connecting science and society as looked at by the Center for Rural Design.

To further expand on the connection between urban and rural futures a chapter for a book, *Balanced Urban Development* (2015), that followed the conference was prepared by John Troughton and me (Troughton presented at the conference). The book chapter, "Rural Design: Connecting Urban and Rural Futures through Rural Design," is summarized here:

> Urbanization has been accelerating around the globe as people move from rural areas to urban areas for economic advancement, creating urban development that sprawls into the countryside, eliminating much of the best farmland surrounding cities. Urban design and urban planning has attempted to shape urban development as cities have expanded, but it has done so solely from an urban perspective. Areas of transition from rural to urban and land uses at the urban/rural edge in the peri-urban landscape require the lens of spatial arrangement from both urban and rural perspectives to shape, manage, and maintain the ecosystems that people depend upon.
>
> Rural areas around the world are undergoing profound demographic, economic, cultural, and environmental change creating considerable challenges and stress for their residents and on the ecosystems upon which they depend for their livelihood and quality of life. The peri-urban landscape is of particular concern because urban expansion has historically been done

at low density, requiring large amounts of land and causing infrastructure and public services to be provided at great cost.

Rural design is the design discipline that brings design thinking and the problem-solving process of design to rural issues at both the macro and micro levels while making connections between urban and rural futures. Rural design is a way to understand the dynamic behavior of natural and human systems, and to unify and conceptualize the complex and dynamic reality of sustainability in integrating humans, animals, and the environment in both rural and urban areas.

Rural design provides a methodology to shape rural and urban landscapes before climate change and concerns for food production and security and water resources become critical for a rapidly expanding world population. Using the lens of spatial arrangement and community engagement, rural design can incorporate agriculture into urban landscapes in existing cities and along the urban/rural edge for food, recreation, economic, and ecological purposes.

Rural design is a process to nurture collaboration and cooperation among rural and urban communities to shape the landscape to make connections and provide an integrated system of human communities, plants and animal production that meets the needs of people, the economy, and the environment in the present without compromising for the future. This is particularly true at the urban/rural edge and the peri-urban landscape.

Design thinking and the problem-solving process of design is a strategic resource and source of creativity, innovation, and entrepreneurship to find ways that limited land and water resources in peri-urban landscapes can be better shaped and utilized. It is a process that can be taught and utilized by human communities to analyze issues, seek solutions, and select a preferred pathway to a better future that does not necessarily require design professionals to generate the solution. It is a process, however, where higher education can work with communities using the design process to bring science to the issue and in turn raise new research questions for scholars.

Rural design is not a science, but a methodology for holistically crossing borders and connecting issues to nurture new design thinking and collaborative problem solving. It recognizes that human and natural systems are inextricably coupled and engaged in continuous cycles of mutual influence and response. As a process rural design brings science to society and in doing so it can identify new research questions.

Rural design can integrate knowledge across disciplines, and while not directly engaged in research, rural designers can translate and apply research knowledge to the design process, helping bridge the gap between science and society, while improving the social, economic, and environmental conditions of human communities on Earth.

Rural design is a problem-solving process and a methodology to bring the evidence of science to help resolve both rural and peri-urban societal needs. Research issues are by nature interdisciplinary and require a dialogue between citizens and the academy for scholars to understand the issues and respond with research and effective solutions. The research, however, must recognize that human and natural systems are inextricably linked and engaged in continuous cycles of mutual influence and response and this requires an understanding of both urban and rural to fully respond to global issues of potable water supplies, energy and food supplies, and the ecosystems services that human and animal communities depend upon.

Urban design and rural design have many similarities in that both embrace those unique characteristics in design thinking that acknowledge social and cultural values to enhance quality of life. Urban design has been taught in university design schools for some time, but rural design is an emerging design discipline that needs to be developed in higher education around the world.

Rural design is a design methodology to address peri-urban issues and resolve peri-urban needs. To be effective and relevant for this task, it must be founded on solid research, and its practice must be based on validated data that will result in transformational changes. Using the lens of spatial arrangement and methods of community engagement, rural design helps citizens manage change and in the process it can help organize peri-urban landscapes and rural regions for recreational, agricultural, cultural, economic, and ecological purposes to enhance quality of life – urban and rural.

(Thorbeck and Troughton 2015)

Figure 7.2 (from the same book chapter) visualizes the dynamic relationships between urban and rural and the potential for maximizing opportunities by making connections. The figure indicates that the design process and design thinking is a way to understand the opportunities and challenges that designers of all kinds can address by bringing forth creative, exciting, and innovative ideas for entrepreneurial development in rural regions.

We are living in a time of rapid change and the problem-solving process of design is needed to make connections between urban and rural futures at the urban/rural edge. Design can help minimize the negative impacts of change while increasing the positive impacts bringing economic resiliency, social interaction, and appreciation for diversity in culture and arts to the process. Urbanization and sprawl into the rural landscape is also increasing people's contact with the natural environment creating concerns for new forms of zoonotic disease transmission from animals to humans that could greatly impact civilization. A sustainable future will require cooperation and collaboration between the private sector in the flow of goods and services and the public sector in defining land uses and infrastructure systems. This will require high level leadership from involved men and women to break down barriers and cross borders to find optimal solutions for the benefit of both urban and rural populations.

7.2
Diagram for book chapter illustrating the relationship between urban design and rural design in shaping the future peri-urban landscape.

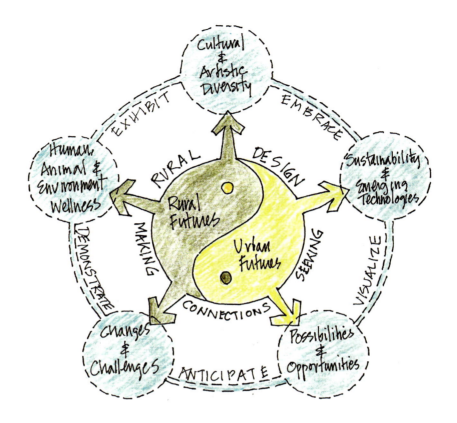

Design disciplines dilemma

The design professions have evolved over time with professional registration requirements for certification defining the scope and characteristics of each profession. As a result the professions have each become protected disciplines (silos?) and deal separately with public safety, health, and welfare. Rarely do the professions step out of their silos and cross borders to work together as peers in multi-disciplinary teams to resolve complex design problems. When they do work together on urban housing and commercial projects, the design team is often organized and controlled by developers whose interests are primarily economic. Under these circumstances the designers are considered as a tool to be manipulated to achieve the developer's vision – usually only based only on profit. When the developer thinks and acts multi-disciplinary with the designer good design and construction can happen.

The design schools have contributed to the isolation of the disciplines with curriculum programs unique to each and educate architects separate from landscape architects or planners or engineers. For example, in the College of Design at the University of Minnesota there are five different disciplines (silos) in three departments: the School of Architecture, Department of Landscape Architecture,

In-between landscapes

and a Department of Design, Housing, and Apparel. Planning is further separated in the Humphrey Institute and engineers are organized in a variety of ways in different schools and colleges. Yet, when the different disciplines start to think and act as designers, rather than as professionals in their individual programs, they start to "energetically think divergently, act creatively, and partner broadly with all who want to join us as we transform the world into a better place" as described by former dean Thomas Fisher of the College of Design in a college publication (Fisher 2011).

There will continue to be great individual buildings designed by individual architects who are very good at designing landmarks and we certainly need to continue to have these buildings around the world. The real action, however, will be in tackling the challenges of the urban/rural edge and peri-urban zone with exciting new developments integrating urban agriculture and densities higher than typical suburbs today into viable and exciting design concepts. The rural zone will remain primarily a food production area, but the buildings constructed in it offer a considerable challenge to architects. They can help shape the character and fit of future production and processing buildings connecting culture, climate, and place to feed a rapidly increasing urban and rural population.

This design dilemma is also impacting how designers think about place. Most of them are often taught about urban problems, work on urban design projects, and design challenges in urban schools as they prepare for their professions in urban universities. As a result they mostly bring an urban perspective to their work even when they are involved in a rural design issue.

It is critical that both urban and rural perspectives be utilized when discussing urban/rural peri-urban land use issues and urban agriculture will become more and more a land use designation for city planning and design. One of my objectives with this book is to help designers look at rural issues with a new rural perspective and think broadly and boldly as they seek design solutions. Too often urban professionals bring their urban perspective with them when they are involved in a rural project. To be most effective they need to develop an understanding about rural and what a rural perspective is.

Through my first book and my work at the Center for Rural Design I am finding more and more graduate students, young professionals, and faculties from around the world who do have a concern for the rural landscape and rural architecture from both a cultural and food production frame of mind. Faculty from China, Poland, and Ireland have sought out funds to come to the University of Minnesota and spend some time seeing what we do and learn about rural issues and how rural design is used as a problem-solving process.

Urban agriculture

Recently architects, landscape architects, and planners are becoming quite interested in the phenomenon of incorporating greenery into their architectural and site plans with a rapidly increasing number of proposals for vertical greenhouses and integrating landscaping into and on top of residential and commercial buildings for absorbing carbon and connecting with nature. This was first defined by Edward O. Wilson as biophilia with the hypothesis that humans have a biological instinct to affiliate with other forms of life, and a number of building projects around the world have incorporated greenery into their design and construction to integrate with nature (Wilson 1984).

Urban agriculture, however, goes beyond biophilia to incorporate food production into the connection with nature and a very good example of architectural exploration of urban agriculture is the award-winning proposal for a Center for Urban Agriculture in Seattle, Washington by Mithun Architects (Figures 7.3 and 7.4). They described their idea for the urban agriculture project:

7.3
Aerial view of Mithun Architects proposal for urban agriculture farm in the State of Washington.

In-between landscapes

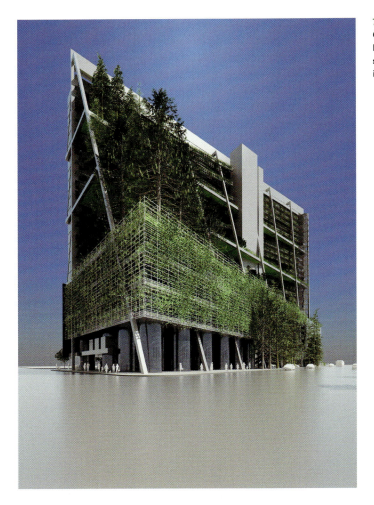

7.4
Ground-level view of the Mithun Architects proposal showing planting integrated into the architectural aesthetic.

The project includes fields for growing vegetables and grains, green houses, roof top gardens, and a chicken farm. The vertical construction allows for more than an acre of farmland on the 0.72-acre site. With the goal of self-sufficiency the project is designed to be independent of city water by treating grey water and collecting rainwater that is treated on site. The project would provide 318 small studios and 1- and 2-bedroom affordable apartments. The entry level would feature a café serving organic foods grown on site. The surrounding community would also be served by the project as a site for stormwater collection and distribution. Produce grown would be distributed to local grocers saving energy reducing transportation costs. The design thinking behind the idea for a "living building" was the desire to design and construct a building that functions like a living organism – able to survive using only the natural environment around it.

(Mithun Architects 2015)

This project is exemplary for what it proposes, but like many other architectural ideas that have recently been suggested for vertical agriculture it does not deal with the broader society goal of "net-zero" meaning zero-carbon and zero-energy in building design. Nor does it deal with the economics of constructing and operating such a facility and the cost of the food produced. It does, however, make steps toward incorporating greenery into the architectural concept to help reduce carbon in the atmosphere – the major cause of global warming – and in the process provides a glimpse of what cities could be like if urban agriculture as well as nature were to become an integral aspect of urban design and architecture.

Landscape architects have also been busy in recent years installing green roofs on existing buildings and working with architects on biophilia proposals for new development incorporating planting into the buildings as well as on the grounds. There have been a number of technical advances on planting systems that make this possible without adding considerable weight to the roof. Often called "green design" it is only partially green because the phrase implies an architectural design that that seeks to be net-zero in carbon and energy, yet green roofs are only one aspect of the issue.

More than anyone the father of the green roof movement was Friedensreich Hundertwasser, the Austrian artist who designed several buildings and developments in Austria in the early 1960s. The most dramatic of his projects is the thermal village of Blumau in the rolling hills of Styria in Austria. For this project he designed and constructed a settlement for people that had as close a connection to nature as possible with curving roofs covered with grass extending up and down from the ground.

Hundertwasser was an eccentric artist who hated conventional architecture and wrote with considerable criticism of modern architecture and architects because he hated straight lines. Here are some excerpts of his writings (the capital letters are the way he wrote it):

> THE HORIZONTAL BELONGS TO NATURE, THE VERTICAL TO MAN, so everything that is horizontal under the sky belongs to vegetation, and man can only claim for himself what is vertical. In other words, this means: FREE NATURE MUST GROW WHEREVER SNOW FALLS IN WINTER.
>
> Government must pass a law that does not allow for a house to be built unless a one meter layer of soil is spread over the entire roof surface and the entire area of the flat soil, on which the house is situated. This also includes gas stations and churches, as well as train stations, official buildings and especially manufacturing plants and their premises.
>
> We must build houses where nature is above us. It is our duty to put nature, which we destroy by building the house, back on the roof. Grass roofs also have ecological, sanitary and insulation advantages. A grass roof produces oxygen and makes life possible. It absorbs dust and dirt and changes earth. Another advantage of the grass roof is the noise-absorbing effect. The grass roof serves as a climate control in winter in order to save heating material and to keep cool in summer.
>
> (Hundertwasser n.d.)

His work has not been widely known outside of Austria, but he did construct buildings that illustrated dramatic ways to incorporate agriculture into the urban and peri-urban landscape as an integral aspect of the design concept for future new development. His project in Styria, Austria clearly reflects his thinking and the fact that it was built with curving green roofs illustrates the impact that creative and passionate individuals can have (Figure 7.5).

Most architecture for urban agriculture today has been constructed independent of urban development in industrial green houses on suburban sites. The amount of fresh food required for the rapidly increasing urban population will require urban agriculture with architectural and landscape integration of residential and commercial development as proposed by Hundertwasser and Mithun with commercial greenhouses for growing food integrated into residential and commercial development in existing urban areas as well as future peri-urban design and construction.

Hydroponics, aquaponics, and indoor agriculture for food production are other forms of urban agriculture that can be integral to the greenhouse. They are an area of expanding interest because of the "locavore movement," which is promoting eating only food that is grown within a 100-mile radius of where you live. Usually operating in greenhouses it uses water to grow food and fish, but it also can be done inside buildings and with the increasing demand for food as the world population expands (Figure 7.6). Hydroponics and aquaponics are an expanding method of growing plants without soil using water and nutrients to support plant growth, and fish. The system offers an economic opportunity for entrepreneurs

7.5
Thermal Village Rogner-Bad Blumau – The Rolling Hills
A Hundertwasser Architecture Project
Bad Blumau, Styria, Austria
1993–1997
Photograph by: Anja Fahrig
© 2016 Hundertwasser Archive, Vienna.

7.6
Large industrial glass greenhouse in Australia. These glass structures are now starting to be constructed on top of existing large roof industrial buildings, and in some cases are using hydroponics and aquaponics for growing vegetables and fish for an urban market.

to grow lettuce, tomatoes, herbs, peppers, and other foods indoors year-round. Some recent installations involve greenhouses being constructed on the roof of warehouses and other industrial buildings using hydroponics and aquaponics for producing food for the urban population.

In many ways the growing interest to integrate agriculture into urban landscapes and development was started by Ebenezer Howard with the Garden Cities movement in England that he outlined in a publication in 1898. The idea was to construct cities that harmonized with nature, yet it remained primarily a utopian idea. Today communities in urban and peri-urban environments do have the choice to include agriculture as part of their landscape with the potential to become resilient in economic, social, and environmental terms. By doing so, they can reinforce their sense of place and strengthen community pride. Urban agriculture should become an integral part of community planning and public policy just as residential, transportation, commercial, parks and recreation, public safety, and health are currently part of city development. Urban agriculture and its architecture have the potential to build upon the ideas of the Garden City movement to redefine the historic relationship between humans and the land and food sources (Knowd et al. 2006).

In a 1925 book, *The Building of Satellite Towns*, author C.B. Purdom discusses the historic relationship between towns and agriculture. He writes:

> No one can study ancient and medieval town-planning without observing the relation of agriculture to towns was of primary importance. Sites were chosen and towns were planned having regard to the need for food supplies. The Greek and Roman city-states were town and country forming an

In-between landscapes

economic and political whole, and what has been called the healthy interaction of rural, urban, and commercial life upon each other is characteristic of civilization at its best.

(Purdom 1925)

He goes on to write:

The antagonism between town and country is fundamentally senseless for the town is the farmer's market and the country keeps the town alive. There should be common interest between the two, and towns should be planned and extended today as in the past having regard to their agricultural requirements.

(Purdom 1925)

Urban agriculture is a form of the Garden City movement as the land surrounding a city or system of agricultural belts as promoted by Purdom, and defined as "An area of agricultural land surrounding a town, with which the town has direct and constant economic relations." The most descriptive current definition of urban agriculture, and much more complicated, was outlined in a conference paper as:

A complex system encompassing a spectrum of interest, from a traditional core of activities associated with production, processing, marketing, distribution, and consumption, to a multiplicity of other benefits and services that are less widely acknowledged and documented. These include recreation and leisure; economic vitality and business entrepreneurship, individual health and well-being; community health and well-being; landscape beautification; and environmental restoration and remediation.

(Butler and Maronek 2002)

They also contend that definitions of urban agriculture should include that it is a response to modernization that has cultural and ethical dimensions. How it might take shape is yet to be seen and will require creative and innovative architects, landscape architects, and planners to work closely with artists and anthropologists and researchers in agro-forestry, agronomy, horticulture, natural resources, ecology, and others to analyze and understand the problem and develop ideas.

Human populations are expected to accelerate until at least 2050 while demand for food from agricultural landscapes may grow even faster. If this process is managed and designed well it may allow for good land to remain agriculture providing the opportunity for widespread ecosystem recovery of rural lands. If these trends can be combined with strong conservation management at appropriate scale it is entirely possible that in the 21st century global trends in species extinction might be reversed at the same time as human populations thrive and reach their expected peak (Ellis 2013).

Urban/rural edge projects

A recent effort in Minnesota to reimagine the urban/rural edge was related to the development of a Concept Master Plan for the Andrew Peterson Farmstead by Thorbeck Architects for the Carver County Historical Society. The farmstead is in Carver County (one of seven counties in the Twin Cities Metropolitan Area) and its location is in the center of the peri-urban landscape zone between the mostly urban area on the east side of the county and the mostly rural agricultural area on the west.

One of the intentions of the plan was for the farmstead to become a public forum for discussion about urban agriculture and the community aspects and impacts of urban sprawl. The vision of the Concept Master Plan is for the historic farmstead to act as a catalyst for discussion as a means to help shape, manage, and maintain the ecosystems that people in Carver County depend upon – urban and rural – today and in the future. A drawing in the Concept Master Plan for the historic farmstead of Carver County illustrates the urban/rural edge and the location of the farmstead on that line (Figure 7.7).

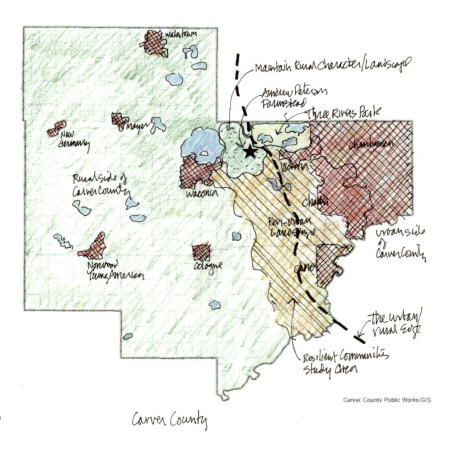

7.7
Drawing of Carver County in Twin City Metropolitan Area showing urban and rural landscape sides with the Andrew Peterson Farmstead in the middle of the peri-urban zone.

In-between landscapes

The proposed site layout for the Concept Master Plan illustrates the many components and opportunities for short and long term public interpretation and education about the history of Carver County and the role of Andrew and Elsa Peterson as immigrant farmers from Sweden to Minnesota in the middle of the 19th century. In addition the plan provides an opportunity to illustrate and demonstrate Community Supported Agriculture and the importance of food supply and food security at the urban/rural edge for a rapidly expanding urban population. The plan envisions an apple orchard, vegetable gardens, and crop plots similar to those grown by Andrew Peterson that would be leased to urban farmers to grow produce for sale at farmers' markets in the Twin Cities. As such the farmstead at the urban/rural edge is as much about the future as it is about the past. I have to add, however, that the plan has received criticism from preservation staff at the Minnesota State Historical Society in that its role as a forum for agricultural discussion in the future does not focus on historic preservation as much as they would like to see and insist upon if they are involved in funding. This is another example of silo thinking.

Nevertheless, the 12.47-acre site is organized to provide visitors a sense of what it was like when Andrew Peterson was living on the farm. He was a Swedish immigrant who settled on the land and kept a daily diary from 1855 to 1898. Fifty years after his death the diary was utilized by the Swedish novelist Vilhelm

7.8
Andrew Peterson and his large family in front of their home in 1885.

In-between landscapes

Moberg for a trilogy of novels about Swedish emigrants including *The Emigrants* (1951), *Unto a Good Land* (1951) and *The Last Letter Home* (1961). Later, two movies were made from these books, *The Emigrants* in 1971 and *The New Land* in 1972. Andrew Peterson was also noted for his horticulturist skills and activity in establishing the Minnesota Horticulturist Society. He married Elsa Ingeman and together they had nine children while living on the farmstead. Figure 7.8 shows the family, in a photograph from 1885, posing in front of their home.

Visitors enter the site off of Parley Lake Road into a parking lot for 80 cars and bus drop-off areas. The site plan (Figure 7.9) illustrates a formal walkway from the entry building to a pivot location providing access to the 1917 Barn (a wedding and event facility) and a new Corn Crib Picnic Shelter where the corn cribs were once located. When visitors proceed into the farmstead the circulation becomes more random and informal much as it was in 1885. This will allow visitors to follow the self-guided tour of the buildings and farmstead site to experience the feeling of the farms when Andrew Peterson lived there.

A new Entry Building (Figure 7.10) will function as a gateway to the farmstead interpreting the historical importance of the Andrew Peterson

7.9
The Andrew Peterson Concept Master Plan for conserving the farmstead and turning it into an urban/rural education center for the 21st century.

In-between landscapes

7.10
The Entry Building to the historic Andrew Peterson Farmstead that will incorporate low and zero-energy design concepts.

farmstead and his legacy. The sustainable design concept for the Entry Building is based on net-zero carbon with a twisted metal roof, metal siding, and a sky-lighted foyer to visually relate to the historic building, but with materials, technology, and forms of the 21st century. The building will provide public information, ticketing, management offices, an orientation theater, interpretive exhibits, public toilets, grounds maintenance garage, and a caretaker's apartment.

Carver County has also received a Resilient Communities grant from the University of Minnesota Humphrey Institute and will be working with students from the University to explore alternative land uses for housing development and open space to maintain rural character and landscape around the farmstead while increasing population and living and working concepts in the peri-urban landscape.

A Center for Rural Design and Metropolitan Design Center proposal to rethink the relationships in land uses at the urban/rural edge is shown by the plan of the Twin City Metropolitan Area in Minnesota (Figure 7.11) that illustrates the seven county metropolitan region and the extent of development in 2015. Up to now the development has been controlled by Twin Cities Metropolitan Council through the extent of the sanitary sewer system serving the seven counties. The peri-urban landscape is indicated in the drawing and its future development might be at a slightly higher density than single family as in the past if current trends are followed. The future of the peri-urban area is the focus of the proposal with an expected transition from rural land use to urban to develop alternative density ideas. The second drawing from the proposal (Figure 7.12) is a transect sketch of the Twin Cities as it is today with the peri-urban expansion area along with a new paradigm transect proposed for 2050 that incorporates urban agriculture as a critical component of the transect.

Although the project was not funded there is ongoing discussion between the two Centers at the University of Minnesota to look again at the peri-urban zone to try to create ideas to help citizens and elected officials determine the best course of action for the future. A critical component of these discussions is the

7.11
Drawing of the Twin City Metropolitan Area showing the 2015 built up area and the peri-urban landscape yet to be developed showing the transect for the proposed Center for Rural Design research study.

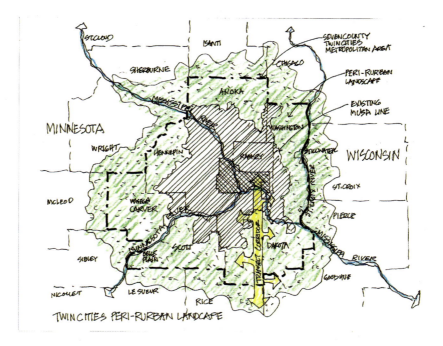

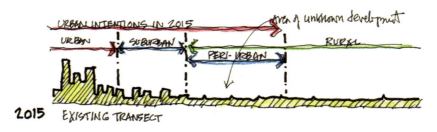

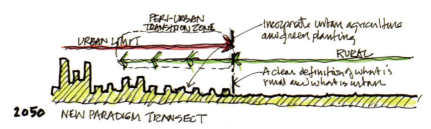

7.12
Transect drawing showing the potential difference in transect densities between 2016 and 2050.

linkages between urban and rural and how land should be shaped to the mutual and sustainable benefit of both.

Urban agriculture may be a key component of future urban land use and a strategic resource that cities, townships, counties, and states can utilize in planning that recognizes the values of agriculture in economic, social, and environmental terms. If they fail to do so they risk denying current and future generations a range of choices in the way land use decisions are made and managed. They also risk

In-between landscapes

the loss of productive land, and social and natural capital through urban expansion into rural areas. This is a time of great opportunity for urban agriculture to redefine urban and peri-urban landscapes. This is indeed a very exciting design challenge yet to be realized and understood, which can have a great impact on global sustainability and resilience – in North America and around the world.

Chapter 8

Rural futures

We abuse land because we see it as a commodity belonging to us. When we see land as a community to which we belong, we may begin using it with love and respect.

Aldo Leopold (1887–1948)

The task before us amounts to relinquishing our attachment to the unhealthy and unsustainable path we have wandered down over the last two centuries and returning to the path we have long been on as a species, remembering what we once knew, and relishing the wealth, now so often overlooked, of all that is free and in infinite supply: family and friends, love and learning, cultivation and co-creation.

Thomas Fisher (Designing to Avoid Future Disasters, 2013)

Today we have an opportunity to unleash the power of design thinking as a means of exploring new possibilities, creating new choices, and bringing new solutions to the world.

Tim Brown (Change by Design, 2009)

Rural regions worldwide are undergoing rapid change raising questions about the future of rural communities and how they link with urban communities and their collective futures. It has been my hope that the reader will be inspired to utilize design thinking and the problem-solving process of design to help resolve any challenge that he/she has along with the opportunity to resolve land use issues in urban or rural areas or the urban/rural edge. Problem-solving is at the heart of the design process that seeks to find the most creative and innovative resolution reflecting the goals and aspirations of the people involved. Peter M. Senge, in writing about leadership in competitive environments, describes the difference between creating and solving problems: "In problem solving we seek to make something we do not like go away. In creating, we seek to make what we truly care about exist" (Senge 2003).

An interesting comparison, but Senge is not a designer. All of the professional designers (architects, landscape architects, planners, graphic designers, industrial designers, engineers) I know see design thinking as doing both – solving a problem and being creative – simultaneously to attain a desired goal. The design process is used in some way by everyone in their daily personal and professional lives – like planning to buy an automobile, looking at alternatives and costs, making the decision, and implementing the plan – they just don't think of it as design or a problem-solving process.

Design as language

In my experience working with rural communities through the Center for Rural Design I always speak as a designer and then later I can work in the architectural ideas along with all of the other issues including land use, transportation, arts, housing, recreation, education, commercial, health, food, energy, water, public services and infrastructure, and economics of contemporary life. Design is a universal process and everyone can relate to it.

Planners might say they do this all the time, but planning is often more connected to public policy rather than the spatial arrangement of things. Architects may say that they are doing this when they design a building and landscape architects may say that they deal with the issue by speaking about the environment and ecosystems, but both may not deal with agriculture and animals for food in competition in land use with natural resources. Engineers might say they deal with the things that make society work, but they might not be dealing with those things impacting quality of life that make life exciting – like arts and culture. The fact is that they are all designers and design is the language that they can all use to nurture partnerships and collaboration to resolve issues for a better future.

The challenges are many as the world adjusts to the rapid shift from rural to urban populations and population increase. The United Nations Department of Economic and Social Affairs projects a population increase that by 2050 we will be living on a planet with roughly 7 billion people living in constructed cities and 3 billion people living and working in rural communities. And by 2100 the world's population may be 11.2 billion, with the largest increase in Africa. It goes on to say that during the years 2015–2050 half of the world's population growth is expected to be concentrated in nine countries: India, Nigeria, Pakistan, Democratic Republic of the Congo, Ethiopia, United Republic of Tanzania, USA, Indonesia, and Uganda. Yet, all of these projections are based on fertility rates and in recent years virtually all regions of the world have declined. Also, people are living longer with higher life expectancy (UN DESA 2015).

In any regard a lot more people are going to be living on the planet which raises the question when we talk about urban and rural futures – what is the future for each and how many years forward do we plan for? When global sustainability is attached to the question the answer must be to improve our quality of life today for everyone, but do it in a way to protect the environment so that future generations have the ability to improve theirs. The global implications of climate change, food security, water resources, renewable energy, and wellness – human, animal, and environmental – must be looked at together from both urban and rural points of view as civilization seeks answers and ways to feed, clothe, and house humanity.

Design is a process to integrate, connect, and cross borders to find new innovative and creative solutions for the future. It is a language that people from different cultures as well as design professionals can utilize to seek solutions that benefit everyone.

City of 7 billion or farm of 10 billion

A 2015 exhibit called *The City of 7 Billion* at the Yale University School of Architecture was organized by researchers and exhibit curators Joyce Hsiang, principal of Plan B Architecture and Urbanism and design critic, and Bimal Mendis, assistant dean and director of undergraduate studies. In an introduction to the exhibit they write that the world has become the most important design problem of our time and the city is a medium to address this problem. The exhibit explores humanity as a geological force in which human activity is permanently transforming the world and the exhibit models the phenomena of global urban development. According to Hsiang, "The show brings together abstract information from across scientific, engineering, and architectural communities, and makes it accessible – it makes the invisible visible, so it can be understood" (Yale News 2015).

The exhibit premise is very intelligent and compelling with its argument that the urban-rural dichotomy has little meaning in that both urban and rural definitions vary in each country, regional authority, or municipality of the world. They go on to argue that the reality of the network and flows of resources between urban and rural implies that every corner of the Earth is urban, "beholden to cultivation, industrialization, drilling, clearing, transportation, and pollution." Further, they write "each country applies different density and total population standards that varies from 200 people per square kilometer to more than double up to 400 or 500 people per square kilometer. For example Australia's minimum definition of an urban area would be considered rural in India or China." Finally, they argue that "the field of architecture is best equipped to comprehensively coordinate the competing and complex issues confronting urbanization" (Hsiang and Mendis 2015).

They are correct in their premise that urban and rural are one issue, and their examination of the entire world as a single urban entity is very challenging, even though I think that it really should be an exhibit called *Farm of 10 Billion* involving land uses in both urban and rural regions around the globe. The real question is how can the world be shaped to be a place where humans, animal, and the environment live and work together and how should it be accomplished?

To say that the architect is ideally suited to understand urbanization as a holistic issue is an expression of arrogance. As good as architects are in their work they are often controlled by developers. Also, declaring that the world is all urban is a mistake. Even if 7 billion people are living in cities another 3 billion are living in rural areas. I would argue that design thinking and the problem-solving process of design is the methodology to address both urban and rural issues and the interrelationships that they have with each other. It is design that brings everything together and a process that is accessible and available for everyone – architects, developers, planners, landscape architects, engineers, and governments and citizens alike.

Nevertheless, this is a very important architectural exhibit at the Yale University School of Architecture that for the first time tries to illustrate ways to understand global land use and density through data mapping using the grid to integrate the multiple systems of information about global land use and densities into three dimensional images. The exhibit is quite dramatic – particularly as it depicts the coalescence of urban regions into a single global city – yet it does not recognize the historical uniqueness of cities and how they developed around the world in response to climate and place. I applaud the exhibit curators for their groundbreaking work.

I think a variation of the exhibit, like *Farm of 10 Billion,* would emphasize that we all – urban and rural – are residents on Earth and adequate water, food, and energy is critical for our collective futures. This idea for the exhibit might emphasize the unique differences of connections between urban and rural and how the agricultural landscape has been historically shaped in different climates in different parts of the world as a model of how the planet might be shaped in the future. With global climate change it is critical to ensure that urban and rural development is integrated and sustainable so that the cultivated and natural landscapes are preserved for future generations. It is unfortunate that the unique, comprehensive, and forward thinking strategy of rural design has not been recognized by design schools and the design professions the same as they have for urban design, and the exhibit *City of 7 Billion* reinforces that impression.

Crossing borders

To cross borders and study issues like water, energy, and food it is critical to have access to ecological data. In the United States it is very difficult to get land use data from one state and coordinate it with similar land use data from another state. It would be very helpful if all states and nations across the globe were to have the same land data format using Geographic Information Systems (GIS) that would be available across the nation and around the globe just as Google Earth makes the whole planet visually accessible. The Minnesota Geological Survey recently distributed a map showing the extent of the County Geological Atlases in Minnesota. Their map illustrates how boundaries (stopping at the state line) control how data is stored with only about half of the eighty-seven counties in the state currently completed or under way. It is this lack of pertinent information that makes design difficult to cross borders within the state as well as between states and the lack of information often leads to citizen mistrust of the bureaucracy and a feeling of arbitrariness by the government in dealing with agricultural land issues.

Globalization has been brought about by improved global communications abilities by innovations such as the internet, social media, and global shipping services. As described by Richard Seline and Yali Friedman in a chapter in the book *Hopes and Visions for the 21st Century* (2007), global trade and communications have always existed, but the modern era of globalizations is unique in its abundance, scale, and degree of integration. They go on to discuss connections and how regions with research strengths can form linkages with regions with development and commercialization strengths to increase the value of each region. They cite the example of the pharmaceutical industry in the U.S. that has research hubs in New Jersey, Massachusetts, and California, while the majority of manufacturing occurs in Puerto Rico. Silicon Valley has a high number of information technology companies but the products are produced in Asia, Ireland, and Scandinavia. This "hub and node" arrangement they say is a direct result of the geographic distribution and globalization of industries, and individuals must be proactive and flexible in their education and career choices to find new ways to extract value from globalization (Seline and Friedman 2007).

In another segment from the same book Jerome C. Glenn, co-founder and director of the Millennium Project, discusses the paradox of our age that as more and more people enjoy the benefits of technological and economic growth, increasing numbers of people are poor and unhealthy, and lacking proper education. He goes on to say: "Although many people criticize globalization's potential cultural impacts, it is increasingly clear that cultural change is necessary to address global challenges." To address these challenges he says: "We need very hardheaded idealists who can look in to the worst and best of humanity, can create and implement strategies of success, and can work with decision makers and educators who fight against hopeless despair, blind confidence, and ignorant indifference – attitudes that too often have blocked efforts to improve the prospects for humanity (Glenn 2007).

Rural design and the problem-solving process of design requires that communities wrestling with a regional issue must embrace the concept of seeking partners to collaborate with while assessing regional assets and defining regional goals and aspirations. Partnering is a way to cross borders and find ways that communities within a region can join with other communities and collaborate and cooperate to create a larger and more meaningful vision for their collective futures – urban and rural – and the quality of life they want. It is these connections across borders that are more likely to help lead to long-term solutions that are sustainable and resilient.

Rural development clusters

In a recent conversation about rural design and its regional approach with Thomas Fisher at the University of Minnesota we discussed groupings of industry with similar products that are called "industry clusters." Perhaps the same concept could be applied to define groupings of rural communities that share assets and economic issues as "rural development clusters." As a rural development cluster the regional communities that formed it can speak with a larger voice and exert more political clout in dealing with federal and state legislation.

Fisher noted that in 1862 the Homestead Act was passed by the U.S. Congress to provide land for farmers (mostly immigrants from Europe) who had to build a residence and live upon the property for five years and pay a very little amount for the land during that time period the land was theirs. This Act allowed immigrant farmers to establish themselves as part of a rural community and in turn to enhance rural economic development all over the United States. It should be noted, however, that the land that was offered to the homesteaders was forcefully ceded to the United States from the indigenous people who had been living on it for centuries.

Fisher went on to speculate that if one were to introduce a 21st-century version of the Homestead Act to enhance rural communities it might be called the "Rural Development Act," and instead of providing land it might loan money to interested entrepreneurs at zero interest for a similar period of time to move to a rural community and try out their idea. This approach to rural development might also help in revitalizing communities, on Native American Reservations as well as rural towns, to help bring in creative people to rehabilitate an existing empty building, and bring their own culture, artistry, technology, and experience or whatever to do their thing and create a new life for themselves and at the same time help revitalize the rural community. This is an idea that should be pursued.

In another segment of *Hopes and Visions for the 21st Century*, Rick Smyre, president of the Center for Communities of the Future in North Carolina, defines the difference between collaboration and cooperation:

> Collaboration occurs when people come together before they start to define their needs and objectives, and develop them together. Cooperation is based on the idea that different groups decide what their goals and objectives are, and then come together to determine the commonalities of their needs and programs of work.
>
> (Smyre 2007)

The Center for Rural Design at the University of Minnesota has used both cooperation and collaboration as an intrinsic aspect of partnering in rural design and in doing so the process reflects design thinking that, in a constantly changing and more complex world, nurtures the notion of people coming together to help each other to achieve mutual success and benefit.

Cooperation and collaboration and clustering are methodologies that historic rural cultures have followed for thousands of years as their way of life. Language and laws developed out of their close connection to family relationships, rituals, land, agricultural production, and the social community. Sometimes this is hard for Americans to understand since rural America is only 400 years old and based on European antecedents, compared to many rural agricultural cultures around the world that are 5,000 years old and developed out of a close working connection with the land for food and shelter and social organization.

In a recent speech to the Public Health Association of Australia, Professor Kerry Arabena of the University of Melbourne, who is one of the Aboriginal and Torres Strait people who now call Australia home, discussed today's complex social-environmental problems in contrast to existing traditional modes of enquiry and decision-making by government leaders:

> Whilst I maintain respect for the contribution of traditional western science, I became keenly attuned to the work of Earth system, environmental and ecological scientists who have tested new waters and are often only tentatively accepted by the established scientific community. From within these sciences we find ways to be concerned with and celebrate the importance and the integrity and diversity of life in all its forms across the entire planet. There are very few places in the academy where I could openly discuss the relationship between human and other species, health and wellbeing, and promote that human health is dependent on healthy functioning ecosystems and all the life those systems contain. This is the first human generation in which the majority will live in crowded cities. Well-founded projections suggest the future supplies of the air we breathe, the water to drink and food to eat are in doubt.
>
> So what can we ask the decision maker of the future? Certainly not to reject the powerful tools that led to the capacity to reduce disease, increase world food production and put a human on the moon. Rather than limiting the focus to any single avenue of enquiry, the requirement here is to be open to different ways of thinking, to use imagination to the full and to be receptive to new ideas and new directions that match the times.
>
> The task therefore is to draw on our intellectual resources valuing the contribution of all the academic disciplines as well as other ways in which we construct our knowledge. And that brings the challenge of developing open transdisciplinary modes of inquiry capable of meeting the needs of the individuals, the community, the specialist traditions and influential organizations and allows for a holistic leap of the imagination.
>
> We know we have capacity to take decisive corrective action and change our practices and social institutions when we learn about perverse outcomes of our management. We must now apply this capacity to the question of health of humans and of landscapes.
>
> (Arabena 2013)

She speaks eloquently about planet Earth and that all human, animal, and environmental creation is interrelated with the sun as a constant energy source. With climate change and population increase our future wellbeing as a species is entirely dependent on our ability to become global in our thinking and actions to transition from a period of human devastation to a period of time when all humans work together in a mutually beneficial way. Now more than ever before humans need to understand and respond effectively to our own human role within this new information.

Net-zero buildings and global warming

Australia's Dr. John Troughton and I have been trying to organize the Second International Symposium on Rural Design in Australia. In his work experience Troughton has been involved in the design and financing of systems that ensure sustainable production within a sustainable biosphere covering air, land, water, and biology. The three areas of the science he has been particularly involved with are the natural resources of CO_2, water, and plants. He was working on research monitoring changes in CO_2 in the atmosphere because of its importance in measuring the changes to determine the sinks and sources of the gas in the global carbon cycle. His first measurements were in New Zealand in 1966 that indicated the CO_2 concentration in the atmosphere was 312ppm, while today it is about 380ppm. This increase has had major implications for plant productivity, melting of the icecaps, and world climate patterns (Troughton, private correspondence, August 8, 2013).

There is growing architectural consensuses that to better deal with global warming architects need to design buildings that are more than sustainable and become buildings that absorb carbon and create more energy than consumed. This is an issue that has lofty goals, but little understanding as to how to achieve it because individual buildings, power systems, and cultural patterns must be integrated as a system in both urban and rural situations to achieve the level of carbon reduction by 2030 that global warming is requiring. Nevertheless, if individual buildings can be designed to absorb carbon and generate electricity through renewable resources and the excess delivered to the power grid we all benefit.

Perhaps the best way to achieve carbon reduction is for communities – urban and rural – to begin to incorporate holistic resilient resource management ideas. The Ecala Group, a restorative infrastructure design, development, and advisory firm dedicated to delivering the world's most advanced developments in sustainability, is currently developing this approach working with cities (San Francisco and Minneapolis) and neighborhoods to rethink how they might organize and manage their communities to achieve this idea. Ecala looks at the entirety of a community and its infrastructure system (social, economic, and cultural) and proposes to manage the system by integrating twelve categories into the process, namely: Energy; Water; Solid Waste; Materials; Food; Information Technology; Access and Mobility; Land Use and Planning; Management and Governance; Health and Well Being; Economy; and Culture and Identity. The goal is assist the community to help manage and coordinate all of the categories so it can become a resilient community. They describe sustainable as being carbon neutral and argue that through proper management the community can go beyond sustainability to a restorative level (meaning to supply energy to the region above what is required for the community) with great beneficial impact.

A project that will attempt to do this was organized by Nordic Business Development, Inc. to work with the small rural community of Tower in northern Minnesota on the Iron Range. By combining smart system designs and modern technology the project will look at the community's infrastructure system to reorganize and utilize community waste to create renewable energy. Orlyn Kringstad of the Tower firm Nordic Business Development, Inc. is leading the effort along with Dr. Terje Kristensen who will lead the analytical work, Jeremy Schoenfelder as master developer and me as architect, to develop a *Tower 2025 Vision Plan* for a new sustainable mixed-use development focusing on a newly created harbor that is connected by a navigable channel leading to the large and beautiful Lake Vermillion. The first phase of the development will be twenty townhouse units using Passivhaus principles for energy conservation that will help lead the way to move forward with the development plan and accomplish the vision that has economic sustainability for the community as an important part of the overall idea.

The intent of the vision plan is to integrate the new sustainable mixed-use development to the existing downtown of the historic mining town along with a long-term program to generate electricity for the development and the community. The Hometown BioEnergy plant in Le Sueur, Minnesota, discussed in Chapter 6, is similar to what might be constructed in Tower using all kinds of organic waste to generate electricity from methane gas from waste. Principles of sustainability, environmental restoration, and economic resiliency will guide the design and new construction of buildings as well as the restoration and remodeling of existing buildings in the rural town over time. The project seeks to develop a framework to coordinate efforts toward a community that stimulates long-term growth in a healthy, resilient, and economically vibrant way.

The framework will serve as the guiding principles in the ten-year *Tower 2025 Vision Plan* with the goal to create a local economy built upon existing strengths and develop economic sectors that fit in with local culture and goals for how the community should develop and prosper. With environmental restoration and economic resiliency as core strategies, the vision proactively focuses on enhancing local natural capital to improve the rural community's ability to adapt to changing economic conditions and developing capabilities for the local government to shape its own fiscal destiny. The goal is to create a realistic and economical vision that is holistic and systemic for the rural community to become a worldwide model for rural sustainability in the 21st century.

Global warming and climate change are critical global issues that can only be resolved by international agreements and cooperation. In an article published by the Associated Press regarding the UN climate summit that took place in Paris in November 2015, the authors describe the questions that the countries are discussing – where the money to combat global warming is going to come from and how much rich countries should invest in helping poorer nations cope with the issue (Corbet et al. 2015). Other sticking points relate to how much should be invested in renewable energy and how much traditional oil and gas producers will lose in countries agree to forever reduce emissions. In December 2015 the agreement was finalized and signed by nearly 200 counties.

A major effort to combat global climate change is a public-private project called Mission Innovation that is being led by at least nineteen governments and Breakthrough Energy Initiative being led by twenty-eight investors including Microsoft founder Bill Gates. Both are investing a great deal of money (billions of dollars) to help lead the world into low- or no-carbon energy over the next five years (Corbet et al. 2015).

Combating climate change is also a design challenge and the design professions need to take a broader view of the ethical impacts of their work. If architects only design individual buildings they will have minimal impact even when designed with green intentions. Architects must begin to think of the design of buildings as part of a global community of humans, animals, and landscapes. If communities – urban and rural – were to take advantage of this design challenge and adopt a holistic and systemic view of their community and infrastructure system they might be able to find a way to provide a more livable resilient community with a higher quality of life at lower cost. Architects may be the most qualified design professional group to lead this effort and the American Institute of Architects is taking steps to enhance resilient design and move away from prescriptive guidelines (like LEED) to performance standards that can be measured.

In 2005 the Center for Rural Design was involved in creating a concept for an energy self-supporting village with the Center for Sustainable Building Research that would be developed by the University of Minnesota for net-zero energy research village. Called UMORE (for University of Minnesota Outreach, Research, and Education) the intent of the village was to integrate environmental, social/cultural, and economic opportunities with specific focus on innovation in health and wellness, renewable energy, and education and life-long learning through integrated sustainable design. For the village sustainability meant an innovative sustainable community that by design:

- uses energy from renewable resources (solar, wind, and biomass from a variety of sources, including waste) to reduce energy consumption from the grid through Net and Gross Zero Energy strategies, including architectural design to reduce energy consumption by 50% over current building code requirements;

- provides for on-site management of storm water such that there is net-zero runoff in comparison with existing conditions and in the process enhance water resources;
- provides for a local multi-modal street network (pedestrians, bicycles, cars, alternative vehicles) and regional inter-modal (transit) access with goal to reduce vehicle miles of travel by one-third in comparison with neighboring cities and towns;
- creates a green infrastructure that enhances bio-diversity and integrates ecological relationships throughout the site and in relationship with neighboring properties to preserve and enhance critical habitats and natural areas;
- integrates active multi-generational living and a matrix of wellness services and employment which are accessible, connected, and integrated into the fabric of the community;
- integrates life-long learning across disciplines developing integrative cultural centers, libraries, and schools while creating the technological infrastructure to use wireless and new net-based communication technologies into the development that build upon university research emphasizing technology transfer, knowledge-synthesis, and global connectivity;
- fosters a strong sense of community through development of a walkable, livable design that promotes human interaction and provides a high quality of life and sense of wellbeing; and
- functions as a good neighbor.

The research village concept was never realized as the University shifted its focus to receiving income from gravel extractions on the site and to sell land to developers without an overall academic purpose as originally contemplated. However, the issues discussed in the planning are pertinent for the way new and renovated communities must be developed if sustainability is going to have an impact on reducing the effects of climate change.

Design thinking

Design thinking and the problem-solving process of design may be the most effective way to address urban and rural futures. Urban design has been taught and practiced for some time and because of that is has a strictly urban point of view. Rural design is a new design discipline that tries to transcend the dichotomy between urban and rural to integrate and make connections at both the macro and micro levels. It is a way to understand the dynamic behaviors of human as well as natural systems, including agriculture, and conceptualize through the lens of spatial arrangement of the land new ideas for sustainability integrating human, animal, and environmental wellness in both urban and rural areas. Design thinking is a way to creatively and innovatively connect the dots to find design solutions that transcend and transform (Figure 8.1).

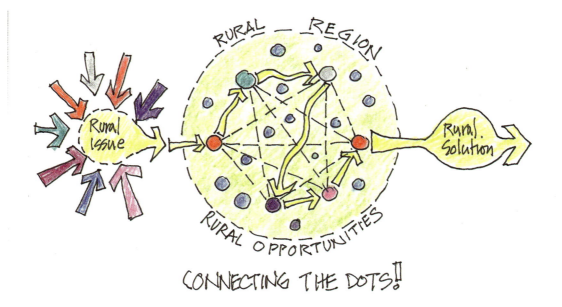

8.1
Diagram by the Center for Rural Design illustrating the innovative potential for creative problem solving by crossing borders and connecting the dots to find optimal solutions.

Global and local initiatives must go hand in hand, and any region in the world that is involved with agriculture and human environments should think about different ways that they can utilize their assets and find things that they need and seek out new ways of addressing them, including these sustainability issues for rural communities developed by the Center for Rural Design:

1. Identify the regional food shed to encourage local food production and process for regional and larger distribution.
2. Enhance regional energy production through wind, solar, and biomass to find ways to take advantage of opportunities in response to climate change and think of renewable energy from these sources as an agricultural process.
3. Ensure high-speed broadband internet accessibility for every household and business in the region along with a coordinated communications plan and regional, national, and global marketing concepts.
4. Organize capital for business and entrepreneurship opportunities using "angel" funding and private equity, specialized education and training for new types of jobs, new technology, new kinds of production and distribution, and create a regional data base for information and sharing ideas.
5. Identify innovative ways to utilize the natural resources of the region (environmental, historical, cultural, aesthetic, water, habitats, and other assets) that can be connected to enhance the region as a tourism destination (remember that tourists like to visit a place for the same reason people like to live there), and find ways to promote economic development to enhance quality of life while crossing jurisdictional boundaries that have traditionally been barriers.

We must find a way to provide enough food, energy, and wellness for people today without destroying the opportunity for future generations to deal with issues at that time. Design education is timeless and as described by Robert A. M. Stern, the dean of the School of Architecture at Yale University, "young designers (architects, landscape architects, planners, engineers, and other designers) must have the intellectual, social, and critical skills to ask the right questions of themselves, the profession and the public" (Stern 2015).

This book is written by an architect who was born and raised in a rural agricultural community and now lives and works in an urban area, yet I maintain a strong passion for the natural and agricultural countryside and the quality and design of buildings that are constructed there as well as in cities. I received my graduate degree in architecture at Yale University and the School of Architecture taught me well to ask questions and try to find the potential of design and design thinking that can bring urban, peri-urban, and rural issues together to resolve issues holistically and systemically. This may be a new way of design thinking for the design professions and how they do their work so that the individual pieces will add up to be a greater whole through integrated and interdisciplinary planning and design rather than working in separate silos.

It is important to remember that humans, animals and environments all equally inhabit our planet Earth. The pictures of a young girl and a calf (Figure

8.2
This small girl with a calf is an image that epitomizes the animal and human bond, and the relationship between humans, animals, and environments on planet Earth.

8.3
Children plowing terraces with oxen in Nepal illustrating the historic working relationship between humans and animals.

8.2) and children plowing terraces in Nepal with a team of oxen (Figure 8.3) illustrate the historic bond between animals and humans and the landscapes we live in – one is about the emotional connection and the other is about the working relationship. These may be images that some architects who are designing buildings in urban settings may think are superfluous, but if they want to be truly meaningful in their design approach and make connections between humans, animals, and nature for a better future they should think about this historic relationship. Humans are part of nature and if cities are going to thrive in the future their designs might be much more admired and cherished if they create architecture that recognizes this innate relationship through design, rather than ignore it. Create cities that are part of nature rather than isolated from it.

    The book is intended to begin a dialog about the connections and interrelationships between urban and rural architecture and agriculture and their impacts on the global environment. My hope is that the book will open the eyes of designers all over the world to the challenges and opportunities that nature and agriculture (urban and rural) have for developing, designing, and constructing resilient buildings and landscapes that are more than sustainable, and indeed become restorative and more livable by 2050 and into the future.

Chapter 9

Epilogue

> *To experience architecture is like going through the ages painting a self-portrait of our spiritual thoughts and feelings.*
> Sverre Fehn (Norwegian architect, 1924–2009)

I have a passion for creating architecture that is connected to nature because a beautiful building may evoke an emotional response, but a beautiful building that is part of nature is poetic. This passion led me to invent and define the idea of rural design to bring design as a problem-solving process to rural land-use issues. I hope that I have elevated the architectural discourse and design thinking about the connections between architecture and agriculture, and between urban design and rural design. The world is changing very rapidly, and vibrant and prosperous futures can only be achieved when urban and rural issues are connected and interrelated in the problem-solving process.

Global issues of climate change, food production and security, potable water resources, renewable energy, and human, animal, and environmental wellness must be vigorously addressed to accommodate a rapidly increasing world population. Architecture that is evidence-based and design thinking are both a methodology and process that can help societies deal with these issues. Urban and rural futures must be interconnected and in doing so there is a great need and a great opportunity for creative and innovative design by architects and other design professions. A sustainable future demands a correlated and integrated evidence-based design approach to define how buildings and landscapes in urban, rural, and peri-urban areas are shaped for a better future while preserving the natural environment for future generations. Meaningful design and strong architectural leadership are critical to this transformation.

The world will become a better place when architects and other design professionals become as excited about opportunities to work in rural landscapes as they are in urban landscapes. It is a mistake for the design schools and design professions to fundamentally ignore rural areas as they generally have done, and as a result when designers and planners do became involved in a rural design issue they usually bring an urban perspective to the issue. This must change and I hope this book helps designers to more fully understand the rural perspective and seek out opportunities to engage with rural communities and agricultural landscapes to seek architectural or planning opportunities. By doing so the design professions can bring interdisciplinary design and design thinking that crosses borders providing opportunities to creatively and innovatively develop solutions that link urban and rural futures.

We all inhabit the same planet that we first saw in pictures from outer space in the 1970s and as designers we must do our design work with both a global and local perspective to make sure we understand and connect the dots to create innovative and sustainable green design. If we only focus, as designers, on the function and form of the individual building or landscape and object we create, we do the world a disservice no matter how beautiful it is. As designers we must work with the clients and communities impacted by our designs to educate and recognize the values of culture, climate, and place. In doing so we may be able to create sustainable and beautiful designs and architecture that helps deal with climate change, food security, preservation of water resources, utilize renewable energy, and seek human, animal, and environmental wellness.

In this book I highlight some of the research and writing about rural issues that is going on around the world. However, most of the writing and research has been from an academic or scientific point of view that becomes published in scientific or discipline journals. This tradition fosters the notion of academic silos as knowledge storehouses filled with scientific evidence and ongoing research that sometimes takes years to have an impact on society.

It is also true for the design professions since designers receive their education in a professional design silo focusing on buildings in mostly urban landscapes. With professional registration and the legal framework of the design and construction system, developed over time to protect public safety and welfare, it is difficult for an architect to make interdisciplinary peer connections with other design disciplines in the problem-solving process. When the focus is on individual buildings on a defined property the system encourages stand-alone structures that have no direct relationship with climate, landscape, or other buildings on adjacent property.

For example, the American Institute of Architects Standard Form of Agreement between Owner and Architect outlines the contractual relationships between the owner, architect and the architect's consultants, the contractor and the construction process. It requires the architect and the architect's consultants to provide services consistent with professional skill and care and the orderly progress of the project and, in the case of a dispute, the legal process usually uses mediation or arbitration to settle the issue and these are defined by well-established construction law and precedent. The level of professional skill is usually defined by the courts as the standard of care that other professionals generally follow on their projects. This interpretation has changed over the years.

In the 1960s the architectural contract had the architect "inspecting" the construction work to see if it was being put together according to the plans and specifications. Due to a landmark legal test in Minnesota the contract language of the Standard AIA Document was changed to have the architect "observe" the construction. This was done to clarify the role of the architect during construction because the word "inspect" implied a level of care in managing the construction process that was not intended in the standard agreement. This definition created a new opportunity for contractors who sometimes became construction managers who overviewed the process for the owner and in other cases they also became the construction manager at risk and became the builder. A few architects do provide construction management services, but not many because of the overlap of professional responsibility.

The long-established legal arrangement with the Standard AIA Document is based on the architect being the leader of the design team (separate from the construction team) and all of the consultants work for the architect on a defined project. There have been efforts to make connections between the members of the design and construction teams through the idea of "partnering" to create an attitude and methodology to improve cooperation and collaboration. However, the economics of controlling costs in the development process is now coming more from the construction side that wants to control the entire process. The traditional design and construction process is organized around the notion of each member of the team operating in a different silo with different responsibilities to meet legal and professional traditions. With this definition of partnering it often leaves design as a means to an end rather than being the creative inspiration for resolving the problem and developing an innovative solution.

To properly address global issues of population increase, climate change, food security, water resources, renewable energy, and wellness the academy and the design professions must find ways to cross disciplines and work together to seek out the most creative, innovative, and entrepreneurial ideas possible. Design and design thinking are powerful tools that can be used by everyone, including scientists and citizens, to solve problems with creativity and innovation and in doing so help find the linkages between urban and rural futures.

While the book focuses on the design of buildings and landscapes in the rural regions of the world it also recognizes that the majority of people on the planet live in cities and as cities change and adjust for the rapidly increasing world population it is critical that rural issues be linked to urban when considering land uses – particularly in the peri-urban landscape. Urban agriculture might become a powerful tool in defining how urban areas expand to avoid loss of agricultural land at the urban/rural edge. It can open up a whole new way of design thinking for architects, landscape architects, and planners to address the global changes that are rapidly taking place.

The current separation of urban and rural design thinking also follows into the business and economic systems for bringing rural products to urban markets that have developed over time. Thomas Foster and Arthur Gets Escudero, writing about the challenges of bringing urban and rural together, point out that the disconnection between urban and rural communities is exacerbated by the fact that many producers of food, fiber, and fuel are selling to intermediaries such as distributers, processors, and manufacturers. In high-income countries most consumer food dollars go to these intermediaries who often have little interest in the urban/rural relationship. Nonetheless, these mostly private sector actors are important to bring to the table because of their power and capacity to either support or hinder progress in finding solutions to interconnected urban and rural challenges (Foster and Gets Escudero 2014).

The sustainability of food, energy, water, and transportation systems cannot be addressed by one sector alone. The flow of food of goods and services from rural to urban and back is critical for linking urban and rural issues. Climate change, food security, water resources, renewable energy, and wellness – human, animal, and environmental – will further impact both urban and rural futures as the world adjusts to rapidly increasing populations and limited land resources for growing food.

Tom Fisher, in *Designing to Avoid Disaster* (2013), writes about designing the future:

> Resilient thinking, like design thinking when done well, ensures that the best possible solution to a problem has the appropriate degree of complexity at the proper scale, while assessing effects at a range of other scales, both smaller and larger than the one the problem seems to involve.

Fisher goes on to outline design strategies to avoid disasters, and asks:

> How would we design the world if the worst was going to happen? How could we live, for example, in a world without affordable oil or available electricity, without global communications or transcontinental travel, without plentiful food or accessible water, without personal safety or political stability, without secure income or a sure job?
>
> (Fisher 2013)

Rural design is a methodology to bring the problem-solving process of design and design thinking to the challenges of rural landscapes and rural people, but it can also be a methodology to help link urban and rural futures. Since rural design is a new discipline it is more free to cross borders and connect the dots. It can provide a fresh new way of using design thinking to find connections between countries, state, regions, cities and towns, and the agricultural and natural landscape to enhance collaboration and partnering. It can encourage creativity and innovation to break down walls and encourage dialog and communication for a better future and quality of life – urban and rural.

Urban agriculture, as it matures, may help in making connections between urban and rural by reminding problem-solvers that future food security in a rapidly changing and increasing world population is critical to the future of mankind on the planet. Around the world there are well-established agricultural cultural heritages with people, animals, and environments living and working together. These indigenous agricultural heritages must become more widely recognized and understood to help the modern world find ways to live in harmony with the planet today in a way that ensures that future generations can also find their ways.

When I was a student at Yale University studying architecture I looked at the idea of urban agriculture in my thesis project where I designed urban houses in vertical towers shaped around gathering place platforms in the sky with plants and open space providing a place to grow food and connect to nature. With new agronomy and urban agriculture insight I would like to explore this idea again to design and construct gardens for growing food in high-density urban housing as well as providing a connection to nature in a way that is meaningful to the people who live there and is economically feasible in the marketplace. This connection must be more than just integrating a lot of plants and trees into the façade or on the roof. If it can be done in a way that is attractive and economical to young home buyers it might suggest a way to develop the peri-urban landscape at densities much higher than normally found in suburban regions in America while preserving existing adjacent farmland for growing food.

Slums as urban models?

In many large cities in developing countries around the world poor humans have become very ingenious in creating places to live. In Caracas, Venezuela 70 percent of its residents live in slums, which are neighborhoods defined by UN-Habitat as "heavily populated urban settlements characterized by substandard housing and squalor" (www.unhabitat.org). These neighborhoods wind among the Caracas hills and have been constructed with salvaged bits and pieces with their own unique social, cultural, and urban organization that holds it together. Caracas is also home to a forty-five story tower inhabited by squatters after the tower was structurally built with a concrete frame and then abandoned. The tower has a collection of shops, grocery stores, and other service businesses. With no elevators, older people live on the lower floors and younger on top. It even has a small dairy farm on the 13th floor. These kinds of horizontal and vertical living situations are often called slums but recent research indicates that they have a high degree of social and cultural organization with neighbors helping neighbors and that new planning and design solutions might come from them for urban futures (Thilla 2015).

At the Oslo Architectural Triennale in 2013 a presenter suggested that city planners and architects need to look more deeply and meaningful at the slum life style to find better ways to redefine urban housing for the poor that reflects the social and cultural heritage of its residents as well as providing fresh water, reliable electricity, sanitation and public services. UN-Habitat say that 33 percent of the population in developing nations is living in slums and the suggestion is that it might be much better and more economical to develop a bottom-up approach to work with the residents in the design and construction of new housing to meet the needs of the rapidly growing urban population. The governmental process today in urban areas is mostly top-down resulting in government designed repetitive buildings in formal patterns that are completely different than the patterns of living and social and cultural connections found in the slums.

It is not hard to imagine that the social and cultural patterns of the slums might be very similar to the social and cultural heritage of indigenous peoples and how they lived on the land for thousands of years without destroying it. Urban agriculture might be a new way to rediscover the relationship between living with the land by incorporating planting for growing food and connection to nature in the architecture of urban housing. It certainly is an exciting design opportunity and one that might appeal to a wide range of home buyers with different economic status.

If new urban housing in America is constructed with urban agricultural ideas, the peri-urban landscape might be developed at higher densities that are more economical with a better life style than traditionally done by developers who generally construct new housing at very low densities in the suburbs. This would allow some of the best farmland surrounding cities to remain agricultural to feed the rapidly expanding urban population as well as preserve natural areas for recreation and habitat for animals. This can only be accomplished if new home buyers, governments, developers, and designers are all in tune with each other and work together to shape the future.

Linking urban and rural issues

The challenges are enormous as we contemplate a future where water, food, and electricity will become increasingly critical as a result of climate change, and where shortages could lead to ecological panic and global disaster. The choice between science and ideology is clear and we must find the courage to base our decisions on science. Timothy Snyder, writing about climate change and food shortages and what it could lead to in America, says:

> The full consequence of climate change may reach America only decades after warming wreaks havoc in other regions. And by then it will be too late for climate science and energy technology to make any difference. Indeed by the time the door is open to demagogy of ecological panic in the United States, Americans will have spent years spreading climate disaster around the world.
> (Snyder 2015)

Evidence-based rural and urban design is a problem-solving methodology that can help find ways to deal with climate change by bringing science to society – urban and rural, local and global – by emphasizing human, animal, and environmental wellness as the fundamental issue facing everyone on Earth.

Regarding science and technological innovations, Larry Downes and Paul Nunes have written that the rapid introduction of new innovative technologies into societies and cultures before they understand the opportunities has led to overzealous regulation to protect old technologies. They identified seven of the most potentially disruptive technologies that are most threatened by premature regulation using old and often broken legal rules:

1. *The sharing economy* – technologies that make it economically efficient for consumers to share, lease, and co-own expensive fixed assets including vehicles, housing, and expertise is bringing to the surface long buried compromises, inside deals, and outright corruption in the mostly local licensing, inspecting, and insuring of transportation companies, hotels, and professional services.
2. *Autonomous vehicles and drones* – self-driving cars and self-flying aircraft will revolutionize the design of cities and roads. They will vastly improve the efficiency of agriculture and public safety by providing new sources of real-time information at minimal cost and reduced human risk.
3. *Digital currency* – much of the financial system has already migrated to electronic formats, but the production of cash stubbornly remains a government monopoly in much of the world.
4. *The internet of things* – the falling cost of sensors will soon connect every one of more than a trillion items in commerce, including furniture, appliances, commercial buildings, and public infrastructure.
5. *The quantified self* – as more devices inside and outside your body collect information about you and your environment, data analytics may radically alter the way we eat, sleep, raise our children, and age with dignity.
6. *Advanced robotics/artificial intelligence* – dramatic improvements in hardware and software are creating a future in which computers will supplant even more human beings in a wide range of dangerous, repetitive, error-prone, or simply boring jobs.
7. *3-D printing* – rapid price deflation for industrial prototyping has led investors to bet heavily on consumer-oriented 3D printers that can make fully functional items – including in the not-too-distant future, food, electronic circuitry, and human tissue.

(Downes and Nunes 2014)

The rapid utilization of new technologies is an economic issue when established businesses become threatened by technologies that can radically transform the way things are done. They can force existing businesses out of business or they need to find new ways to incorporate the technology into their businesses. For example, in America the online purchase of goods and services has forced major retail companies to redefine how they sell, and those that are creative and innovative, like Target, are reacting to the new phenomena with innovation by incorporating online technologies to reinforce traditional retail sales. Certainly the use of cell phones to communicate, take pictures, pay bills, purchase tickets, use as boarding passes at airports, and the like is having a huge impact on both urban and rural life worldwide. Some have predicted that the cell phone in the near future may replace the use of cash and credit cards.

It has become quite clear to those who travel that people everywhere are rapidly incorporating new technologies into their daily lives. It is not clear that architects, landscape architects, and planners who are mostly involved in the make-up and construction of the built environment are responding the way they should in the design process to incorporate these technological phenomena. I see very interesting and beautiful buildings in the architectural magazines, but as it is done so often the building is presented as an isolated object.

As a practicing architect I feel that far too often the design professions and the design schools hang on to the old ways of professional certification and function in silos of knowledge exclusive to their domain. They may design and build beautiful buildings that are objects, but often accomplished with an attitude that protects the profession. Architects and the other design and engineering professions must become innovative and daring in putting forth design proposals that cross borders, incorporate agriculture into urban life, initiate new kinds of linkages and connections, and emphasize interdisciplinary design thinking and problem solving.

I was interviewed recently by a young architecture student from Iowa State University who was meeting with a number of prominent architects in the Twin Cities and he asked me if there was anything in my career that I regretted and would like to do over. I responded no, because I have always tried to follow my passion for connecting buildings and landscapes in everything I do. In some cases I did it better than others, however, it is that pursuit that has guided my career. I also told him about my experiences working as an architect with rural communities where I discovered that if I talked to them about rural design as an architect they would think of buildings rather than the problem. I quickly learned to talk as a designer because as a designer I can cross borders and make connections that I could not make if I only spoke as an architect. In my presentations I encourage design students and design professionals that I am in contact with to think of themselves first as designers and second as professionals if they want to make real connections with people and have a real impact. So, my advice to the student was to be a designer first and follow your passion!

Working on this book has been a wonderful opportunity to make contact with people all over the world who are now beginning to get involved in rural issues. Since my first book *Rural Design: A New Design Discipline* was published in 2012 it seems that the academy, as well as governments and individual citizens, are starting to recognize that urban and rural futures must be connected if we are going to design and shape resilient communities and create a resilient planet. I have had the opportunity to engage in dialog with architects and landscape architects around the world about rural design and how it can help them deal with rural change in their countries. I have written about some of those experiences in this book and I am hopeful that rural design will eventually be taught in design schools at the same level as urban design. I am also encouraged about the emergence of sustainable green design as a way to articulate and help resolve issues of climate change, food security, renewable energy, water resources, and wellness.

One result of this new awareness is that my first book is now being translated and will be published in China in December 2016. Also, an exciting new organization has been created in China and the European Union called the World Rural Development Committee that will focus on rural development and rural design worldwide. I believe this new Committee can have a profound impact in finding ways to cross borders and share ideas, promote partnering and collaborating, and research better ways to preserve agricultural cultural heritage areas around the world as a means to discover new ways of working with the land that 21st century farmers, producers, and consumers can embrace while preserving the natural and cultivated landscape for future generations.

Innovation and new design thinking

Perhaps the most exciting new architectural design thinking that offers great design opportunity is the integration of urban and rural design by bringing agriculture and greenery into the built-up human urban environment while adapting to climate change. Architects have been very successful at integrating new materials into their building designs, but as Blaine Brownell, in his book *Material Strategies,* writes about innovations and the kinds of construction and use of materials impacting urban and rural development he has this cautionary statement about the future:

> Presently, the world faces a series of fundamental challenges that define a new context for architecture. The scale and pace of environmental, technological, and social change today is remarkable. Population growth and accelerating urban migration outpaces the carrying capacity of the earth's resources.
>
> (Brownell 2012)

If architects and other designers were to engage in design thinking about new materials, along with a broader view of architectural and agricultural heritage and with new insight in how indigenous peoples around the world lived with nature without destroying it, more important and innovative ideas might emerge. As expressed by Tom Fisher:

> We have come to see those older ways of living as primitive or impoverished. But we need to see the work of our ancestors anew, not as more rudimentary that are own, but quite the contrary as more resilient and resourceful, and more flexible and dependable than the extremely fragile, fracture-critical world that we have since created.
>
> (Fisher 2013)

The fracture-critical world and extreme climate differentials are becoming issues that highly creative architects are trying to find answers to. The current building codes and engineering of public infrastructure deal with averages in terms of wind and snow loads guiding the design of buildings, but are silent about how to design and construct buildings and communities that can adjust to extreme climate differentials. Research has shown how our changing climate can alter atmospheric circulation and weather patterns such as the jet stream affecting the frequency and location of extreme weather. While these extreme events naturally occur, recent scientific evidence indicates that the probability and severity of some type of events has increased. These include high winds and tornadoes, heavy rain storms and immediate flooding, severe snowstorms, droughts, more intense lightning strikes and resulting fires causing great damage to rural as well as urban areas.

One methodology that is receiving some interest by architects is biomimicry, where unique natural traits formed by an evolutionary adaption to an environmental challenge or limitation of food, light, water, reproduction, etc. are being mimicked in human design of buildings. An example of this was an early scheme for the Bell Museum of Natural History at the University of Minnesota

9.1
Design sketches illustrating the diatom as the inspiration for architectural form for the new Bell Museum of Natural History at the University of Minnesota to express a design concept for the museum in which humans are part of nature rather than in opposition to nature. The diatom is one of the most significant groups of organisms on Earth.

where I, as the design architect, developed the building concept using the diatom (one of the largest and most significant groups of organisms on Earth) to reflect an architectural idea in which humans are part of nature rather than being in opposition to nature. This idea expressed the philosophy of the museum and its connections to natural world and human, animal, and environmental wellness (Figure 9.1).

In a recent design discussion about the architectural impacts of climate extremes with Dr. Terje Kristensen, a native of Norway who is an expert in managing and monitoring sustainability efforts, we speculated how architects can better design buildings to cope with these weather extremes that have the greatest negative impact on buildings and communities. If the buildings could be designed to be dynamic and adaptable to protect life and property from these extremes as well as be adjustable for natural ventilation while using solar heating and daylighting to reduce energy it could bring about a cost saving in insurance and maintenance costs as well as a reduction in the use of fossil fuels. Dr. Kristensen pointed out that sustainable energy design in housing is also beneficial from an economic perspective and that on average a 10 percent reduction in energy use in could show an increase in market value of 1.1–1.2 percent.

Over the past 60 years modern buildings in America have been mostly designed with material systems and heating and cooling systems in a way that the buildings would function well anywhere in any climate. In colder regions you pump in more heating and in warmer areas you just make the buildings cooler and that is why so many of these buildings look the same whether constructed in Mississippi or Minnesota. This is a very wasteful energy approach in terms of cost, but also in carbon emissions. If we are serious about climate change then design and engineering with measurable and interrelated performance metrics for environmental and human health to guide the design of sustainable buildings and communities is critical.

In Europe over the past ten years contemporary urban architecture has become much more adjustable with façade systems utilizing natural ventilation and solar heating and daylighting so that the energy required has been greatly reduced. As American architects work to realize the goals of the American Institute of Architects 2030 program I believe you will start to see a dramatic shift in the character of new buildings to reflect the idea of architectural form following function – and climate, place, and culture. These will be contemporary buildings that look quite different in Minnesota that those constructed in the southern or southwestern parts of the United States with facades that change depending on where the sun is in summer and winter.

According to Dr. Kristensen the construction sector worldwide accounts for more than a third of all resources consumed, including 12 percent of fresh water and nearly 16 percent of energy. He pointed out a recent report by McKinsey & Company that suggests that if buildings in America were upgraded to sustainable levels total energy would decline by 23 percent, yielding more than $23 trillion in savings for an investment of $520 billion. It makes economic sense to be sustainable.

For new housing developments Europeans have created the notion of "Passivhaus" that provides a high level of comport while using very little energy for heating and cooling by utilizing more insulation and thicker walls, reducing air infiltration, and careful attention to window and door placement in the façade. Norway has mandated that all new home construction must follow these standards after 2015. This idea is starting to catch on in America, but the current energy codes do not mandate such a low energy use requirement in housing developments. That may be changing, unless the politics around the reality and impact of climate change stymies any significant steps in that direction. As I write this the U.S. House of Representatives is planning to vote on legislation that will set back efforts to design and build energy saving federal buildings. The legislation includes a repeal of the 2030 targets in place to reduce and ultimately eliminate the use of fossil fuels in new and renovated federal buildings, and instead replacing them with weaker efficiency standards that fail to address the issue of carbon emissions.

That would be a shame considering that the United States helped draft and sign the 2015 World Climate Change Summit in Paris to build international consensus to limit the Earth's rise in temperature due to climate change to an average 2.0 degrees centigrade. Even with nearly 200 nations signing the agreement, time will tell if nations can join together in some equitable fashion to limit carbon emissions through architectural and community design and construction that is near net-zero energy and net-zero carbon.

Sketching and the design process

In many of the developing nations raising domestic animals or growing food adjacent to the family home is an integral part of their culture and village life. I saw this very clearly when my wife and I visited some rural villages in Myanmar in 2014 with their simple bamboo-supported houses, with humans living on a second level and animals below. I also enjoyed the opportunity to see young school kids excited by my sketches of their village after we saw a presentation of music and dance in their school. It was wonderful to see the children eager to learn about the future as well as their cultural heritage (Figures 9.2 and 9.3).

Designers who draw and record their travels in sketches have a special way of seeing the world. It is a methodology where images are engraved in the mind rather than in the camera. The photograph shows you the reality as seen through the lens of the camera, while the sketch records the emotion and character of place as seen through the eyes and hand of the artist. In a time where digital cameras and computer renderings dominate the design professions, the tradition of hand drawing what one sees and experiences is a way to communicate inherent ideas about people and cultures and landscapes. Drawing can be used to promote human understanding and appreciation of the incredible and exciting diversity of the world we live in.

9.2
A traditional Myanmar house in a rural village with animals below and living quarters for humans above on the second floor is typical of the close connection between humans and animals that rural villages have.

9.3
Dewey Thorbeck showing fascinated school children in a Myanmar village his sketches of the students and village his tourist group visited. The students had put on a dance presentation because the cruise operator, Viking River Cruises, was donating new sanitary toilets to the school.

Many of the places around the world that my wife and I have visited express diversity in the relationships between buildings and landscapes, as reflected in sketches I made at the time. They include a sketch of the river entry pathway to the village of Minhia on the Ayevarwaddy River in Myanmar (Figure 9.4); a sketch of a sheep farm in Patagonia and the demonstrations of the variety of activities on the farm and connections with agriculture and the unspoiled landscape (Figure 9.5); a sketch of buildings and streets in the 13th-century rural town of Scanno, Italy (Figure 9.6); a sketch of Vedema Resort on the Greek island of Santorini built around an ancient winery and cave (Figure 9.7); and a sketch of the wooden church of Borgund from the 11th-century near Laerdal on Sognefjord, Norway, where my father's mother emigrated from (Figure 9.8).

9.4
Sketch of the pathway up the river bank to Minhia village along the Ayevarwaddy River in Myanmar.

9.5
Sketch of a sheep farm in Patagonia showing the variety of activities on the farm including a sheep shearing demonstration.

9.6
Sketch of the Italian rural town of Scanno, established in the 13th century showing a variety of town scenes and the wonderful Italian integration of architecture and community.

Epilogue

9.7
Sketch of the Vedema Resort on the Greek island of Santorini constructed around an ancient cave for aging wine. It is a modern resort that feels quite at home on the ancient island.

9.8
Sketch of the Borgund Stave Kirke near the rural town of Laerdal on Sognefjord in west Norway. This is the town my father's mother emigrated from.

Shaping urban and rural futures

In Norway, scholars at the Barents Institute in the far north area of the country have been studying the reasons why people choose to live in rural areas in remote parts of northern Scandinavia and northern Russia. They call the phenomenon "lust for rural living." It is this passion that rural citizens have about their place, their landscape, architecture, climate, and quality of life that makes the discipline of rural design meaningful, challenging, and exciting as a design process that architects and the other design professions can utilize to help shape sustainable rural futures.

As I travel the world and meet people who have a lust for the rural it is apparent that there is a growing academic and political understanding that urban and rural issues must be integrated for a viable and sustainable future. The global crisis in climate change, fresh water, and food security makes it imperative to find land-use solutions that can feed the rapidly growing world population while reducing poverty and improving quality of life.

As I stated at the end of my first book, the only effective way to deal with these global land-use issues is to look at them systemically and holistically from both an urban and a rural perspective. Rural design offers a new way of design thinking in creating ideas to shape land use for agriculture at a wide range of scales to preserve rural cultural, architectural, and agricultural heritage. It is also a methodology for finding creative and sustainable transformative concepts and innovations for a healthy and prosperous future for everyone in North America and around the world.

Because of their skills and experiences architects should be global design leaders in this transformation process while integrating and innovatively designing human, animal, and environmental wellness into their architectural projects – urban, peri-urban, and rural.

References

Arabena, K. (2013) *Regeneration: Healthy People in Healthy Landscapes – Addressing Wicked Problems of Our Time.* Speech to the Public Health Association of Australia.

Brown, F.E. (1961) *Roman Architecture* (New York: George Brazilier).

Brown, T. (2009) *Change by Design* (New York: HarperCollins).

Brownell, B. (2012) *Material Strategies: Innovative Applications in Architecture* (New York: Princeton Architectural Press).

Butler, L. and Maronek D.K. (2002) *Urban and Agricultural Communities: Opportunities for Common Ground.* Paper for Agricultural Science and Technology, Ames, Iowa.

Corbet, J., Ritter, K., and Borenstein, S. (2015) A "victory for all of the planet": Nations pledge to slow global warming in historic pact, *Associated Press* article, December 12.

Curry, A. (2013) Archeology: The milk revolution, *Nature,* 500: 20–22.

Design Futures Council (2013) *Leadership Summit on Sustainable Design,* www.designfuturescouncil.org, accessed September 17, 2013.

Downes, L. and Nunes, P. (2014) *Big Band Disruption: Strategy in the Age of Devastating Innovation* (New York: Portfolio/Penguin).

Ellis, E.C. (2013) *Sustaining biodiversity and people in the world's anthropogenic biomes, Current Opinion in Environmental Sustainability,* http://dx.doi.org/10.1016/j.consust.2013.07.002.

Endersby, E., Greenwood, A., and Larkin, D. (1992) *Barn: The Art of a Working Building* (Boston: Houghton Mifflin Company).

Falk, C. (2012) *Barns of New York* (Ithaca: Cornell University Press).

Fisher, T. (2011) The Divergent College of Design, *Emerging* (College of Design at the University of Minnesota), Spring.

Fisher, T. (2013) *Designing to Avoid Disaster* (New York: Routledge).

Florida, R. (2002) The rise of the creative class: Why cities without gays and rock bands are losing the economic development race, *Washington Monthly*, May, www.washingtonmonthly.com/features/2001/2005/florida.html, accessed September 17, 2013.

Foster, T. and Gets Escudero, A. (2014) *City Regions as Landscapes for People, Food, and Nature* (Washington, DC: EcoAgriculture Partners).

Gjerde, J. (1985) *From Peasants to Farmers: The Migration from Balestrand Norway to the Upper Middle West* (Cambridge: Cambridge University Press).

Glenn, J. (2007) Global prospects, in *Hopes and Visions for the 21st Century*, ed. T.C. Mack (Bethesda, MD: World Future Society).

Heinberg, R. (2010) What is sustainability? In *The Post Carbon Reader: Managing the 21st Century's Sustainability Crisis* (Healdsburg, California: Watershed Media with Post Carbon Institute).

Howard, E. (1898/1902) *Garden Cities of Tomorrow* (Swan Sonnenschein and Co.).

Hundertwasser, F. (n.d.) Hundertwasser Non-Profit Foundation, Vienna, Austria, www.hundertwasser.com.

Hsiang, J. and Mendis, B. (2015) *The City of 7 Billion: An Index*, Association of Collegiate Schools of Architecture Annual Meeting 2013, apps.acsa-arch.org.

IBC (2006) *International Building Code* (Country Club Hills, IL: International Code Council, Inc.).

iCOMOS (2016) *2nd International Conference on One Medicine One Science*, University of Minnesota, April.

King, V. (2012) Quinta Do Vallado Winery, *ArchDaily*, www.archdaily.com.

Knowd, I., Mason D., and Docking A. (2006) *Urban Agriculture: The New Frontier*. Paper presented at the Planning for Food Seminar in Vancouver in June 2006.

Koohafkan, P. and Altieri, M. (2011) *Globally Important Agricultural Heritage Systems: A Legacy for the Future* (Rome, Italy: UN FAO).

LEEDv4 (2016) *Reference Guide for Building Design and Construction* (Washington, DC: U.S. Green Building Council).

Mileto, C., Vegas, F., Soriano, L.G., and Cristini, V. (2014) *Vernacular Architecture: Towards a Sustainable Future* (Leiden: CRC Press).

Midwest Plan Service (n.d.) *Swine Growing and Finishing Buildings* (Ames, IA: Iowa State University).

Mithun Architects (2015) Center for Urban Agriculture, http://mithun.com/centerforurbanagriculture.

Moberg, V. (1951) *The Emigrants* (Stockholm, Sweden: Bonniers).

Moberg, V. (1951) *Unto a Good Land* (Stockholm, Sweden: Bonniers).

Moberg, V. (1961) *The Last Letter Home* (Stockholm, Sweden: Bonniers).

Murakami, H. (1989) *A Wild Sheep's Chase*, trans. A. Birnbaum (New York: Kodansha International).

Niedźwiecka-Filipiak I., Potyria J., and Filiipiak, P. (2015) The current management of the green infrastructure with the Wrocław Functional Area, *Architektura Krajobrazu/ Landscape Architecture*, 2/2015, 47: 4–25.

Peri-Urban (2014) *International Conference on Peri-urban Landscapes: Water, Food and Environmental Security*, University of Western Sydney, Australia, www.periurban14.org.

Purdom, C.B. (1925) *The Building of Satellite Towns* (London: J.M. Dent & Sons Ltd).

Roos, S., Hellevick, W., and Pitt, D. (2003) Environmental practices on dairy farms (unpublished CRD report for the Minnesota Milk Producers Association as part of their Environmental Quality Assurance Program).

Rostovtzeff, M. (1957) *The Social and Economic History of the Roman Empire*, 2nd edn (Oxford: Clarendon).

ROTOR (2014) *Behind the Green Door: A Critical Look at Sustainable Architecture through 600 Objects* (Oslo Architecture Triennale).

Rudofsky, B (1977) *The Prodigious Builders* (New York and London: Harcourt Brace Jovanovich, Inc.).

Scully, V. Jr. (1960) *Frank Lloyd Wright* (New York: George Braziller, Inc.).

Seline, R. and Friedman, Y. (2007) Hubs and nodes: how I learned to stop worrying and love globalization, a chapter in *Hopes and Visions for the 21st Century*, ed. T.C. Mack (Bethesda, MD: World Future Society).

Senge, P. (2003) Creating the desired futures in a global economy, *Reflections of the Society of Organizational Learning*, 5, 2.

Smyre, R. (2007) The three triangles of transformation, in *Hopes and Visions for the 21st Century*, ed. T.C. Mack (Bethesda, MD: World Future Society).

Snyder, T. (2015) *Black Earth: The Holocaust as History and Warning* (New York: Penguin Random House).

Stern, R. (2015) Letter from the dean, *Retrospecta* 38 (Yale School of Architecture).
Taylor J. (1993) *Complete Guide to Breeding and Raising Racehorses* (Neenah, WI: Russell Meerdink Company, Ltd.)
Thilla, R. (2015) Solutions can come from slums, *The Hindu*.
Thorbeck, D. (2012) *Rural Design: A New Design Discipline* (New York: Routledge).
Thorbeck, D. and Troughton, J. (2015) Rural design: connecting urban and rural futures through rural design, in *Balanced Urban Development* (New York: Springer).
Troughton, J. (2014) *Australia 21 Shaping the Future Landscape,* a curriculum program for rural primary schools. From a proposal for curriculum change in Australia.
UN DESA (2015) *United Nations Department of Economic and Social Affairs 2015 Population Predictions*, www.un.org/development/desa/en/.
UN-FAO (2002) *Globally Important Agricultural Heritage System,* www.fao.org.
UN-Habitat (2015) *United Nations Sustainable Development Summit to adopt the 2030 Agenda for Sustainable Development*, www.unhabitat.org.
United Nations World Commission on Environment and Development (1987) *Our Common Future.* Brundtland Report (Oxford: Oxford University Press).
WGDO (2015) World Green Design Organization overview of the World Rural Development Committee inaugural ceremony in Beijing.
Wilson, E.O. (1984) *Biophilia* (Cambridge: Harvard University Press).
WRDC (2015) *Charter* approved by committee vote at October 25, 2015 meeting in Beijing, China.
Yale News (2015) *City of 7 Billion* exhibit by J. Hsiang and B. Mendis in School of Architecture, http://news.yale.edu/2015/05/27/yale-architecture-exhibition.

Illustration credits

All the photographs and sketches in the book were taken or drawn by the author unless otherwise noted below:

1.1	David and Claire Frame
1.3	Kathy Imle
2.1	Bardo Museum, Tunis from Ben Abed (2006)
2.2, 2.3	National Trust, Swindon
2.4	Otter Tail County Historical Society
2.7	Jim Gallop
2.10, 2.11, 2.12, 2.13, 2.14, 2.15, 2.16	David and Claire Frame
2.17, 2.18, 2.19	Andrew Wald
2.20, 2.21	Xiaomei Zhao
2.22	Yue Jia
3.2	Metal Sales Company
3.3	Center for Rural Design
3.11, 3.12	Laura Donnell
3.15	Duncan Taylor
4.6	Wensman Company
4.7, 4.8, 4.9, 4.10, 4.11	Jeremy Bitterman
4.12, 4.13, 4.14, 4.15	Michael Nicholson
4.16, 4.17, 4.18, 4.19	Jiri Havran
4.21, 4.22, 4.23, 4.24, 4.25	Roberto de Leon
4.26, 4.27, 4.28, 4.29, 4.30, 4.31	John Lin
4.32, 4.33, 4.34, 4.35, 4.36, 4.37	Alberto Placido
4.38, 4.39, 4.40, 4.41	Qingyun Ma
4.43	St. Paul's Farmer's Market
4.48	U of MN Center for Sustainable Building Research

5.1. 5.2	Midwest Plan Service
5.4, 5.5, 5.6	Riverview Dairy
6.1, 6.2, 6.3	Mary Ann Ray
6.4, 6.5	Jeff McMinenum
6.6, 6.7	Avant Energy
6.8, 6.9, 6.10, 6.11	Irena Niedźwiecka-Filipiak
7.3, 7.4	Mithun Architects
7.5	Anja Fahrig, © 2016 Hundertwasser Archive, Vienna
7.6	John Troughton
7.8	Carver County Historical Society
8.2	David Hanson, UMN Experiment Station
8.3	David and Claire Frame
9.3	Evelyn Kolditz, Viking River Cruise

Every effort has been made to contact and acknowledge copyright owners, but the author and publisher would be pleased to have any errors or omissions brought to their attention so that corrections may be published at a later printing.

Index

Figures in **bold** refer to illustrations

Aboriginal and Torres Strait people (Australia) 175
Abu Dhabi (United Arab Emirates) 126
academic silos 155, 184
Ag Reliant Genetics (Minnesota) 67
AIA Standard Form of Agreement 184
Allied Works 68
American Academy in Rome (Italy) 7
American Institute of Architects (AIA) 124, 193
Amish farmer plowing with three horses (Pennsylvania) **64**
Andrew Peterson Historic Farm (Minnesota) 163
    Entry Building **166**
    historic picture of home and family **163**
    Master Plan **165**
aquaponics 161
Arabena, Kerry (Australia) 1, 175
architects 121, 181, 199
architecture and agriculture 1
Architecture and Agriculture: A Rural Design Guide 11
Architecture without Architects 3
Avant Energy, Inc. (Minnesota) 136
Ayevarwaddy River (Myanmar) 196

Bagley (Minnesota) 5
Balanced Urban Development 152
bank barn in Pennsylvania **13**
Barents Institute (Norway) 199
Barn: The Art of a Working Building 2

Barns of New York 2
BASEBeijing study (U of MI) 133
beef/sheep barns 60
Behind the Green Door conference (Norway) 125
Behind the Green Door: A Critical Look at Sustainable Architecture through 600 Objects 126
Beijing (China) 12
Bell Museum of Natural History (U of MN) **192**
Belluschi, Pietro 3
Best Management Practices 51
Blumau Thermal Village (Austria) 160
    aerial view of thermal village **160**
Borgund Stave Kirke (Norway) **198**
Breakthrough Energy Initiative 178
Brooklyn Park Historical Farm (Minnesota) 25
Brown, Frank E. 18
Brown, Tim 169
Brownell, Blaine 191
Brundtland Report 123
building code issue 108
Building of Satellite Towns, The 161
Bulls Run Property (Australia) 72

Caracas (Venezuela) 187
Carleton College (Minnesota) 49
Carlowitz, Hans Carl von 123
Carver County Historical Society (Minnesota) 163

drawing of Carver County and urban/
    rural edge **163**
Center for Rural Design (U of MN) 10, 58,
    96, 113, 115
    rural design as link between science
        and society **152**, 166, 170, 174, 178
    rural design connecting the dots **180**
Center for Sustainable Building Research
    (U of MN) 101, 115, 178
Center for Urban Agriculture (Seattle)
    157, 158
centuriation 19
Chaplin, Jonathan 197, 113
Chiloe Island (Chile) 4
    village on water **4**
China 2, 11, 48, 124
Chinese architecture 87
Chuan Di Xia (China) 12
    photo **28**
    sketch **12**
City of 7 Billion (Yale University) 171
*City Regions as Landscapes for People, Food,
    and Nature* 148
Civil War in America 26
Clearwater County (Minnesota) 5, 6
Clearwater River (Minnesota) 49
climate change 11, 33, 186
Cloepfil, Brad 68
Clos, Dr. Joan 127
Codex Alimentarius Commission 121
College of Design (U of MN) 10, 155
College of Food, Agriculture, and Natural
    Resource Sciences (U of MN) 10
Community Supported Agriculture (CSA)
    45, 104, 164
*Complete Guide to Breeding and Raising
    Racehorses* 49
corn crib (Iowa) **66**
County Geological Atlases (Minnesota) 172
Coxwell Tithe Barn (England) **20, 21**
Cristini, V. 2
crossing borders 172, 186, 190
Currie and Ives 25
Curry, A. 18

Dalaker/Galt Farmhouse (Norway) 76
    corner detail **78**
    house and existing barn **76**
    house on former pigsty **77**
    house and rocky landscape **77**
    Michael Darling 76
    Turi Dalaker 76

Deepwater Woolshed (Australia) 72
    detail of overhang **75**
    end view of building **73**
    interior with sheep **74,**
    side view of building in grasslands **72**
De Leon & Primmer Architecture Workshop
    79
Design as Language 170
Design Futures Council 126
design guidelines for agricultural
    buildings 115
*Design Guidelines for Worker and Animal
    Health and Safety in Animal
    Production Building Systems* 114
Designing to Avoid Disasters 169, 186
design professionals 183
design professions 155, 190
design thinking 4, 63, 179, 183, 185, 191
Devilieger, Lionell 126
disease transmission
Dong Community (China) 41
    dancers under drum tower **42**
    family dinner around drum tower **42**
    village of Dali **41**
Douro River (Portugal) 89
Downes, Larry 188

Earth 17
East Africa 29
Ecala Group (Minnesota) 176
Eidem, John farmstead (Minnesota) **25**
Emerson, Ralph Waldo 1
Emigrants, The 165
Endersby, E. 1
engineers 181
England 27
Environmental Quality Assurance Program
    (Minnesota) 97
Eri, David 5
Eri, Nils 6
Eri, Synneva 6, **6**
Escudero, Arthur Gets 148, 185
ethnic tourism 43
evidence-based design 188

fabric-roofed dairy barn 96
    architectural drawings **96**
factory farming 16, 104
Falk, C. 2
farm buildings 24
Farm of 10 Billion 172
farmsteads 23, 24

farm worker hazards 107
Federal Farm Service Agency 51
Federal Natural Resources Conservation
    Service 51
Fehn, Sverre (Norway) 78, 183
Fergus Falls (Minnesota) 24
Fisher, Thomas (Tom) 146, 156, 169, 174,
    186, 191
Florida, Richard 147
food security 11, 15, 12
Fosse, Burton 7
Foster + Partners 67
Foster, Thomas 148, 185
Frame, David and Claire 29
free-stall dairy barn 59
Friedman, Yali 17

gable barn in Illinois **24**
Galta, Tom 76
Garden Cities 161
Gates, Bill 178
Gehry, Frank 67
Geographic Information Systems (GIS) 172
Gjerde, Jon 22
Glacier Museum (Norway) 78, **79**
Glenn, Jerome C. 173
Global Footprint Network 125
global issues 183
global sustainability 168
global warming 176, 178
Globally Important Agricultural Heritage
    Systems (GIAHS) 3, 129, 131
Gonvick (Minnesota) 6
Graftaas, Oscar 6
Grandfather Hanson farm **5**
Grandmother Eri farm **6**
green design 4, 124, 191
Green Valley, Inc. (Japan) 38
Greenwood, A. 1
Gropius, Walter 3
Guggenheim Foundation 3

Hadid, Zaha 67
Hanson, Emma 5
Hanson, Olaf and Hilda 5
Haoshu, Jiang 130
Heinberg, Richard 123
Highspeed Internet Access in China 133
    CLOUD at twilight **135**
    CLOUD at night **136**
    CLOUD concept over village **134**
Hjeltnes, Knut 76

hog facilities 60
Homestead Act (1892) 23, 174
Hometown BioEnergy project (Minnesota)
    136
    back side of completed building **138**, 177
    early site plan drawing **137**
    entry side of completed building **138**
    site elevation drawing **138**
Hopes and Visions for the 21st Century 173
horse barn (Tennessee) **66**
House for All Seasons (China) 85
    above view of house **88,**
    aerial view of Shijia village **86**
    house in field **87**
    interior courtyards **88**
    stages of construction **89**
Howard, Ebeneezer 161
Hsiang, Joyce 171
human, animal, and environmental
    wellness 118
    children plowing with oxen in Nepal
        182, 193, 199
    young girl and calf **181**
Hundertwasser, Friedensreich 159
hydroponics 161

Ichiu (Japan) 36, **37**
immigrant farm workers 111, 117
in-between landscapes 150
indigenous agricultural heritage 187
Ingeman, Elsa 165
Integrated Performance Metrics 101
Integrated Performance Metrics for
    Sustainable Animal Production
    Buildings 16, 115
interdisciplinary design 183
International Building Code (IBC) 108, 121
Iowa State University 104
Irodori Project (Japan) 38
Italian hill towns 7, **8**

Jacobson, Larry 113
Jade Valley Winery and Resort (China) 93
    entry to Well House **95,**
    resort adjacent to winery **95**
    Well House for father **94**
    winery in rolling hills **94**
Janni, Kevin 113

Kamikatsu and Kamiyana (Japan) 37
    Engwa House **39**
    old shops renovated **38**

Kentucky 49, 53
King, Andrew 72
King, Victoria 89
Koohafkan, Parviz 12, 131
Kosciuszko Foundation (Poland) 139
Kringstad, Orlyn 177
Kristensen, Dr. Terje 177, 193

Laerdal (Norway) **28**
land grant universities 26, 58
landscape architects 121, 181
Larkin, D. 1
Last Letter Home, The 165
Leadership in Energy and Environmental Design (LEED) 84, 126, 178
Leopold, Aldo 169
Le Sueur (Minnesota) 136
Liberri Villa floor mosaic (Tunisia) **19**
Lin, John 85
linking urban and rural 14, 188
Locavore Movement 160
Luke Him Sau Charitable Trust (China) 85

Ma, Qingyun 93
Maasi (Tanzania) 34, **35**
MADA 93
Malawi (East Africa) 29
　　corn storage **31**
　　farm on ridge **31**
　　farmer selling potatoes **32**
　　rural Malawi village **29**
Mangurian, Robert 133
manure digester system 97
Masdar City (Malawi) 126
Mason Lane Farm Operating Center 79
　　end view of Barn B **83**,
　　interior of Barn A **80**
　　interior of Barn B **83**
　　Operating Center overview **80**
　　side view of Barn B **84**
Material Strategies 191
McMenimen, Jeff 136
McKinsey & Company 193
Mendis, Bimal 171
metal grain bin **61**
Metropolitan Design Center (U of MN) 146, 166
Midwest Plan Service 104, **105**, **106**
Mileto, C. 1
Millenium Project 173
Miller, Dunwiddie Architects 26
Minhia (Myanmar) 196

Minnesota 48
Miller, Eleanor Bingam 79
Ministry of Culture (China) 130
Minneapolis and Saint Paul (Minnesota) 26
Minneapolis Farmers' Market 46
Minnesota Dairy Association 58
　　Geological Survey 172
　　Horticultural Society 165
　　Municipal Power Association 136
Minnesota State Historical Society 164
Minnesota State Legislature 58, 97
Mithun Architects 157
　　aerial sketch of urban agriculture farm **157**
　　ground level view of farm **158**
Moberg, Vilhelm 164
Moon, Ban Ki 127
Mongolia 29
　　ger (yurt) **36**
　　herdsmen on the move **35**
　　Maasai village **35**
Montepulciano (Italy) 8
Murakami, Haruki 40
Museum of Modern Art (New York) 3
Myanmar 194
　　Dewey Thorbeck showing his sketches to school kids **195**
　　sketch of pathway to rural village **196**
　　traditional rural Myanmar house **195**

Nantucket Principles 126
National Institute for Occupational Safety and Health (NIOSH) 114
National Landmarks 1
National Registry of Historic Places 1
Nepal 182
net-zero 176
Neutra, Richard 3
New England 27
new innovative technologies 189
New Land, The 165
Niedźwiecka-Filipiak, Irena (Poland) 139
Nordic Business Development Inc. (Minnesota) 177
North Central Sustainable Agriculture Research and Education Program 115
Norway 5, 22, 194, 199
nsima (food from maize in Malawi) **31**
Nunes, Paul 188

Occupational Safety and Health Administration (OSHA) 112
odor and manure management 113
Ohno, Akira 37
Ominami, Shinya 39
One Medicine One Science (ICOMOS) 118
Oslo Architectural Triennale 2013 (Norway) 125, 187

partnering 185
passion for architecture 183, 198
Passivhaus 177, 194
Patagonia **197**
Peace Corps 29
Peasants to Farmers 22
Penn State University 9
Pennsylvania 64
Peri-Urban 2014 (Australia) 151
peri-urban landscapes 150, 185
Peterson, Andrew and Elsa 164, **164**
Pine Lake Wild Rice Farm (Minnesota) 49
   architectural relationships **52**
   central building **51**
   chemical building **52**
   equipment **53**
   Paul and Kathy Imle 49
   shop complex across field **50**
   three generations of Imle family – Paul, Peter and Sara **53**
planners 121, 181
pole barns 14, 47, 50
   post-frame construction systems 46, **47**
   pre-engineered building systems **47**, 48, 58, 102
Pomeroy Alumni Center (U of MN) **26**
Ponti, Gio 3
Post Carbon Institute 123
poultry facilities 60
Prodigious Builders, The 3
Public Health Association of Australia 175
Public Land Survey System 19
Purdom, C. B. 161
Purina Farms 9
   humans and animal bond exhibit **9**

Quinta do Vallado Winery (Portugal) 89
   entrance terrace **90**
   entry to visitor center **91**
   interior of visitor center **92**
   interior of Production Room **92**
   wine aging cave **93**
   winery in Durou River valley **90**
Quonset building 50

Ralston Purina Company 9
Ray, Mary Ann 133
Red Lake Indian Reservation (Minnesota) 5
Red Lake River (Minnesota) 5
Rennesoy Island (Norway) 76
Resilient Communities Grant 166
resilient design thinking 186
Riverview Dairy (Minnesota) 111
   aerial view of dairy farm **111**
   interior view of animal stalls **112**
   rotary milking parlor **112**
robotic milking 59
Rome (Italy) 12
Rome Prize in Architecture 7
Roos, Stephan 59
Rostovtzeff, M. 20
ROTOR (Belgium) 126
round barn near New Prague (Minnesota) **14**
Rudofsky, Bernard 3
rural design and urban design relationships **155**
   architectural heritage 44
   architecture and rural design 45, 101
   building design guidelines 62
   change 11, 13, 46
   design 14, 101, 146, 173, 179, 186
   development 147
   development clusters 174
   futures 145
   rural architecture 2, 44, **48**
Rural Design: A New Design Discipline 10, 190
Rural Design: Connecting Urban and Rural Futures through Rural Design 152
Rural Development Act 174
Rural Renewal Program (Poland) 139

Saint Paul Farmers' Market (Minnesota) 45
   farmers selling products **46**, 98,
   historic public market **98**
   proposed new market **99, 100**
Scanno village sketch (Italy) 197
Schonfelder, Jeremy 177
School of Architecture and Landscape Architecture (U of MN) 10
Scully, Vincent Jr. 65
Seline, Richard 173

Senge, Peter M. 169
Sert, Jose Louis 3
Shaanxi Women's Federation 85
Shang Shui Guo (China) 133
sheep research (Italy) **109**
Sherping farmstead (Minnesota) **23**
Shija village (China) 86, **86**
Shikoku Island (Japan) 36
sketching and the design process 194
slums as urban models 187
Smyre, Rick 174
Snyder, Timothy 188
social conflict potential **48**
Sokol Blosser Winery (Oregon) 68
    Alison and Alex Sokol Blosser 70
    deck terraces **69**
    interior **71**
    main entrance **68**
    open space between parts **71**
    seating terrace **70**
Sonstegaard family 112
Sorianno, L.G. 1
Southern California University School of Architecture 93
Steel, Carolyn 125
Stern, Robert A.M. 181
Stifter, Charles 7
stonehouse and attached barn (Iowa) **65**
Study of the Cultural Landscape of the Pazkow Municipality, The (Poland) 143
    Cultural landscape presentation board **144**
Stutchbury, Peter 72
Styria (Austria) 159
Sunrise Farm (Iowa) 112
sustainability 183, 186
Sustainability Performance Metrics 85, **102**
sustainable animal housing 115
Sustainable Development Goals (2015) 128
Swanson, Dr. Katherine M.J. 120
swine post-frame barn (Minnesota) **14**

Taliesen 64
Tange, Kenzo 3
Tanzania 34
Target 189
Taylor Made Horse Farm (Kentucky) 53
    breeding center **54**
    horse stable **56**
    horse stall **57**
    Joseph Lannon Taylor and sons Frank, Ben, Mark and Duncan **57**
    stud barn **54**
Thief River Falls (Minnesota) 5
Thorbeck Architects 98
Thorbeck, David 6
Thorbeck, Dewey 152
Thorbecke, George 6
Tower (Minnesota) 177
Tower 2025 Vision Plan 177
Troughton, Dr. John 116, 152, 176
Tunisia 19
2030 Commitment (AIA) 124, 193
Twin Cities (Minnesota) 25, 166, **167**
Twin City Metropolitan Council (Minnesota) 166

UMORE (U of MN) 178
UN-Habitat 127, 187
United Nations Climate Summit 178
United Nations Department of Economics and Social Affairs 170
United Nations Food and Agriculture Organization (UN-FAO) 3, 131
United Nations Sustainable Development Summit 127
United Nations World Commission on Environment and Development 123
university research 58
University of Cambridge 125
University of Hong Kong 85
University of Michigan 36
University of Minnesota 27,
    Center for Sustainable Building Research 101
    College of Design 10
    College of Food, Agriculture, and Natural Resource Sciences 10
    Department of Bioproducts and Biosystems Engineering 115
    Grand Challenge 148
    School of Architecture 10
University of Western Sydney (Australia) 151
Unto a Good Land 165
Upper Midwest 23, 24, 26, 59, 111, 114, 117
urban agriculture 156, 162, 167, 186,
urban agriculture and building code 116
urban architecture 44
urban design 14, 179
urban futures 199

urban greenhouse in Australia **161**
US Centers for Disease Control 121
US Department of Agriculture 115
US Food and Drug Administration 121
US Global Positioning System (GPS) 51
Uthinia region (Tunisia) 19

Vedema Resort sketch (Santorini) **198**
Vegas, F. 1
vernacular architecture 3
Vernacular Architecture: Towards a Sustainable Future 2
vibrio 121
Viero do Compos, Francisco 89
vineyard farm (California) **65**

Wagga Wagga, New South Wales (Australia) 72
Wald, Andrew 36
Walter Davidson Little Farms Project 65
Webster American Dictionary 25
Wensman Seed Plant (Minnesota) 67, **67**
Whole Earth Catalogue 126
Wilson, Edward O. 157
World Agricultural Heritage Foundation (Italy) 12, 131
World Climate Change Summit 194
World Future Society 173
World Green Design Forum 124
World Green Design Organization (WGDO) 124
World Rural Development Committee (WRDC) 128, 190
Wright, Frank Lloyd 64
Wroclaw Functional Area (Poland) 140
  green infrastructure map **142**,
  simplified green infrastructure map **143**
  study area in Poland **141**
Wroclaw University of Environment and Life Sciences Inst. of Landscape Arch. (Poland) 139

Yale University 7, 18
Yale University School of Architecture 171, 181, 187
Yamhill countryside (Oregon) 68
Yangzhou (China) 124

Zhao, Dr. Xiaomei 41
Zhaoxing Dong Community (China) 42